PLAY ALL NIGHT!

T0248382

UNIVERSITY PRESS OF FLORIDA

Florida A&M University, Tallahassee
Florida Atlantic University, Boca Raton
Florida Gulf Coast University, Ft. Myers
Florida International University, Miami
Florida State University, Tallahassee
New College of Florida, Sarasota
University of Central Florida, Orlando
University of Florida, Gainesville
University of North Florida, Jacksonville
University of South Florida, Tampa
University of West Florida, Pensacola

Play All Night!

DUANE ALLMAN AND THE JOURNEY TO FILLMORE EAST

BOB BEATTY

University Press of Florida

Gainesville · Tallahassee · Tampa · Boca Raton

Pensacola · Orlando · Miami · Jacksonville · Ft. Myers · Sarasota

Library of Congress Control Number: 2022942176
ISBN 978–0-8130–6950–0 (pbk)

The University Press of Florida is the scholarly publishing agency for the State
University System of Florida, comprising Florida A&M University, Florida Atlantic
University, Florida Gulf Coast University, Florida International University, Florida
State University, New College of Florida, University of Central Florida, University of
Florida, University of North Florida, University of South Florida, and University of
West Florida.

University Press of Florida
2046 NE Waldo Road
Suite 2100
Gainesville, FL 32609
http://upress.ufl.edu

Dedicated to a brother and a sister: Brian Beatty and Gwynne Beatty

CONTENTS

PREFACE

Before you start reading you need to know one thing. I am far from unbiased when it comes to Duane Allman and the Allman Brothers Band. Though I am an academically trained historian who has worked in the field of history museums since 1999, my dyed-in-the-wool, unabashed, hardcore Duane Allman fandom led me to this project. I rank the Allman Brothers Band among the greatest, most significant rock bands in history. Their third album, *At Fillmore East*, is why we remember them as such.

Blame the BMG music club's "Twelve-CDs-for-One" deal for this book. Actually, fault their liberal policy of allowing folks with the same address to benefit from their "refer-a-friend" policy, as the Allman Brothers' *Decade of Hits 1969–1979* came addressed to my roommate, I. M. Fletcher. It was 1993, the moment I discovered the Allman Brothers Band (ABB). Since that day, I have not gone a week of my life without listening to *something* Allman Brothers–related, including this very moment.[1]

Yes, a greatest hits collection changed my life.

I use quotes around "discovered" because everyone who came of age in the seventies or later knew the Allman Brothers Band. Even in the pre-classic rock era, they were a stalwart on FM radio. Most stations favored their 1973 number 2 hit "Ramblin' Man," but I also remember "One Way Out," "Midnight Rider," and the bouncing, western swing-inspired instrumental "Jessica" on the radio. I assumed it was the Grateful Dead as they were the only band I knew of that played music that was mysterious and fun and serious all at the same time.

Sometime in the mid-1980s, I bought *At Fillmore East* on cassette at Spec's music in Jensen Beach, Florida. I was a new guitar player, twelve or thirteen at most and I was consumed by the blues. Muddy

Waters led me to Robert Johnson who led me to Eric Clapton who led me to seek out Duane Allman.

Given where things ended up, it astonishes me to this day that *At Fillmore East* went completely over my head. In the years since, the album has given me everything I had hoped to find when I first purchased it. But my ears weren't ready for it. Duane's masterpiece fell flat.

Fast-forward a decade. I was in my twenties when *Decade of Hits* arrived in the mail. The title is a misnomer. The Allman Brothers were never a singles band, and very few songs were actual "hits." Instead, the album offered a good overview of the band's first ten years. Its tracks introduced me to a sound that was, to my ears, wholly original to the Allman Brothers Band: blues covers and originals, a country influence, haunting ballads, and gorgeous instrumentals (including "Jessica," the song I originally thought was the Grateful Dead). I was awestruck then; I remain so now.

"What band combines all of this in one place so brilliantly?" is a question I've pondered for many more hours than I'd care to admit. Ultimately, I chose to write a book answering that question for myself.

If the ABB's music was incredibly interesting and genuinely unique to me, the band's history opened up an entirely different way for me to understand it. It fascinated me then; still does. Duane Allman looms large throughout: His single-minded pursuit of music, his openness to the ideas of his bandmates, his band's virtuosity, his loyalty to the South and its musical influences, the supporters he picked up along the way, the families who loved them, and the family he and his bandmates created together.

I consider myself a son of the South and I have spent much of my life making meaning from its past. To me, the Allman Brothers are a rich well of southern history. Their story, their music, their inherent southernness resonates with me. They built their aesthetic on excellence in the moment, which they defined as "hittin' the note." I hear it as authentic. It has touched my soul deeply for my entire adult life.

On November 13, 1993, I attended my first Allman Brothers Band concert at the Palm Beach County Fairgrounds. I went expecting nostalgia and I left a lifelong convert. If the CDs I'd been listening to nonstop for most of the year already hadn't done it, seeing the band live sure did! I was so flabbergasted I bought *Wipe the Windows, Check* the Oil, Dollar Gas, a live collection from the post-Duane era I'd casually dismissed as inferior. "If they're this good in 1993," I remember thinking, "they had to be great in 1973!" They were.

You can blame BMG Music Club for providing the bait, but it was the Allman Brothers Band that set the hook. The music has offered me endless hours of joyous listening. I love how the musicians integrate themselves into the whole, how soloists conjure up astounding riffs on the fly, how the band plays behind the soloists—pushing and prodding them forward, backwards, even sideways. At times the guitars stand out; at other times, it's the drums. Sometimes it's Gregg's vocals or the magnificent, swirling sound of his Hammond B-3. Undergirding it all is a rock-solid foundation of ensemble playing, each musician making up his part as he goes along. It is a musical conversation. And the Allman Brothers Band are among the premier musical conversationalists in the history of rock music.

As of this writing, I've been unpacking what the Allman Brothers Band mean and why their music struck me like it did (and when) for twenty-nine years. I knew the music was special to a lot of people. I wanted to explain why I found it particularly fascinating.

I knew going into my research that Duane Allman begins, and remains, at the center of the story. He set the model in with his choice of players and the band's improvisational intent. After his death in October 1971, his surviving bandmates followed this model (to varying degrees of success) for forty-three more years. They built their career on maintaining a level of excellence that reflected the standard Duane and the band set with *At Fillmore East*.

This worked for the band because *At Fillmore East* is the truest fulfillment of Duane's musical vision. The album is an honest look at Duane as an individual artist and, more importantly, as a bandleader. More than just seventy-eight minutes of live improvisational music, the record is the definitive artistic statement of the original Allman Brothers Band. "The Fillmore days are definitely the most cherished memories that I have," Duane's guitar partner Dickey Betts said. "If you asked everybody in the band, they would probably say that." Listening to *At Fillmore East*, it is easy to see why. The album sounds like a group of gifted musicians having the time of their lives communicating with music.[2]

In 1993 I began the journey of trying to understand why the Allman

Brothers Band captivated me like they did when they did. It was 1998 when I formally wrote down a goal to write a book on the band. By 2004 the goal turned into "Write a book," which I did two years later. I had given up on the "Write a book on the Allman Brothers" goal when I lost my mom suddenly to cancer in 2012. It was about a week shy of my forty-first birthday and caused the kind of reassessment that a parent's death often brings. I went back to graduate school. I sat down with Tennessee State Historian Van West, and said, "I want to write a book on the Allman Brothers." He said yes, and here we are.

My initial goal was to understand Duane Allman's influence on American music. I find the Allman Brothers Band unique, a very special musical brew of disparate influences distilled into something distinct to them. I sought to demonstrate how that manifested Duane's vision. This ideal attracted me, and still does, but a historian has to work with his sources. And those just weren't there. I find the Allman Brothers Band unique. Way more people acknowledge their influence but find the ABB interesting at best. Still others—my wife Candy and daughters Ryan and Tyler included—don't care for them much at all.

Proving something is unique is simply impossible. Instead I wrote a book on how *At Fillmore East* demonstrated Duane Allman's musical vision. It was not "a live album by the Allman Brothers Band," but was instead the *next* ABB album, recorded live. The distinction was important in helping me understand the album as more than a concert document, but as an artistic statement.

At Fillmore East was the band's third album, and it was their breakthrough. Without it, Duane's career might have been a mere "What if?" Duane is remembered because of *At Fillmore East* and the success of the Allman Brothers Band after his death. Here is my take on that story.

A few final notes to three specific groups of readers:

To my friends who are neither ABB fans nor historians, I hope this book makes you think, while also giving you some insight into your friend Bob's obsession with the ABB, history, place, and music.

To my fellow ABB fans, I approached this book with you in mind. It was my goal to offer some new insights, and to aggregate the personal stories with some historical context and material that has yet to make it into other books about the band. Though you'll see some familiar quotes and stories, I left many more on the cutting room floor. I beg your forgiveness for those omissions. My goal was to do something different. We already have three biographies of the ABB and two on Duane. This is a biography of Duane's music.

To my fellow historians, you will understand why I say this has been the most challenging book I have ever written. I did my best to walk the line between historian and fan carefully. But in the end, I was simply unable to fully extricate myself from the love of my subject matter. I hope what you perceive as gaps in this book's analysis inspires thought, and perhaps additional research opportunities for you.

INTRODUCTION

"Berry Oakley, Dickey Betts, Butch Trucks, Jai Johanny Johanson, Gregg Allman, I'm Duane Allman!" the leader of the Allman Brothers Band exclaimed as the band wrapped up nearly an hour of nonstop improvisational music playing two songs, "Whipping Post," a ferocious blues, followed by "Mountain Jam," a tour-de-force instrumental based on the melody to folksinger Donovan's "There Is a Mountain."

"Mountain Jam" closed a six-show run at Bill Graham's Fillmore East. Four of the March 1971 shows served as sessions for the band's third album, *At Fillmore East*, the success of which validated Duane's pursuit of musical excellence on his own terms in a music business that prioritized conformity and record sales over individuality and live performance.

The album appeared just two years after Duane turned his back on a successful career as a studio guitarist to develop and nurture a band that did not chase pop hits but instead focused on musical virtuosity and improvisation, qualities he best presented live. Duane forged an uncompromising musical path as the ABB's front man despite neither singing nor writing songs. And Duane, a white man, made this journey in an integrated band from the South, a group of fellow southerners whose sound melded strains of southern music in ways that reflected their collective vision of what music could and should be.

Improvisation, virtuosity, and live, organic, communal, experience are what Duane Allman valued most in music. It took him time to sift out these values, put them into action with the Allman Brothers

Band, and capture the dynamic on record. And despite critical acclaim, the group remained firmly a part of the American rock underground for most of Duane's lifetime. Success eluded them until the July 1971 release of *At Fillmore East*.

Within two months the record reached number 13. By October 1971, it hit Gold, for 500,000 units sold. The album spent forty-eight weeks on the charts and has remained in the rock canon ever since its release, with historians, musicians, fans, and critics all considering *At Fillmore East* one of rock's best albums and among the best live albums ever recorded. In 2004 the Library of Congress added it to its National Recording Registry. *Rolling Stone* magazine's 2003 and 2012 lists of "500 Greatest Albums" ranked *At Fillmore East* number 49 and number 105, respectively, in its 2020 list.[1] How this happened, why it happened, and why it is important are the central themes of this book.

At Fillmore East is the most significant recorded work by a band regarded as one of the most important bands of its era. The Allman Brothers Band represents the fulfillment of Duane Allman's musical vision: a brotherhood of virtuosos playing improvisational, often extended songs and jams in front of audiences. *Fillmore*'s original compositions and covers offer the ABB's distinct blend of southern music: driving psychedelic blues-rock, played with the improvisational freedom of jazz.

The record is Duane's masterpiece not only as a guitar player but also as band leader. Duane chose bandmates who pushed musical boundaries and drew inspiration from the guitar-based, freeform attacks of British blues groups, most notably Cream. To this mix he added an important new element: dual lead guitars. In Dickey Betts, Duane brought in a player he and everyone else acknowledged as his equal. Bassist Berry Oakley, himself a former lead guitarist, commanded the bass as a third lead instrument, gave the band three guitar soloists. Two drummers, a rare combination in rock, provided a foundation that simultaneously grounded the band rhythmically as it propelled the music forward with an unusually powerful sound.[2]

Although he was its star, Duane built the Allman Brothers Band as a band of musical equals. On *At Fillmore East*, Duane's bandmates play precise, intentional improvisations unconstrained by form or format. Throughout the record's seventy-eight minutes, each musician plays with a confidence that belies the tightrope he walked. They were collectively composing complex music in the moment while recording live in front of an enthusiastic audience they held in thrall. They played what they felt, they depended on each other to hear their cues; each responded accordingly.

Though *At Fillmore East* captured this dynamic and propelled the band to massive success, Duane did not live to see its triumph. He died in a motorcycle accident on October 29, 1971, just four days after the record hit gold. His bandmates responded with *Eat a Peach*, a double album of studio and live tracks that was the last to feature Duane. Together, *At Fillmore East* and *Eat a Peach* represent the apogee of Duane's vision. The former demonstrates the fullest expression of Duane as an artist, the latter new directions his band was exploring.

Duane's career demonstrates his exceptionality as a musician and bandleader, but his success happened also because of his sheer determination to play music when, where, and most importantly, *how* he wanted to. By the time he was twenty-two he had already auditioned and failed in three of America's music hubs: New York, Nashville, and Los Angeles. Though he garnered some interest, Duane's sound was still too indistinct, and the music industry saw little market potential in his ideas to expand it. All of that changed when he founded the Allman Brothers Band in March 1969. Two years later, the band's sound matured into *At Fillmore East*.

The album presented a different approach to what the music industry had forced Duane to follow in New York, Nashville, and Los Angeles. His bandmates expressed themselves freely, improvising in conversation for and with an audience. Record buyers loved it, and *At Fillmore East* was a remarkable commercial breakthrough for a band without a hit single, much less an integrated band of southerners with a predilection for jamming.

The record's success is the pinnacle of Duane Allman's musical journey but marks only the beginning of his enduring influence. *At Fillmore East* also birthed an explosion in southern music, with Duane's surviving bandmates at the forefront of the "Southern rock" genre.

At this point, I need to offer a quick note of important clarification. In simplest terms, the Allman Brothers Band were the embodiment of "southern rock"—a rock band from the South. Yet the ABB were a part of the "Southern rock" genre that emerged in the wake of the success of *At Fillmore East*. For the purposes of this book, where I use "southern rock" (lowercase "s"), think "rock band from the South." Where I capitalize "Southern rock," I am referring to the record-industry term that came of age with the Allman Brothers Band's 1973 album *Brothers and Sisters* and the emergence of the proto-Southern rock band Lynyrd Skynyrd. Southern rock soon exploded in popularity, forever tethering the ABB to the genre.

Southern rock was part of an effort to market and codify the mostly white rock bands from the American South who emerged in the wake of the ABB's breakthrough: Lynyrd Skynyrd; the Charlie Daniels Band; Capricorn label mates the Marshall Tucker Band, Wet Willie, and Grinderswitch; and countless others. All cite Duane and the Allman Brothers Band for their pathbreaking roles in creating opportunities for southern musicians of their era.

Defining "Southern rock" is difficult in part because the influences that converged into rock 'n' roll in the mid-1950s were all southern to begin with. Subsequent generations of southerners, Black and white, adopted, adapted, and expanded these forms. Far from the first southerners to play rock, the Allman Brothers were just the first southern *band* to do so successfully from the South in the rock era. Their success opened the floodgates of opportunity for southern musicians of the rock idiom.

"Southern rock" as a musical genre rather than descriptive term emerged around 1973. Prior to the invention of the term, the Allman Brothers Band were simply a rock band from the South. That they were also among the first to be marketed as "Southern rock" complicates matters. The band members themselves disliked the term, yet it became part of their legacy.

By the 1980s, Southern rock evolved in American culture to represent something beyond describing white southerners playing rock music. For example, in his 1976 review of *Gimme Back My Bullets*, critic (and unabashed Allman Brothers fan) Lester Bangs called Lynyrd Skynyrd "crude thunderstomper hillbillies whose market value rested primarily on the fact that they could play their instruments about like they could plant their fists in your teeth." Journalist W. J. Cash identified a similar archetype in 1941, the southern "hell-of-a-fellow," a man whose life's goal was "to stand on his head in a bar, to toss down a pint of raw whiskey in a gulp, to fiddle and dance all night, to bite off the nose or gouge out the eye of a favorite enemy, to fight harder and love harder than the next man, to be known far and wide as a hell-of-a-fellow." Southern rock brought this southern stereotype into the mainstream.[3]

More troubling, by the 1970s, the years immediately following the passage of the 1964 Civil Rights and 1965 Voting Rights Acts, many Southern rock bands began to use Confederate flags in their stage backdrops and marketing. Some, including the ABB, prominently displayed on stage the "rebel" flag that legislators incorporated into the Georgia state flag in 1956 in protest of the modern civil rights movement.

Southern rock bands seemed to pay little attention to the reality that flying the rebel flag redeemed the racism in their midst. Fifty years later, the condemnation of such imagery is near universal in the music community. But even in the 1970s, the prominent display of the rebel flag led critics and fans to dismiss the South and Southern rock as preternaturally backwards, behind the times, and racist.

And displaying the rebel flag was exactly those things. Southern rock's embrace of Confederate imagery signaled public acceptance of segregationist ideals. But band members, almost all educated in southern schools, considered their flag waving as an expression of regional pride and defiance. Some southern schools taught that the Confederate cause was just and that its flag signified rebellion in the spirit of the American Revolution rather than an act of treason against the United States to create a southern slave nation. The acceptance of the flag was a success of the Lost Cause narrative that framed the Civil War as a valiant defense of southern virtue against overwhelming odds. To those critics and fans who condemned the public embrace of Confederate imagery in the 1970s, we can only say amen.[4]

Racially integrated from their founding, the Allman Brothers Band publicly pushed back against affiliation with the rhetoric and symbols of the Lost Cause. Betts explained,

We had nothing to do with that whole ideal, "the South will rise again." We did appreciate our culture, and a lot of people in the South were proud of the Allman Brothers, because we were typically and obviously Southern. That was part of our aura. But beyond that, I don't think we were part of what was changing the South. It was people like Jimmy Carter and Martin Luther King Jr. and John F. Kennedy who helped affect Southern attitudes. We were just a good thing for some people to identify with, and obviously, we influenced the music from the South a great deal. A lot of musicians thought, "Hey, they're speaking for or representing the way I feel"—and that was a cool thing.[5]

"Southern rock" was also inaccurate, drummer Jai Johanny "Jaimoe" Johanson remarked: "We didn't invent something that was already there. I'm proud of our achievements, but, shit, southern rock was going on fifty years before we came along." Gregg called the term redundant. "All rock 'n' roll came from the South, it is southern by definition," he said. "You might as well call it Rock rock."[6]

Despite how individual band members felt about the term, the band as a business entity embraced Southern rock. People lump the Allman Brothers together with the Southern rock stereotype because they promoted themselves that way. The Great Southern Company handled the band's merchandise. The rebel flag was part of the band's "Campaign '74" promotional campaign, which featured an image of Robert E. Lee on horseback. Promoters used the rebel flag on Allman Brothers posters and advertisements throughout the 1980s and even into the early 1990s.

Toward the end of his life Gregg Allman shared what many white southerners of his era have also since come to understand about the flag's sinister meaning. "My best friend in the world, Chank Middleton, is a black man. If people are gonna look at that flag and think [slavery was a positive], then I say burn every one of them."[7]

I found no reference to the Allman Brothers Band as "southern rock" in Duane Allman's lifetime. The first use I found of the term was from musician and writer Robert Palmer, in a 1969 article, to describe southern musicians, not their music. That same year the British critic Nik Cohn called rock 'n' roll pioneers Little Richard, Elvis, Buddy Holly, and Fats Domino "southern rockers [who played] a mixup of Black and white music. . . . Southern rock is hard rock." The only other mention I found before 1973 was in a 1971 review of *At Fillmore East* in which Al Rudis identifies the band as "a funky bunch of southern blues rockers." And while many accounts from the band's earliest days reference the group's southern roots, they describe the music as "heavy," "experimental," and/or "progressive" blues rock, never "southern." Southern, it seems, was a given.[8]

I agree with writer Scott B. Bomar that the Southern rock genre is music "rooted in a specific time, belonged to a particular place, created by musicians with similar formative and cultural experiences, [that] served as a key expression of a uniquely countercultural movement of the South."[9] Following Bomar's template, Southern rock began in 1973 and lasted through the early 1980s, when a new southern rock sound, more punk- than country-influenced, emerged in Athens, Georgia, with R.E.M., Pylon, and the B-52s.

The South is important not just because it influenced the music. This was true of all popular music of the era. Southern rock is instead the sound of southern musicians making music at home. Choosing to stay in the South, Rankin Sherling argues, represented "a defiance . . . in the face of overwhelming disdain from the rest of the nation for the South and its culture."[10]

These frameworks—music rooted in place and a sense of defiance—make the Allman Brothers Band a prototypical southern rock band, that is, a rock band from the South. But because they formed four years before the Southern rock genre exploded, they are not its exemplars. That crown belongs to Lynyrd Skynyrd. The Allman Brothers Band was a different animal altogether, blazing trails that generations of southern musicians of all genres followed. This sets Duane and the Allman Brothers Band apart from southern bands of the rock era as musicians from the South before the 1973 marketing term "Southern rock" was used.

Before any of this happened, however, Duane had to gain the attention of the music industry. He first made his name as a session guitarist for Rick Hall's FAME (Florence Alabama Music Enterprises) Studios in Muscle Shoals, Alabama. Following a star turn on a Wilson Pickett session, Duane's contract landed with a partnership of two men: Jerry Wexler of Atlantic Records and Phil Walden, former manager of Otis Redding. Their belief in Duane's vision led the men to found Capricorn Records, a subsidiary of Atlantic Records.

Over the course of several months in early 1969, a band of players coalesced around Duane in Jacksonville in northeastern Florida. The group included African American drummer Jai Johanny "Jaimoe"

Johanson and five white musicians: bassist Berry Oakley and guitarist Forrest Richard "Dickey" Betts of Jacksonville's Second Coming and drummer Claude "Butch" Trucks, an old friend from the Sunshine State circuit. On March 26, 1969, brother Gregg (on organ and vocals) joined the other five at 2844 Riverside Avenue in Jacksonville. The jam birthed the Allman Brothers Band.

Each member of the new band was a road-hardened professional musician. Duane and Gregg had been touring musicians in a variety of bands since 1965. Jaimoe, Duane's first recruit, was a jazz man at heart who had carved out a career in the touring bands of rhythm and blues stars Percy Sledge, Arthur Conley, and Otis Redding. Bassist Oakley, a Chicago native, first took to the road in the band of pop star Tommy Roe before relocating to Sarasota, Florida, and founding the Second Coming with guitarist Dickey Betts. Betts had regularly crossed paths with the Allmans at roadhouses and nightclubs throughout Florida. Drummer Butch Trucks, too, knew the Allmans from their home state, where his bands, most notably the 31st of February, enjoyed a modicum of regional success, including a short stint in tandem with Duane and Gregg.

Duane and his mates joined a long lineage of southern musicians who changed musical history by incorporating diverse sounds and influences to create distinct musical forms. Duane is both benefactor and heir to the cultural inheritance of southern music, which, like the music of the Allman Brothers Band, kept one foot firmly rooted in the past and the other in the present. The ABB sound typifies what historians Bill C. Malone and David Stricklin describe as core to southern musical tradition, music as "a means of release and a form of self-expression that required neither power, status, nor affluence . . . a body of songs, dances, instrumental pieces, and musical styles—joyous, somber, and tragic—that simultaneously entertained, enriched, and enshrined the musicians and the folk culture out of which they emerged."[11] The Allman Brothers Band played contemporary American music that built on southern musical traditions and trends in improvisation-heavy attack favored the ultimate American musical melting pot: jazz.

When he formed the Allman Brothers, Duane had already earned renown as a guitar hero in the mold of British guitarists Eric Clapton and Jeff Beck and Americans Jimi Hendrix and Mike Bloomfield.

The comparison is somewhat apt in that all gained their renown as groundbreaking electric blues guitarists. Duane stands out in two ways: in making his name in the confines of a stable group of equals rather than being billed as the show's star and in the complexity of his vision. Duane's music transcended electric blues. It was jazz-fueled and psychedelic, with improvised solos that extended well beyond the constraints of AM radio. Somehow Duane found a way to make this work.[12]

Duane was more than a guitar hero; his impact is equally great as a bandleader. His significance reflects southern forebears like Jimmie Rodgers, Robert Johnson, Louis Armstrong, the Carter Family, Bob Wills, and even Elvis Presley. They were musicians who incorporated a variety of sounds and played wide-ranging repertoires that included not only their home styles of music but also elements of mountain music, minstrel, blues, Tin Pan Alley standards, gospel, jazz, ragtime, and pop—exactly what Cohn called "southern rock" in 1969. Allman did likewise in the Allman Brothers Band; his life's work reflected his ancestors not only as a native of the South but in the wide range of styles his band played.[13]

This book is not a biography of Duane Allman nor of the Allman Brothers Band. It is the story of how *At Fillmore East* fulfilled Duane Allman's musical ideal. Duane's journey from one-nighters on the southern touring circuit to the pinnacle of success contained its share of failure. He learned vital lessons that informed his approach with the Allman Brothers Band. Setbacks honed in Duane a decision to put his vision first, to the near exclusion of a successful career by traditional means.

This choice was counterintuitive. He abandoned a promising career as a Muscle Shoals session guitarist to form a new band of relative unknowns. Duane enjoyed the attention and the money sessions brought, but he missed the excitement of playing live with a killer band, and he was determined to put one together. The band would operate without a designated front man or a declared leader, though everybody knew he played the role. They would share "that goal, that attitude," he said, a fierce, uncompromising approach to music.[14]

In this book I focus on the music and musical roots of Duane Allman and how they revealed themselves on *At Fillmore East*. I won't address in more than a cursory fashion the familiar tropes of sex and drugs in rock music. There is plenty of material available discussing those issues as they relate to Duane and the band, and this well-trod ground only interests me as it affected the music, and it did. I also avoid detailing the money-related troubles the band had with Phil Walden in the years after Duane's death. This is not because I find the story immaterial. Indeed, it is significant and indicative of a changing music industry, when rock music became a more complex, lucrative business. I avoid it here for two reasons. The first is because the relation between Walden and the band was relatively stable in Duane's lifetime. Second is that others have covered the story pretty thoroughly, and I simply don't have much to add to it. My focus instead is on Duane Allman, his music, and how *At Fillmore East* represents his artistic vision.[15]

A Note on Terminology and Sources

When I refer to the South, I am referring primarily to the states of the former Confederacy, though southern culture extends well beyond those geographic boundaries. In this book, southerners are those born in the region or transplants who adopted southern culture as their own. Thus, though he was born in Chicago, Berry Oakley is a southerner because he made the South his permanent home and identified as such, moving South, he said, "as soon as I had enough sense."[16]

The book covers the original era of the Allman Brothers Band, which I date from Gregg's arrival in Jacksonville on March 26, 1969, to Berry Oakley's death on November 11, 1972, and Linda Oakley's eviction from the Big House in Macon the following January. My focus is on Duane Allman and the band he created, so I will avoid discussion of the band's career after Oakley's death except as those discussions add context to the original era of the band.

Names and terminology prove somewhat difficult at times, and I've done my best to formalize nomenclature. Though Jaimoe used several monikers over the years, liner notes of this era list him as Jai Johanny Johanson. For the most part, I call him Jaimoe or Johanson. It's the same person. In addition, for consistency's sake, I have corrected the spelling of guitarist Dickey Betts's first name in each case I encountered it. In the band's early days, writers used "Dicky," "Dickie," and "Dick," and he later went by Richard Betts when touring and recording. I have done likewise with the spelling of Gregg Allman's and Berry Oakley's first names and various other inconsistencies. My renditions of other names include these:

It's Hour Glass, not *the* Hour Glass.

I know the official name of the venue on 1820 Tchoupitoulas Street in New Orleans is *A* not, *The* Warehouse, but I'm using the latter because that's how everyone else referred to it, and it just flows better.

The official album title is *At Fillmore East*, not *Live at Fillmore East*. I use *Fillmore* and *Fillmore East* for variety from time to time.

To build this narrative, I primarily consulted three band histories: Tom Nolan's *The Allman Brothers Band: A Biography in Words and Pictures* (1976), Scott Freeman's *Midnight Riders: The Story of the Allman Brothers Band* (1995), and Alan Paul's *One Way Out: The Inside History of the Allman Brothers Band* (2014). Nolan's book is the earliest full history of the band. His work consists of interviews conducted at the peak of the band's fame; the book is a remarkably candid early look at the band's history. Journalist Freeman based much of *Midnight Riders* on interviews he conducted with band members at the nadir of the ABB's popularity, in the early 1980s after their second acrimonious breakup. With the band's reputation in tatters, the book carries with it an uncertainty about the band's legacy. Unlike Freeman, whose book highlights a band whose legacy was still in flux, Paul's work covers the breadth of the group's forty-five-year career. That the band played its final note in the wee hours of October 29, 2014, was fitting. It was the forty-third anniversary of Duane's death.

There are two biographies about Duane, though I find it hard to affix a "biography" label to the book by his daughter, Galadrielle Allman, *Please Be with Me: A Song for My Father* (2014). Part biography, part memoir, and all heart, it's a wonderful tale about Duane Allman as a human being and as an artist. It also shares a part of the rock 'n' roll story too often ignored: the lives of the wives, girlfriends, and children of rock musicians. Randy Poe's *Skydog: The Duane Allman*

Story (2006) is a more traditional biography, to date the only one of its kind.

An important way this book differs from these others is that I've included the fan voice as much as possible. Personal accounts from the band and the insiders are excellent, and ABB-related memoirs from Gregg Allman, road manager Willie Perkins, Duane and Gregg's Hour Glass bandmates Johnny Sandlin and Paul Hornsby, ABB keyboardist Chuck Leavell (1972–1976), roadies Joseph "Red Dog" Campbell and Kim Payne, and friend Jan Marks have all helped me understand how the principals felt about any number of things. But without an audience to appreciate and support the Allman Brothers Band, *At Fillmore East* would never have broken free, and their voices are important when considering the album.

I have meticulously documented every quote and every source in this book. I did this for a reason: you should expect historians to show their sources. But I also did it because of how helpful it would have been for me when I started this journey. Though I have made slight alterations to quotes to help them read better, I have strived never to change the original intent.

The Chapters

Now, to the book. I approached the task as a story in three acts. Act I (chapters 1 through 6) describes Duane's development as a musician and a bandleader. Duane's career pivots in Act II (chapter 7), with the founding of the band that made Duane's vision come alive. Act III (chapters 8 through 14), traces the phenomenon that was the ABB in the wake of *Fillmore*'s success.

Galadrielle Allman calls her father's life a love affair with music. I examine that romance in chapter 1 as I explore Duane's ethos as a man, a musician, and a bandleader. Duane was dedicated to his craft and hyperfocused on achieving his artistic vision. In the first chapter I describe Duane's artistic commitment to music and how that commitment manifested with the Allman Brothers Band.

Chapter 2 provides an overview of the musical culture Duane emerged from. It highlights two important factors in his development: the influence of southern music and the importance of originality. The South was crucial because it was his home. Its sounds shaped Duane's listening habits and his playing. Originality was important because it was how musicians separated themselves from the pack and made more money playing music. In this chapter I trace the lessons Duane learned about the value and importance of original material and original arrangements.

In summer 1965 Duane and his brother, Gregg, hit the road as the Allman Joys, the subject of chapter 3. Among the many lessons he learned, touring taught Duane that successful bands had two characteristics: they were great live and had hit singles with something new, an original composition or a unique take on someone else's song. Duane succeeded as a live player, honing his talents leading one of the southern roadhouse circuit's hottest bands. He failed miserably, however, at recording hits, the first of several disappointments he would experience.

Chapter 4 covers Duane's third attempt at stardom, his time in Los Angeles with Hour Glass. Under an onerous contract with Liberty Records that gave him no creative control, the label forced him to abandon the bluesy, southern R&B he had mastered for a pop-psyche-delic sound that didn't sell. Worse, Liberty restricted the band's live dates, leaving Duane broke and despondent. The Hour Glass experience proved formative, as it dictated the terms under which Duane pursued record-industry support in the future. He never again ceded control of creative direction.

In chapter 5 I track Duane's 1968 return to the South from Los Angeles, first for a session at FAME Studios with Hour Glass and later for good. The Hour Glass session proved a turning point. It revitalized his spirits, and his playing thrived in the less rigid environment of the southern studio. He soon quit Hour Glass and returned to Florida, where he and Gregg briefly joined with drummer Butch Trucks in the 31st of February. The group was the first musical project to include a member of the Allman Brothers Band not named Allman.

By fall 1968 Duane's career appeared to be failing. He had lost two bands and had abandoned his contract. His move to Muscle Shoals, covered in chapter 6, allowed him to regroup and reconnect as he settled into a brief, well-regarded tenure as an A-list session player. But Duane's spirit proved too restless for studio work. He missed playing live, and he longed for the creativity of a band. In early March 1969 he left northwestern Alabama for Jacksonville to build a band that could play the sounds he had in his mind. He assembled the band within two weeks of his arrival.

In chapter 7 I describe the founding of the Allman Brothers Band. I focus on the careers and musical influences of each band member and highlight how each contributed to the group's overall sound. In particular, I underscore the importance of the first two members of the ensemble, drummer Jai Johanny Johanson and bassist Berry Oakley. Johanson and Oakley inspired Duane to find players who similarly pushed him creatively. After several weeks of jam sessions in Jacksonville, guitarist Dickey Betts and drummer Butch Trucks signed on to Duane's new band. A few days after that, Gregg did too.

Macon, Georgia, home base for manager Phil Walden, is the subject of chapter 8. The band relocated from Jacksonville to Macon in May 1969, and from there the musicians grew into the Allman Brothers Band as players and as people. Far removed from the star-making machinery of the big city, the middle-Georgia town shaped the band in multiple ways. Their families soon joined them, and Macon provided a quiet, comforting backdrop, a home that supported the band's decision to present themselves and their musical values as those of ordinary, everyday people.

Duane's band was foremost a live band, one whose creativity and improvisation thrived in front of audiences, and the group was on the road for nearly three hundred days per year in Duane's lifetime. In chapter 9 I examine the first nine months of that journey as the band coalesced its sound, built a reputation live, and released a debut album. Reviews of *The Allman Brothers Band* reveal there was much to like about the record. Sales told another tale: it failed miserably, a frustrating setback for the band and its management. That the band was unable to capture the same force in the studio as it did playing live remained a frustration for the ABB, its label, and audiences for two more years.

The Allman Brothers Band spent most of 1970 on the road and ended the year determined to record their third album live. I discuss this transition in chapter 10. In December 1969 the band began its association with Bill Graham, whose Fillmore West in San Francisco and Fillmore East in New York City were rock's premier theaters. Graham's support helped the band move from shows at clubs, bars, and even school gymnasiums to theaters and ballrooms. The ABB also released *Idlewild South* in 1970. Like its predecessor, it failed to sell. By the end of the year, Duane hinted at the band's response: its third album would be live from Graham's famed Fillmore East in New York's East Village.

In chapter 11 I look at the decision behind recording and marketing *At Fillmore East* and argue for Phil Walden's importance to the album's ultimate success. Walden founded Capricorn Records in 1969 as a vehicle for Duane's artistic vision and fought repeated attempts by his partner, Jerry Wexler, to move the band from the South. Duane wanted to stay in the South, and Walden supported the decision. With the Fillmore album, Walden's gamble on Duane was to pay off.

The album *At Fillmore East*, Duane Allman's masterpiece, is the subject of chapters 12 and 13. Chapter 12 traces the decision to record and issue a live record in lieu of a third studio record and the March 1971 recording sessions in New York. In chapter 13 I recount Walden's marketing genius in calling the ABB "the People's Band" and releasing the record as a double album for a single-album price. The chapter concludes with the overwhelmingly favorable reaction of critics and fans.

Duane Allman died on October 29, 1971, while the ABB was in the middle of recording its fourth album, *Eat a Peach*. In chapter 14 I discuss the album and how the five-man band regrouped in the wake of Duane's death. The band members channeled their grief the only way they knew how, through music. They finished the album and embarked on a nationwide tour in tribute to their fallen leader and his musical vision. Berry Oakley's death on November 11, 1972, added finality to the story. It was the end of the original era of the Allman Brothers Band and how I end this story.

I conclude with an epilogue in which I consider the role *At Fillmore East* played in creating Duane Allman's legacy. I discuss the Allman Brothers Band's career in the years after Duane Allman's untimely death and its enduring influence, including the triumphant end to the band's career on October 29, 2014, forty-three years to the day of Allman's passing. Though Duane Allman and the Allman Brothers Band were groundbreaking and important before the release of *At Fillmore East*, it is because of this record rock audiences and music fans revere them.

Duane Allman was a singular force in American music and southern culture. Despite his untimely death at age twenty-four, his accomplishments dwarf those of his contemporaries. *At Fillmore East* is how he is best remembered. This book is a story of how that happened.

CHAPTER 1

DUANE'S MUSICAL ETHOS

You gotta strive to play a kind of music that's honest to yourself.
Duane Allman

"My father is killed in the first paragraph of every article ever written about him," Galadrielle Allman wrote in 2014. "His life story is told backwards, always beginning at the end: in the road, his motorcycle down, his body broken. People linger over the wreckage as if it says something meaningful about his life." Focusing on Duane's death, she argues, misses the point altogether. "Duane Allman's story is more than a tragedy. . . . It is a true romance. He fell in love with his guitar and gave his heart away."[1]

Duane's legacy, therefore, isn't the "what if" of his tragically rock 'n' roll death at twenty-four; it is what he accomplished in music. It is larger than just the accomplishments of *At Fillmore East*; it is how he conceived of and built a band that fulfilled the sound he heard in his head. Here's my understanding of the origins and manifestations of Duane's musical philosophy and artistic vision.

Duane's career prior to forming the Allman Brothers Band was that of a talented musician and bandleader whose abilities were a poor fit for a music business focused on hit-making. Duane was not a traditional front man; he neither wrote songs nor sang. He valued live improvisation, not rote recitation, and he sought other musicians who shared that value. By March 1969 he found them: the Allman Brothers Band.

The first son of Geraldine Robbins and D-Day veteran Willis Allman, Duane was born in Nashville on November 20, 1946. Brother Gregg arrived December 8, 1947. Willis's murder in a botched robbery attempt in December 1949 left Geraldine a single mother who never remarried). By fall 1955, she enrolled her sons at Castle Heights Military Academy in Lebanon, Tennessee, while she studied to become a certified public accountant. The family relocated to Daytona Beach, Florida, two years later. Though each brother returned to Castle Heights in separate stints between 1961 and 1964, Daytona Beach remained home base for the rest of their lives. Geraldine lived in the house at 100 Van Avenue in Daytona Beach until her death in 2015.

Duane was forever the leader. Gregg explained, "Duane was only a year older than me, but in his mind it might well have been twenty years. He was a world traveler, even at age five."[2] Music forged the brothers' relationship. Duane joined the Uniques in 1961. Two years later, he and Gregg played a brief stint with the House Rockers, a white band that backed a group of African American singers called the Untils. The integrated combo was the house band at the whites-only Surf Bar on Daytona Beach Pier.

Duane formed his first true band, the Escorts, in 1964. Following Gregg's graduation from Seabreeze High School in 1965, they hit the road as the Allman Joys and within a year had moved to Nashville, writing and recording under John D. Loudermilk's guidance. Their efforts failed to inspire interest, and by 1967 the Allmans joined forces with the Alabama-based band 5 Men-Its and moved to Los Angeles to record as Hour Glass. The resulting two records, *Hour Glass* (1967) and *Power of Love* (1968), failed to chart. Producer Dallas Smith's heavy hand grated on Duane. He abhorred Smith's choice of material and took great offense that the producer ignored him. The experience provided an important lesson in creative control, one he never forgot.

In September 1968, Duane quit Hour Glass. He moved back to Florida and found himself in a thriving scene in Jacksonville that circled around the Second Coming, a band with two virtuosos, bassist Berry Oakley and guitarist Dickey Betts, whose playing and musical values complemented Duane's own.

Simultaneously Duane began garnering a reputation as a session guitarist in Muscle Shoals. By January 1969 he relocated to northwest Alabama to work at Rick Hall's FAME Studio. Drummer Jai Johanny "Jaimoe" Johanson, a veteran of the R&B touring circuit, would soon join him.

In March 1969 Duane and Jaimoe decamped to Jacksonville, where they joined community jam sessions that Oakley organized. From this wider group emerged a core group of players who met at the Second Coming's communal home on March 23, 1969: Duane, Jaimoe, Oakley, Betts, and Butch Trucks. Reese Wynans joined on keyboards, filling in for Gregg, who arrived from Los Angeles three days later. It was the birth of the Allman Brothers Band.

Only twenty-two when he founded the band, Duane seemed destined for stardom. "Duane walked to a different beat," early bandmate Sonny Fussell recalled. Ted Petrucciani, another friend from Daytona Beach, said, "I don't know too many people who had more direction than he did. "He just didn't waste time talking with people about trying to make his decisions. It was already made in his mind. Duane was music, music, music. The focus, the concentration was phenomenal."[3]

Duane left his hometown in 1966 and pushed himself hard with each musical project he pursued. "The qualities he emanated were strong and unique," ABB biographer Tom Nolan observes, "and those who associated with him seem certain Duane would have excelled at whatever task or occupation he approached." Duane, former bandmate Paul Hornsby said, "would never have been ordinary."[4]

Gregg, Duane's first musical partner, carried the weight of his brother's dreams and musical aspirations from an early age. He was a reluctant convert. "He had more faith in us than I ever did," Gregg recalled. "He would push me and push me. He would say, 'No, man! We're better than all of them!' and I would say, 'Fuck you, man! How can you sit here and say that? Every corner you turn, man, someone's gonna wipe your ass playing music.' And he didn't seem to think that way."[5]

Friends from Daytona Beach describe Duane as a wild child with extreme self-confidence bordering on recklessness. "When he first came into town," Jim Shepley said, "nobody really liked the guy. He had a cocky attitude, and he was kind of an aggressive, brazen type." Duane could also be self-destructive. "I always sensed that he was gonna have his problems," Shepley continued. "I just had a bad feeling about the outcome of his life." Van Harrison, bass player for the Escorts, recounted, "I think he was suffering from all these conflicts. Some days he was really high on doing music and then some days he'd get so damn depressed, he would disappear for a while and you wouldn't know where the hell he was." Fellow musician Sylvan Wells recalled, "He was absolutely on a self-destructive path. The only question was how much life before he killed himself."[6]

"Duane would have become a killer if he hadn't found that guitar," his mother said. Duane said so as well: "The guitar saved me from so much grief. . . . I was a hoodlum. . . . Then that old guitar came along and I had something to do. When I get pissed off I just sit down and beat the fire out of some old Jimmy Reed shit instead of going out and drinking and fighting and falling down and going crazy. It would take me all the way, man, and put me on a good note."[7]

Music calmed and focused Duane. "Duane was an absolute driver. He would go after what he wanted with a vengeance," Wells said. His reckless approach to life masked a ferocious drive and determination, a stubbornness that served him well as he steered the career of the Allman Brothers Band. "You couldn't talk Duane out of anything once he made his mind up. He was so intense. When he decided to do something, he did it. He didn't let anyone tell him otherwise, and that is probably the thing I loved most about him."[8]

Duane's output as a working musician was the sum total of his engagement with the era's social and political upheavals. Though his professional career coincided with some of the most tumultuous years in American history, 1965–1971, he shunned contemporary issues. Yet he didn't claim immunity from the forces around him. "I understand the need for a lot of changes in the country," Duane remarked, "[but] I'm a player, and players don't give a damn for nothing but playing and what playing entails." For him, music helped people "see just a little bit better and get a little hipper to what's going on."[9]

A carefree, friendly personality influenced Duane's playing just as his playing reflected that personality. "You can either have yourself a good time or a shitty time," he remarked. "Why not have a good time? Don't surround yourself with things that bring you down, don't dig nothing that brings you down. Just dig yourself for the beautiful thing you are."[10]

Duane was introspective and wise. He sought "to have a good life and be on a good note, [to] be true to yourself and other people around you, true as you can be. You've got to learn to be nice to everybody, and show everybody respect. That's the only way people respect you." Duane was fearlessly authentic. "Don't be afraid to share what's inside of you with other people. That's the only way you're ever going to get free or have any fun at all."[11]

Commercialism irritated the guitarist. He found the very idea of selling music abhorrent. "[Money] squashed out a lot of people that was really good folks" from the world of music. Money also brought obligation. Duane preferred to play for free "because people don't even expect you to be there. And if you're there to play, that's really groovy. . . . About the nicest way you can play is just for nothing. And it's not really for nothing—it's for your own personal satisfaction and other people's, rather than for any kind of financial thing. . . . I quit doing sessions because of that. I was getting to like it too much."[12]

Geraldine said this was her son's approach from the beginning. "I would go hungry to play this guitar," Duane told her. "I knew he was dedicated," she said. "I knew that he had picked his way." He told her, "I never want a hit record. I do not want that wherever I go, I have to play the same song. I want to do whatever I want to do; I want to be free. I don't want fame and fortune. I just want enough money to eat regular, and to pay my bills, that's all I want out of life; and to play my guitar." Because he never sought fame, Geraldine concluded, "that's why he attained it. Duane didn't ever want nothing but to play his guitar and make enough money to keep himself clean and fed. He didn't ask too much out of life."[13]

Duane was generous in spirit, particularly toward other musicians. He had broad likes with one requirement: "Anybody that's playing good, I admire them." He cited the inspiration of jazz and blues masters Miles Davis, Roland Kirk, Muddy Waters, and B. B. King. But he didn't just emulate his heroes, he explained: "Being influenced shouldn't mean sounding like or copying anyone else." He instead made his own sound from their inspiration. As ever, Duane's greatest influence was in-house, his Allman Brothers bandmates. "I don't know how much other musicians have influenced the sound of the band, but probably not very much. I think the guys in the band have influenced each other a lot."[14]

Despite his magnanimity, Duane's ego was widely acknowledged. "He was pretty arrogant sometimes," Cameron Crowe wrote in the early 1970s, "but he had a talent to match." Nolan notes, "Duane had a confidence in his talent and his purpose in life that struck some as blatantly conceited. Others argue that Duane's seeming arrogance was an uncontrived expression of his ability and personality."[15]

Artifice drew attention from the music, and Duane sussed out other musicians not by their chops, but by how they approached their craft. "You can find out real fast who's got respect for music and who don't by just listening," he remarked. "Like who's into it for what reason. People aren't aware that there's different motivations to making different people play. It's important to know what is the driving force behind it and what makes it happen." Fellow white blues guitarist Johnny Winter played "good bottleneck" and was "good all around," but overly reliant on flash. "I prefer his music to his show," Duane said. "I prefer music to any show."[16]

Winter served as a benchmark for Duane's aspirations. They played a similar circuit and collaborated together onstage several times in Duane's lifetime. The Texan came to renown a little more than a year before Duane, and contemporary observers regularly compared the two white, southern, slide-guitar phenoms. Winter was Duane's barometer, and Duane knew he measured up. "Johnny is really good, but I can cut him," he told guitarist Jimmy Johnson while watching Winter perform at Fillmore East in January 1969. "You see that stage down there? Next year by this time, I'm going to be down there." Duane proved prophetic, as the Allman Brothers Band made their Fillmore East debut in December 1969.[17]

Most musicians found Duane exceedingly encouraging and kind. "Duane was a creator and motivator," Daytona Beach bandmate Floyd Miles recalled. "One of those people that would get the best out of you. It was always, 'You can do it, let's work on it and we can do it.'" Another former bandmate, Johnny Sandlin, remarked, "Whenever anyone played with Duane, he would bring out the best in them. Not that it was a competition, but he was an inspiration."[18]

Joe Marshall, a friend from Duane's early touring days, said, "He was the first person I knew, musically, who always found something good to say about fellow musicians. Whenever he and I would hear another musician or group who maybe wasn't so great, he would always find something positive to say, even if it was just, 'Hell, Joey, at least they're trying.'" Duane's largesse extended to the avant-garde blues-rock Hampton Grease Band of Atlanta jam-band stalwart Bruce

Hampton "Duane liked our band. He liked the spirit of it," Hampton said. "Did the big brother act and took us under his wing. Without him I doubt if anybody woulda ever had a music career."[19]

Atlantic Records executive Jerry Wexler, famous for coining the phrase "rhythm and blues" for *Billboard* in 1949, was among Duane's earliest supporters. As writer Jon Landau put it, Wexler instantly recognized the "long-haired wild man as a true son of R&B and Southern music." Wexler called Duane "a complete guitar player, no end to his resource [who played with] originality, taste, sensitivity. Great acoustic, he could play bossa nova, he could play jazz." Duane was, he concluded, "a great session man, and a great 'feel' man."[20]

Music promoter Bill Graham heard in Duane's guitar a deep connection to African American music. Duane's playing didn't mimic Black influences. Graham heard in it "the essence of what the Black musician gave us. The soulful aspect, [which all] the technical prowess in the world doesn't give you." Wexler described it more succinctly: Duane played "no-bullshit blues phrased like the authentic black guitarists."[21]

Electric slide guitar is what even the most casual of music fans associate with Duane Allman. While slide guitar was a relatively novel concept when Duane popularized it in rock music, country and blues musicians had long used metal, glass, or a knife along a guitar's strings to mimic the human voice or a harmonica. Slide became Duane's calling card, and he was among a very small number of guitarists of his era who played it on electric guitar, which offered wider tonal possibilities than on acoustic instruments.

Though Duane didn't introduce the technique to rock music, he was among its earliest proponents, and he used slide to great effect throughout his career. "On slide he had *the* touch," Wexler remarked, "one of the very, very few who played clean, sweet, and to the note." His playing was different because he looked beyond guitar for inspiration as well. Bluesman Elmore James was certainly an influence, Dickey Betts remembered, but "Duane played slide guitar more like a harmonica than he did a guitar."[22]

Duane picked up slide while in Los Angeles with Hour Glass. Stories conflict about his first exposure to the technique. Some cite Jeff Beck's "Beck's Bolero," a 1966 recording that appeared on *Truth* in 1968. The most common understanding is Jesse Ed Davis on Taj Mahal's cover of Blind Willie McTell's "Statesboro Blues." Hornsby remembered that Duane picked up the slide after seeing Taj Mahal live, while Gregg said Duane's inspiration came from the Taj Mahal's self-titled debut album. "I took him a bottle of pills for a cold he had, plus a copy of the first Taj Mahal album with Jesse Ed Davis playing slide," Gregg recalled. "About three hours later he called me and said, 'Baby brother, get over here.' And he'd dumped all the pills out of the bottle, washed the label off, and was playing bottleneck." The slide, Gregg said, "put a new charge in him."[23]

At the expense of those around him, Duane mastered the technique. "He drove us crazy," Hornsby recalled. "There's nothing in the world worse than hearing somebody learn how to play the slide guitar, unless it's hearing somebody learn how to play the fiddle." Duane said, "Everybody was looking at me and thinking, 'Oh no! He's getting ready to do it again!'" Eventually, he said, "I got a little better at it." It was an understatement.[24]

Duane valued making music with others and eschewed talk of competition. He said, "I'm with the other guitarists, not against them. I know there's always gonna be somebody better anyway, so why fight that?" Graham recalled, "Duane had the technical proficiency, but never sold it. There was no, 'Can you top this?' He never tried to beat you." Tommy Talton of Cowboy said Duane "always wanted to play with you. He had flames coming out of every note he played; but he didn't throw it at you. He just did what was necessary at the time."[25]

The restraint is notable. Yes, Duane was an amazing guitar player. But his virtuosity extended beyond mere technique; he regularly demonstrated an uncanny ability to know when and how to unleash. This is particularly evident in his studio playing at FAME beginning in late 1968 and continuing through March 1969, when he formed the Allman Brothers Band.

Recording studios are often awkward environments, particularly for musicians who thrive on improvisation. The precision and time constraints of the studio often hamper and stunt in-the-moment creativity. Such was not the case with Duane. "Duane would do things that were not extremely difficult," Sandlin recalled, "but were so appropriate, so fitting, and so tasteful. Somebody with all that power, all that ability and technique, and he could sit there and play a simple rhythm part. . . . He was into the total concept of the song." Phil Walden said Duane "just had impeccable taste. He only played what needed to be played." Duane was a "consummate musician," the writer and musician Tony Glover observed, "totally dedicated to music and playing it right. He had a real passion for it and intensity." Jaimoe summed it up well: "Duane just loved to play. He was not the type of cat who would try to intimidate someone or whatever—he just played."[26]

On the cusp of stardom as a solo artist, Duane pulled together a group of musicians. His new ensemble was a *band*, foremost. Duane would not dominate the group. "They never ceased to be a band, or became a vehicle for Duane Allman," critic Jon Landau remarked. They were, Landau argued, "a pure music band that would work hard, work honestly, but would not compromise for anyone, no matter what the cost." They were "a band he could play with, not over or against, or through: a group of partners."[27]

In founding the Allman Brothers Band, Duane carved a niche that allowed pursuit of his musical vision, one based on his band members' abilities and an original take on their combined musical roots. The arrangement, he remarked, was egalitarian, a band of "allies working together, sharing a mutual love."[28]

In his bandmates Duane found musicians whose musical ideas, values, and abilities reflected his own. The original musical vision was Duane's, but his personality was such that he allowed each musician wide berth in how he incorporated his own vision into musical mélange. Though he rarely had to assert his leadership, and band dynamics from 1969 to 1971 were remarkably calm, he was the ABB's undisputed leader. "Duane was the Douglas MacArthur of that band," said Bruce Hampton. "It was his band and he let you know that you were in his band." ABB roadie Joseph "Red Dog" Campbell noted, "There was no question that it was his band, even with Dickey, who was a pretty strong character in his own right."[29]

Like most musicians of his era, Duane indulged in his share of the drugs and alcohol that were prevalent, acknowledged, and accepted in the world of music. He had been sniffing glue and drinking since his days in Daytona Beach, and he soon graduated to pills and marijuana.

As he got older, psychedelics came into the mix, drugs such as LSD and psilocybin that Dickey remembered as an important bonding element in the ABB's earliest days. "Those drugs opened up one's life and enlarged your life experience," Betts said, contrasting them with alcohol, cocaine, and heroin, which he called "hiding away, escape-type drugs" that sapped the band's creativity and energy.[30]

Marijuana and psychedelics expanded the band's creativity, and alcohol blurred it. "Booze affected the band a lot more than anything else we did," harmonica player and unofficial band member Thom Doucette said. Jaimoe recalled, "When Duane wasn't clear-headed to me, it certainly wasn't from doing heavy drugs. Duane did not need to drink alcohol. He would become a different person. Duane could be so fucking nasty you wouldn't want to admit you knew him."[31]

Gregg said Duane "lived hard, fast, and on the edge . . . [and] you could tell he had a little taste for speed." He liked heroin, Gregg wrote, "but blow [cocaine] was much more his thing, and he did a lot of it." Writer Joel Selvin reported a day Duane began with cocaine after a December 1970 show. "I met Duane at his hotel room, waited in the hallway an hour," Selvin wrote. "I was ushered in to a naked Duane, just getting out of bed at four in the afternoon. Comes out with a pile of cocaine, snorts it up, repeats. Puts away bottle and brush, pounds chest, and says, 'Ah, I feel like a white boy again!'" The drug was the last step in the day's preparations.[32]

In October 1970 Duane overdosed on barbiturates and opium. He survived, though he missed a few shows as he recovered. A year after Duane's overdose, *Rolling Stone* reporter Grover Lewis trailed the band for a November 1971 profile. Lewis wrote of a band too drugged to care: "'Coulda been a dynamite gig, too, man,' Berry Oakley said after one show. 'It wasn't,' Duane snapped. 'Maybe it was the audience, but then again . . . it coulda just been too much fuckin' coke.'"[33] Lewis's article blasted the band as zonked-out rednecks, a somewhat mean-spirited depiction that *Rolling Stone* published in the same issue that announced Duane's death. It was a slight the band never forgave.

Around the same time, Wexler lectured Duane and Gregg about their heroin use. "Do you have any fucking idea what you're messing with?" he asked. "It killed Charlie Parker, it killed Billie Holiday, and it will kill you too. No one survives the fucking shit." ABB producer

Tom Dowd admonished the brothers as well: "You're throwing your fucking life out the window. Worst of all you're fucking up your music, and you're wasting my goddamn time. If you don't fucking listen and stop now, you're not going to be able to." The warnings came far too late. The brothers were deep in the grip of heroin addiction.[34]

Heroin's impact on Duane's playing became evident during his final West Coast run with the Allman Brothers in October 1971, the tour Lewis documented for *Rolling Stone*. "I saw Duane declining," John Carter of Atlantic Records said. "Dickey Betts seemed to be taking over the band musically." Such was Dickey's talent that the passing of the baton was indiscernible for most listeners. But the band noticed, as did Duane. Things finally came to a head when Duane confronted Butch after a show. "I'm pissed off!" he said to Butch. "When Dickey gets up to play, the rhythm section is pumping away and when I get up there you're laying back and not pushing at all." The drummer yelled back, "You're so fucked up on that smack that you're not giving us anything!" As Butch recalled, Duane "looked me in the eye and walked out the door. I think he knew I was telling him the truth. He needed someone to tell him what he already knew." Duane decamped to a rehab in upstate New York shortly after the tour concluded. While he successfully kicked heroin, he did not stop using drugs. He returned from New York with a vial of pharmaceutical-grade cocaine.[35]

While drugs and alcohol seemed to have a mostly deleterious effect on Duane, Jaimoe found that Duane's heroin use slowed the guitarist down considerably. "Duane moved five times faster than normal anyhow, heroin might have normalized him a little bit," the drummer said. But ultimately, Jaimoe knew that drugs hampered the music. "I think about how great a band this was, how great the sound was and it makes me think how great it could've been if we hadn't slowed ourselves down with all that shit." Gregg said if Duane had not been killed in the motorcycle accident, their addictions "would have torn us apart."[36]

Duane thrived in a variety of musical settings throughout his life. While he left full-time session work to found the ABB in March 1969, he remained an in-demand session player. He saw work outside of the Allman Brothers as another way to express himself artistically while also helping others fulfill their own aspirations. "I like to work in other people's context, help them highlight their own work," he remarked. "But I prefer to be included in the sessions as part of the band" rather just adding to tracks as a session man.[37]

After the formation of the Allman Brothers Band, Duane nurtured prominent partnerships with two musicians, Delaney Bramlett and Eric Clapton. Both relationships came by virtue of his association with Atlantic Records.

Wexler introduced Duane to Bramlett, a Mississippi native who fronted, along with his wife Bonnie, the soul-rock band Delaney & Bonnie & Friends. Based in Los Angeles, Delaney sought a slide guitarist for his band's 1970 album *To Delaney from Bonnie*; Wexler suggested Duane. From their instant and intense musical bond sprang a fruitful, short-lived partnership between the two southerners.[38]

Duane appeared regularly on record and onstage with Delaney & Bonnie. "Delaney Bramlett is a partner of mine," Duane said, "and I go play with him and his band whenever I can." Bramlett said, "We got to be best friends, and if you saw one of us you saw the other." Saxophonist King Curtis rounded out the trio of southern musical legends. Delaney said, "Me and Duane and Curtis, we hung together and we made some real good music."[39]

Listeners appreciated the alliance. "Guitarist Duane Allman, moving with agility, skill, and taste from bottleneck to feedback was probably the Friend who fitted best into the D&B format," Ian Dove observed in his review of an October 1970 Delaney & Bonnie show. "He moved easily into and out of the blues, gospel, country, rock, and revivalist strains that they [Delaney & Bonnie] mix and merge, and then tie together into a working entity."[40]

In May 1970 Duane played on Delaney & Bonnie's *Motel Shot*, an album featuring a formidable assemblage of southerners and southern-influenced musicians, including Leon Russell, Gram Parsons, Joe Cocker, and Dave Mason. The album was an acoustic affair, the title a reference to a term familiar to road-weary musicians: the "motel shot" of laid-back music at the end of the night. "Sometimes it happens in somebody's game room, sometimes in a backstage dressing room, sometimes on a tour bus," the liner notes say, "but the 'motel shot,' wherever it is played, is always characterized by the nonelectric, no strain, no pain, soft easy sound that Delaney & Bonnie—and their talented friends—bring you in this record."

Recorded in May 1970 but not released until the following year, *Motel Shot* includes traditional spirituals such as "Rock of Ages" and "Talkin' about Jesus"; a song whose melody the Allman Brothers often riffed on in "Mountain Jam," the Carter Family's "Will the Circle Be Unbroken"; "Goin' Down the Road Feelin' Bad," first made famous by Woody Guthrie; Robert Johnson's "Come on in My Kitchen"; and several Delaney Bramlett originals, including "Never Ending Song of Love," which peaked at number 13 on the *Billboard* chart.

Following the *Motel Shot* sessions, Delaney & Bonnie bassist Carl Radle and organist and vocalist Bobby Whitlock left the Bramletts to join forces with Eric Clapton in Derek and the Dominos. By late August 1970, Duane had joined Clapton's band in the studio as well.

Clapton first met Radle and Whitlock when Delaney & Bonnie opened for Blind Faith, the short-lived supergroup he formed in 1968. Already uncomfortable with the level of fame he had achieved in Cream, which disbanded in August 1968, Clapton found Blind Faith similarly dissatisfying. The guitarist reveled in Delaney & Bonnie's musical mélange and approach; he often joined them for their opening sets. "Their approach to music was so infectious," Clapton wrote. "They would pull out their guitars on the bus and play songs all day as they traveled. . . . I took to traveling with them and playing with them. I was irresistibly drawn to it." He recruited Whitlock, Radle, and drummer Jim Gordon from Delaney & Bonnie for his new project.[41]

Duane Allman's involvement with Derek and the Dominos and the role he played on its epic *Layla and Other Assorted Love Songs* is a story often told. By all accounts, Duane's playing and infectious personality brought a renewed vigor to the project and to Clapton in particular. Whether or not Duane was a full-fledged member of Clapton's band during the sessions is immaterial; he was offered a permanent role shortly afterward and declined. *Layla* remains among rock's most famous one-off collaborations.[42]

"I was mesmerized by him," Clapton wrote. "Duane and I became inseparable and between the two of us we injected the substance into the *Layla* sessions that had been missing up to that point." Tom Dowd, who produced the sessions, recounted the guitarists' intense mutual attraction. "They were switching guitars, fingerings, it was like a marriage made in heaven," Dowd said. Keyboardist Bobby Whitlock said, "They had the same authority, and they dug from the same well,

Robert Johnson, Elmore James, Sonny Boy Williamson, Bill Broonzy. Something deeper was happening right away with Eric and Duane, who were like two long-lost brothers. Those two guys started bouncing back-and-forth on each other and it was an amazing experience."[43]

"We fell in love. And that was it. The album took off from there," Clapton said. "Because of Duane's input, it became a double album. Because of the interest in playing between his style and my style, we could actually have played any blues or any standard and it would have taken off." Robert Johnson, Clapton recollected, "Was where we connected. We didn't really talk about the modern players much at all. It was really the roots that we were meeting on."[44]

When the ten-day *Layla* sessions concluded, Dowd called it "the best damn record we've [Atlantic] made since *The Genius of Ray Charles*." Yet *Layla* was far from an instant classic. "For a year, it didn't sell," Dowd noted. "I was embarrassed. I thought this was insane—we'd spent that much money and I'd had such a good time doing it, and the guys were playing so incredibly well—it's pitiful that with all that love and energy and everything that went into creating it, it wasn't getting the recognition it deserved."[45]

Layla finally broke through in 1972 when the title track appeared on two compilations: Clapton's *The History of Eric Clapton* and Duane Allman's posthumous *Duane Allman: An Anthology*. As the albums gained attention, Atlantic rereleased "Layla" as a single. It reached the top 10 in both the United States and Britain and has since remained among the most popular tracks of the rock era.

Layla gave Duane the opportunity to play with one of his heroes, Eric Clapton, and he shone brightly in the moment. "That's my lick," Duane told Sandlin of the opening notes of the title track that he'd culled from Albert King's "As the Years Go Passing By." "I can play with the big boys now!" he remarked to musician John Wyker. "There was no denying that Duane and Clapton had really cooked up something special and Duane was like a proud papa," Wyker recalled. "Nobody could blame him at all for all the chest beating he was doing after a session like that. He had arrived and he knew it! We all knew it."[46]

Clapton asked Allman to join the Dominos, an offer Duane seriously considered. The opportunity was enticing, and he was genuinely torn. "I really don't know what to do," he wrote his wife, Donna Allman. The money he stood to make dwarfed what he was earning in the ABB. "It would mean about $5,000 a week to us, as well as a home in England and a lot of things we'd like to have. . . . I'm really up in the air right now." Butch urged Duane to stick with the Allman Brothers: "Duane, look, what we've got going—and it's yours. Are you ready to give this up to join someone else's thing?"[47]

Before he made his final decision, Duane appeared twice live with the Dominos. "I was thinking about trying to make the whole tour. But it was ten weeks long and I had my own fish to fry," he said. Duane "figured out what I already knew," Jaimoe said. "Shit, Eric Clapton should be opening for us. That was the kind of attitude we all had. I just simply thought Duane had more going playing with us than with Eric."[48]

Duane had put together the ABB exactly how he wanted it, Jaimoe said, "and playing those dates with Eric helped him realize that." Clapton called Duane "the musical brother I've never had but wished I did; more so than Jimi [Hendrix], who was essentially a loner, while Duane was a family man, a brother. Unfortunately for me, he already had a family."[49]

With *Layla*, Duane understood that the Allman Brothers Band provided him the vehicle to best express himself musically. To succeed on this path required two things: music industry support and finding the right bandmates. The industry backing followed his November 1968 performance on Wilson Pickett's cover of "Hey Jude." Duane's playing and help with the arrangement earned him a contract with FAME Studios head Rick Hall, who sold the contract to Jerry Wexler and Phil Walden soon afterward. Their support for Duane's vision in the band's early, lean years proved vital.

Next, Allman assembled a band of players who could add more originality to the music than he could on his own. Combined with artistic freedom, great players afforded the opportunity to "go ahead and do what you please." The problem with Hour Glass wasn't the combination of musicians; it was his dissatisfaction with their musical direction. That wasn't the case with the Allman Brothers—"five of the smokin'est cats I've ever met in my life."[50]

Duane's new bandmates had all experienced much dissatisfaction with the music industry. All expressed a desire to move beyond those constraints and try something new. They succeeded in the ABB. "Music is constantly around them and they are constantly making music,"

Gary Wishik observed. "It's their life, not just their jobs and they put everything into it. The music flows spontaneously created." Berry Oakley said, "Music is all we do. If we're not practicing or playing, we're going someplace or making arrangements to make a record."[51]

The band described its musical philosophy as "hittin' the note." It was music free of artifice, sounds composed in the moment for appreciative crowds whose enthusiasm impelled the band to greater heights. Oakley explained,

> All of us like to play to an audience and get response back. Hittin' the note is hitting your peak, . . . the place where we all like to be at, you know? When you're really feeling at your best, that's what you describe as your note. When you're really able to put all of you into it and get that much out of it. We just found it out along as we did it. We learned some from the audience, and they learned some from us, and things came together that way. It happens, I'd say, 75 percent of the time. There's some special places we play where we've done it before, and every time we go back, the vibes are there and it ends up happening again. We'll end up playing three or four hours, and when we finish, I'll be so high I can hardly talk. When you start hitting like that, the communication between the members of the band gets wide open. Stuff just starts coming out everywhere.[52]

The audience was vital to this equation. "Whatever you're doing, if you get a little encouragement, you're going to do it better," Duane said. "You're gonna think 'I'm hittin' a note' and you're gonna try and perfect it, work it on out. So when we started getting a little response, it regenerated itself back around again. When you feel you're doing right, you got plenty of power, you have people behind you, you can do whatever you want." Duane wanted his music to mean more than mere entertainment. "We want people to listen with their eyes closed," he said, "to just let the music come inside them and forget their worldly cares. We just want to make music that makes people feel it's easier to go on than they did before they heard us."[53]

Duane felt he best expressed himself musically in the ABB and it remained his most important musical project. When asked why, he answered, "I don't know, it's just part of my life. That's the only way

I can describe it. It's just a reflection of what happens to us." When pressed, he pointed to the stage. "You'll hear it all man, in just about a half an hour. I don't want to be evasive man, but there are just no words. I don't even want to try and explain. I don't believe I could."[54]

Pete Kowalke of Cowboy recalled another encounter. "The Allman Brothers were up on stage just lettin' it eat. They take a break, Duane stops right in front of me and says, 'This band only knows how to play one way, full tilt!'" Kowalke's bandmate Tom Wynn recalled, "It was always mighty impressive to watch them totally dominate an audience. They made a point of getting up on the tightrope every night, and people had no choice but to watch—and try to keep breathing. It was powerful."[55]

Duane may have been the Allman Brothers Band's biggest fan. "I like to jam with anyone who likes to play, and anybody who likes to can come around to our set anytime," he remarked, "but I'd rather jam with my own band than anybody alive! I've got the best players there are. . . . Everybody in the band can smoke me. That's why we're in the band together—to keep each other kicking." He thrived on his bandmates' energy and commitment to the music. "You wanna play in my band," Duane said, "you'd better come to pick, not to show off your clothes. It ain't no fashion show."[56]

Ultimately, the players in the Allman Brothers Band were simpatico in both musical ability and temperament. What resulted was a six-way musical conversation between players passionate about music and the music they made together. Each added his own element as the discussion evolved. Even while Duane and Dickey were soloing or Gregg was singing, the band rarely laid back. Rhythm parts added subtle "Amens" and "Yeah mans" from the band, simultaneously supporting the soloist and pushing him and the music further. "They seemed to goad each other pretty aggressively," Wynn of Cowboy reflected, "but it always seemed good-natured and positive at heart. They had much more of a warrior feel among themselves than Cowboy ever dreamed of." This fearlessness demonstrated Duane's confidence in his bandmates and theirs in him. The ABB's music, Oakley said, was "whole and spontaneous. It's like everyday living, like conversation. Our songs are about getting messed up, love troubles, the kinds of troubles most people seem to have."[57]

Of all of Duane's musical partners, Dickey Betts was one of the most important. While it was not unprecedented for a band to have two lead guitarists, a vast majority of the two-guitar bands of the era featured one player primarily on rhythm and the other on lead. The Allman Brothers' dual lead guitar approach was an outgrowth of each guitarist's virtuosity and the equal time they afforded one another as soloists. Indeed, each played lead guitar on nearly every Allman Brothers Band song, often in tandem.[58]

Duane and Dickey shared a profound "musical love," longtime collaborator Thom Doucette recalled. "They were very tight and they had a lot of unspoken communication." Duane held Dickey in thrall. "Duane played music the same way that he rode his motorcycle and drove his car. He was a daredevil, just triple-Scorpio, God's-on-my-side wide open. That was part of the romance. And I loved Duane."[59]

It was a collaboration the guitarists honed on stage, in rehearsals, and in private conversation. "What struck me when I first heard them playing together was how they didn't try to outdo each other, but instead supported one another," Doucette remembered. "I had worked with the Butterfield Blues Band in Chicago and all Butterfield and Bloomfield thought about was wasting one another."[60]

Some of this dynamic was built on mutual esteem, some on self-confidence, and much on approach. "Duane and I had an immense amount of respect for each other," Betts recalled. "We talked about being jealous of each other and how dangerous it was to think that way—that we had to fight that feeling when we were on stage. He'd say, 'When I listen to you play, I have to try hard to keep the jealousy thing at bay and not try to outdo you when I play my solo. But I still want to play my best!' We laughed about what a thin line that was." There was jealousy, Betts acknowledged, "but it was so honest that it was healthy; and it just *fired* the energies that we did have. We just *fired* each other off." The competition was by design. "We can make each other better and then do something deep," Duane said. "He was probably the most honest player I've ever played with," Betts reflected. "Man, he could get what was in his heart to come off the neck of his guitar."[61]

Betts said the connection between the two guitarists transcended music.

There are very few times two musicians come together who understand each other in that fashion, the same as two people having a real conversation, and truly understanding each other, the same as a man and a woman making love. This is the kind of thing that me and Duane had. I *knew* the dude. I knew him all the way through. I admired him. I learned from him. He learned from me. . . . To experience that with a musician the caliber of Duane Allman is one of the greatest gifts that I've received and been able to share.[62]

The band noted the synergy. "Duane played guitar better than anybody out there—except maybe Dickey Betts," "Red Dog" said. "Many nights Duane walked off stage and said to me, 'Goddamn, he ran me all over the stage tonight. He kicked my ass.' It's not that they were trying to outdo each other, but Dickey would come up with off-the-wall shit and Duane would have to keep up."[63]

Duane was his partner's biggest evangelist. "Duane had a real spearhead effect in that he was a super-positive, anything-can-be-done kind of inspiration," Betts recalled. "Duane was the flashier player and he'd get more attention. But he used to get mad when they'd overlook me."[64] "There ain't no way I can fail," Duane remarked. "Not only do I got it coming on two fucking ends, but Dickey's doing at least half the shit they think I'm doing."[65]

Duane sang Dickey's praises whenever he had the chance and identified Betts's authorship of the instrumental "In Memory of Elizabeth Reed" in nearly every live recording that exists. He encouraged Dickey's songwriting efforts and urged him to sing "Blue Sky," which Betts composed with Gregg in mind. "This is your song," he said. "It sounds like you, and you need to sing it." It was Betts's first recorded vocal with the ABB.[66]

Duane's support of Betts demonstrates that he was acutely aware of his band's internal dynamics. He was its founder, its leader, and the one with the most star power. In addition, as the band's singer and main songwriter, younger brother Gregg was an ideal front man and the band carried their name. "He really had a lot of problems with the name the 'Allman Brothers Band,'" Butch remembered. "He didn't want to call it that. He really wanted to find a name for the band that didn't call attention to himself, and we couldn't come up with anything." Trucks recalled, "Duane was going to start a band with himself as the leader, but once we started playing this music, he said, 'This is incredible. This is a band. This is not a star with a backup group.'"[67]

That the Allman Brothers Band functioned as a *band* was important to Duane. "My brother strived to make sure there was a comfort zone in our gang at all times," Gregg wrote. "There wasn't going to be any bullshit about Duane Allman and his sidemen. We were all equal, all together. A band means a bunch of guys working together for the same goal—that's what the word 'band' means, and we defined that."[68]

Duane despised being singled out from his mates. "I don't think anybody who's ever heard us would get on that trip," he remarked. "Our band is a band, and we work like a band. In a way though, I actually hope people get a delusion like that, if it'll get them down to hear us—and then we'll open up their eyes right." Jon Landau observed that "Duane did not so dominate that group that they ceased to be a band or became a vehicle for Duane Allman. It was one of the things he had most in his mind when he conceived of the group; he wanted a band he could play *with*, not over or against, or through. He wanted a group of partners, and that's exactly what he got."[69]

Thus, Duane's greatest legacy is the Allman Brothers Band itself. Though he only played in the group for less than three years, the ABB outlived him by more than four decades. The band's survival without him, Cameron Crowe contends, "is one of the modern miracles of rock."[70]

The band endured because Duane Allman found a particular way to express himself musically. That included his decision to subsume his own abilities within the group context, an ideal Jaimoe said was core from the founding:

> When you have one or more people trying to do something, you either have a team or you have nothing. The Allman Brothers Band was a team from the day we became a band. Duane Allman was the guy who had the vision, who saw what he wanted—two drums, two lead guitars, Gregg singing—and knew which musicians could make it happen. There's no question he was the leader, but Duane understood for it to work, everyone had to

have their voice and express their personality. Duane never dictated what anyone else played. He wanted a *band*. . . . Duane had the vision from the start.[71]

"You gotta strive to play a pure form of music," Duane remarked, "a kind of music that's honest to yourself. If you got that attitude and feeling about what you play, you'll be a lot better off. That's the kind of attitude that makes a great performing band."[72]

It took time for the band Duane formed in March 1969 to catch fire. The original ABB spent an estimated three hundred days a year on the road through 1971, building an audience for its unique blend of southern music, of American music. Though Duane died before he reaped much success for these efforts, the band persevered. Duane's initial vision of individual expression through live improvisational music remained the band's foundation, and subsequent players, most notably guitarists Warren Haynes and Derek Trucks, adopted this mindset in their own bands and careers. That is Duane Allman's ultimate legacy; *At Fillmore East* is the album that secured that legacy.

LIVING AND PLAYING MUSIC IN THE SOUTH (1960-1965)

Little brother we've got to get into this.
Duane Allman

As Duane developed his musical vision, two things loomed large: the influence of the South and the evolution of his understanding of the importance of originality in music. The lessons were not mutually exclusive. The South mattered as home to a rich musical and cultural heritage and strict racial hierarchy that Duane navigated in pursuit of music. Originality proved much harder; it continued to elude him.

Duane launched his career from Daytona Beach, a small Florida town on the Atlantic coast about one hundred miles south of Jacksonville. His path tracked that of thousands of like him, men and women who formed garage bands playing wide-ranging cover repertoires at schools, teen clubs, and backyard parties. Some graduated to low-fidelity recordings in local, ad hoc studios, while others grew into regional touring ensembles. A few, including Duane, left the South to pursue greater fame and fortune. Many more disbanded before they had the opportunity.[1]

White musicians barnstormed the region, playing first in white teen clubs and white high schools and gymnasiums. The more successful, like Duane and Gregg, graduated from racially segregated venues to bars and nightclubs that served both Black and white patrons. Eventually, a community of musicians across the South formed around Duane and his band, a fellowship that blossomed into a full-fledged musical movement.

The milieu centered not in dense urban areas but instead in and around southern cities such as Daytona Beach, Jacksonville, and Tampa, Florida; the Quad Cities in Muscle Shoals, Alabama; and later in Macon, Georgia. Each of these cities had strong connections to federal programs. Daytona Beach, Jacksonville, Tampa, and Macon all hosted military bases. The Muscle Shoals region was powered by Wilson Dam, a part of the Tennessee Valley Authority.

Duane was part of the third generation of American rock 'n' roll musicians to emerge in less than a decade. The first era began in 1954 when Elvis Presley, Buddy Holly, Carl Perkins, and many others merged Black music and culture with country-and-western music and culture and helped launch the rock 'n' roll revolution alongside contemporary Black stars such as Little Richard, Fats Domino, and Chuck Berry. The second, the teen idols, gained popularity in the late 1950s early 1960s. They tended to be younger, clean-cut males (nearly always white and not always teenagers) singing pop songs written by professional songwriters. Many adopted Americanized stage names: Fabian (Forte), Frankie Avalon (Francis Thomas Avallone), and Bobby Vee (Robert Thomas Velline), the protégé of record producer Dallas Smith. The teen idols were the music business's reaction to rock 'n' roll's quick ascension into the minds and wallets of America's youth.

Duane's era began in the early 1960s and explodes after the Beatles broke in America in 1964. Unlike the antiseptic pop of Fabian, Avalon, and Vee that scrubbed the music of most of its racial undertones, Duane's generation made no attempt to hide the Black influence of their music; they highlighted it.

Neither did the musicians hide their southern roots. How could they? Music is one of the South's most significant resources, the taproot from which nearly all popular American music emerged. Southern music is where, historians Bill C. Malone and David Stricklin argue, British and African folk traditions first intersected in a southern society "long defined by its limitations: a social context of poverty, slavery, suffering, deprivation, religious extremism, and cultural isolation." Southerners transcended these limitations with music, the Allman Brothers among them.[2]

Although the modern civil rights movement had secured multiple victories against segregation, southern society remained racially divided. Black music permeated southern culture and life as the region's racial mores hampered interactions between Black and white musicians. Crossing boundaries was a fraught proposition, easier for whites than African Americans, for whom it was often quite dangerous.[3]

Though very few bands were racially integrated, the music always was. Black music held sway in these cross-cultural communications, but its reach was somewhat limited. Many white southerners remained entrenched in their belief in segregation, as they compartmentalized their love of Black music from their disregard of African Americans in general. "Send all the n——rs back to Africa," read a handwritten sign posted in New Orleans in the late 1950s, "except for Fats Domino."[4]

In addition to these Black roots, Duane and his contemporaries drew inspiration from Britain. Beginning in 1964, bands such as the Beatles, the Rolling Stones, the Kinks, and the Dave Clark Five sparked a revolution in American youth culture. Dubbed "the British Invasion" by the American press, these British musicians expressed a reverence for the music of the American South, particularly the blues and early rock 'n' roll. Many of the bands, most notably the Beatles, also wrote their own music, a rarity in American popular music, which had long been dominated by professional songwriters.[5]

The British invasion also ushered in a new chapter in contemporary music in which the *band*, not the singer, received top billing. From their British counterparts, American musicians learned of the possibility of making music as a unit of equals rather than as backing musicians in support of a singer. In such bands, no single performer had to carry the entire ensemble. Musicians typically followed the Beatles' formula: two guitars, a bass, and a drummer, often with more than one person handling vocals. Many also added keyboards.

The Beatles burst into the American consciousness on February 9, 1964, with their first appearance on the *Ed Sullivan Show*. It was a cultural touchstone. An estimated seventy-three million people watched the performance that inspired a generation of American musicians. Tom Petty of Gainesville, Florida, recalled, "The minute I saw the Beatles on the *Ed Sullivan Show*—and it's true of thousands of guys—*there* was the way out. *There* was the way to do it. Everything changed. I wanted a group."[6]

Just as significant was a second wave of British bands, musicians who adhered much more closely to the repertoires and sounds of

American bluesmen Muddy Waters, Robert Johnson, Son House, Howlin' Wolf, and others. These British blues bands such as the Yardbirds, John Mayall's Bluesbreakers, Fleetwood Mac, the Animals, Cream, and Led Zeppelin reintroduced the blues to the American public.[7]

This zeitgeist was particularly important to Duane, who had already developed an affinity for electric blues directly from the source. The success of the British blues players offered opportunities for the music he loved to play. "It widened the whole thing to the point where we didn't have to be restricted," he said. The British blues players showed him something else: others liked the music too. And they liked it a lot. "Everyone began to dig the blues."[8]

The blues offered Duane the freedom to play what and how he wanted to play. To make a living, he had to first find an audience. Duane learned early on one of the best ways to do that was to play live and play regularly. Duane loved both equally.

Southern musicians fused their sounds in rehearsal spaces, on the bandstand, and in studios throughout the South. Their musical palates were catholic, befitting a region that had given America a wide variety of sounds, styles, influences, and musical traditions. They were unconcerned with labels or nomenclature. Southern musician, music critic, and blues historian Robert Palmer explains, "We didn't talk about what a contemporary music critic might call the astonishing eclecticism of our musical offering. There we were, stirring Dixieland and surf music, rockabilly and R&B, pseudo-jazz and honky-tonk country and western into a big gumbo. We had no idea we were breaking down barriers and cross-fertilizing genres. In those days, the definitions were not so firmly fixed."[9]

The brothers' musical ambitions began when a Nashville neighbor of their grandmother's introduced Gregg to the guitar in 1960. "My life changed that day," he wrote. That same summer, Duane and Gregg caught a revue show featuring Jackie Wilson, B. B. King, Johnny Taylor, among others. The concert enraptured Duane, Galadrielle Allman says: "Everyone rocked in their seats, all except Duane. Gregg says his brother sat forward on the edge of his seat perfectly still, transfixed. The music had energy, and it captivated Duane. 'Little brother . . . we've got to get into this.'"[10]

Having lost interest in trumpet and piano lessons, the guitar was

Duane's and Gregg's third attempt at music. "I'll never need this damn music," Duane told his piano teacher when he quit. "Take it and keep it." It was a statement he came to regret. "She died before I could get back and apologize to her. I always regretted that really bad." Gregg financed his first guitar delivering newspapers. The instrument became such a bone of contention between the brothers that Geraldine purchased a second guitar for Duane. Natural lefties, both played right-handed.[11]

"Musicians find musicians," Gregg recalled. "And I met every one of them in Daytona." The brothers were eager students. "Somebody would show you a lick, and that would open up a whole can of worms of licks," Gregg continued. "I was really studying them, and by this time, Duane was too."[12] Duane came under the tutelage of another Daytona Beach musician, Jim Shepley, "the coolest thing that ever walked," according to Gregg. Shepley was "the cat that actually taught me how to play," Duane said. "If you wanted to learn to play something right, anything, you'd go to him."[13]

Shepley introduced Duane to bluesman Jimmy Reed, whose songs were standards for southern bands of the era. One of the most popular blues artists of the 1950s and early 1960s, Reed was in regular rotation on WLAC, a Nashville-based radio station that highlighted blues, R&B, and other Black-influenced music. WLAC's 50,000-watt signal covered much of the eastern United States, and its broadcast sometimes reached as far north as Canada and as far south as Jamaica. Shepley and Duane also bonded over a love for B. B. King. "I showed Duane as much B.B. King as I knew," Shepley recalled, "because I was a pretty big fan of B.B. And so was Duane." King remained a major influence.[14]

In 1961, Duane Allman joined the Uniques. He played lead guitar, Sonny Fussell and Gregg played rhythm guitars, and Ted Petrucciani played piano. (The band's drummer's name is lost to history, and the Uniques never had a bass player.) Playing a repertoire of music they heard on WLAC, the group performed at school dances and school assemblies and even won a local talent show.[15]

Interest in African American music led Duane and his bandmates to the Black neighborhoods of segregated Daytona Beach. Covenant and custom had restricted African Americans from living on the beach side east of the Halifax River. Black neighborhoods such as

Waycross, Midway, and Newton were on the mainland, west of the railroad tracks that run parallel to U.S. 1.[16]

Venturing to the African American side of town was dangerous for Duane. Floyd Miles, an African American singer who befriended the Allmans, remembered the tension as "frightening." Duane was "one of the few white guys that would go in the Black neighborhood and play. Well, he was one of the few guys that would go into the Black neighborhood to a nightclub, period, back in those days."[17]

These interactions happened coincident with the events of the modern civil rights movement, a time of great social and cultural change for the South and the nation. Crossing color lines was an act of rebellion. To Duane, it was worth the risk.[18]

Miles met the Allman brothers in 1963 when Duane and Gregg played a brief stint in the House Rockers, a band that also included Shepley. The all-white House Rockers backed the Untils, a group of Black singers that included Miles, at the whites-only Surf Bar. It was where, Shepley reported, "we all got schooled in music."[19]

White musicians playing Black music in integrated bands and segregated venues weren't an anomaly. Sylvan Wells recalled, "White musicians could go to any of the Black clubs, and you were treated with respect and invited to come in as long as you wanted to sit in and play. So it wasn't unusual at all for white musicians to run around with Black musicians."[20]

Unwelcome on the white side of town after their sets ended, the Untils and other Black musicians retired with the Allmans in tow to Black clubs such as George's Place on Campbell Street or the Paradise Inn on Alabama Street. Miles remembered that Duane would "play there for free, just to play the blues for the Black people and with the Black people. Most of the people got to know him as the white guy that plays blues, that plays the guitar so well. So he was accepted. He was just another one of the guys after a while." Black musicians in and around Daytona Beach, Miles said, viewed the Allmans as "those white boys who can play that funky music."[21]

The musicians bonded in the after-hours sessions. "They were called hippies because they had long hair and were weird," Miles recalled. "The bond was built between us because we all experienced some kind of discrimination." "We had each other and we had the music," Gregg recalled. "Miles caught a lot of hell from his friends for hanging out with a white boy." Geraldine also gave her sons grief about their new friends. "We had to turn my mother on to the Blacks," Gregg concluded. "Took a while, but now she's totally liberated."[22]

Miles "took me across the tracks, literally," Gregg said. There, in a combination barbershop, pawnshop, and record shop, Gregg and Duane bought records as Miles supplemented the playlists of WLAC. From James Brown, B. B. King, Sonny Boy Williamson, Elmore James, Ray Charles, Howlin' Wolf, and Little Milton, the Allman brothers gained a deeper understanding of the African American music that had so inspired them. Joining forces briefly with another of Miles's bands, the Universals, the brothers added to their repertoire the Isley Brothers' "Twist and Shout," the doo-wop hit "Daddy's Home," and two Hank Ballard songs, "The Twist" and "Thrill on a Hill."[23]

Tired of playing in other people's bands, Duane formed the Escorts in 1964. The Escorts' lineup mirrored the Beatles': two guitars (Duane and Gregg), bass (Van Harrison), and drums (Maynard Portwood). Its repertoire featured songs they'd played in the Uniques, the House Rockers, and the Universals and in after-hours sessions in Daytona Beach's Black neighborhoods. The band played covers; it was what venues and audiences demanded. "Clubs just wanted us to be a juke-box on stage," Gregg said, "and we were a great one." They covered songs by white artists including "Pretty Woman" by Roy Orbison and "You've Lost that Loving Feeling" by the Righteous Brothers and by Black musicians such as "I've Been Trying" by the Impressions and Tommy Tucker's "Hi-Heel Sneakers." The Beatles' "That Boy" rounded out the set because, Gregg noted, "We had to play a Beatles song." The Escorts gave Duane his first taste of playing music beyond Daytona Beach as the group picked up gigs in other Florida towns. This, too, inspired him. "He was a little too ambitious to stay in one place," Miles recalled. "He wanted more."[24]

The cover-only repertoire proved a detriment when the Night-crawlers' single "A Little Black Egg" crept into the local charts. The Nightcrawlers recorded the original song at the makeshift studio of Lee Hazen, in Ormond Beach, fifteen miles north of Daytona Beach. At the time of the recording, Duane was giving Nightcrawlers guitarist Sylvan Wells lessons. "Duane could play circles around him," Hazen said. Wells agreed. "We were not near the musicians they were, but we started writing our own material very early, largely because if you tried to play covers, then everyone who heard you would compare you to the record and we couldn't be as good. So we were playing about 80 percent original material and people liked it. We got the jobs and breaks early because of that. Duane and Gregg were still playing basic old R&B. They were great, but they were not getting the recognition because they were a cover band." Wells learned that originality was key. Duane had yet to discover it. "It used to drive them crazy," Wells continued. "We were getting all the jobs and all the recognition."[25]

Duane may have wanted to play original music, but hits were how bands made money and honed their chops. "When you didn't have any records out," Miles explained, "you had to duplicate those cover tunes, and that is what made you good or bad" in the eyes of the audience.[26] These are the songs the Escorts recorded sometime in early 1965 at Hazen's studio. Tracks included Roy Orbison's "Pretty Woman," the Righteous Brothers' "You've Lost that Loving Feeling," Ray Charles's "Don't Let the Sun Catch You Crying," and two cuts from the British invasion, the Searchers' "Love Potion No. 9" and "Ferry 'Cross the Mersey" by Gerry and the Pacemakers.[27]

Fame as original artists eluded most southern musicians of this era, and most who achieved success had to leave the South to do so. Nashville was the closest music-industry city, but it remained a country-music town that only dabbled in rock music until the late 1960s. The other centers of the American music industry—Los Angeles, New York, and Chicago—further stymied southern musicians, Black and white.

Robert Palmer observed in 1969 that making a living playing music in the South "meant playing Top 40, and that's why southern bands have always been known for incredibly exact, mimetic renderings of the latest Beatles, Stones, and whatever. It is also why southern rock bands have been comparatively late getting into their own music and their own stylings; they simply had to live, and just having hair below your collar was enough of an impediment. In many ways, the Black music, rhythm and blues, was more vital than rock in those days." Familiar songs paid the bills, and Duane and Gregg were particularly adept at playing them. They had to be as the Escorts played no originals. "We never even thought about it," Gregg recalled. Their well-executed repertoire of covers earned the Escorts a regular engagement at the Daytona Beach Pier.[28]

In April 1965 the Escorts and the Nightcrawlers co-opened for the Beach Boys, the most popular American band of the era. The gig was a turning point for the band's leader. "If this works out," Duane told bass player Van Harrison, "we can make it big. We can go on the road." Harrison, who had yet to graduate from high school, bowed out. "There's no way in hell I can go on the road except for weekend things," he remembered thinking. Worse, Duane had to wait to leave until Gregg graduated high school that summer. It was Geraldine's prerequisite.[29]

Two things are apparent from Duane's early efforts in music. First, the South was important to him as the wellspring of most of his musical influences, most notably the blues. Duane made common cause with Black musicians; they accepted him as a musical peer. The second lesson was that cover songs earned paying gigs, but original songs earned radio play and more attention.

That Duane spent the first few years of his musical career as a cover artist is far from unusual. It is how most musicians' careers begin. What Duane had yet to discover was how to create an original sound out of his influences. Musical fulfillment eluded him until he did.

CHAPTER **3**

ALLMAN JOYS TAKE THE HIGHWAY (1965-1967)

Get your ass out of here and get to the coast.

John D. Loudermilk

Soon after the 1965 Beach Boys show, Duane and the Escorts returned to Hazen's studio. They recorded two R&B staples, "Turn on Your Love Light" by Bobby "Blue" Bland and "What'd I Say" by Ray Charles, and an unnamed original instrumental. That summer, the band changed its name to the Allman Joys, and Duane began his professional career.[1]

Life as a touring musician is a grind under the most ideal situations, and conditions in the mid-1960s South were particularly harsh. The going was rough. Nightclub owners and audiences demanded bands that played precise covers of current hits under the ever-present threat of violence. Black musicians faced Jim Crow segregation. White musicians were harassed for their long hair.

Duane picked up two important lessons from his early days on the road: playing in a great live band was critical to his satisfaction and success as a musician, and the music industry cared little about a band's onstage prowess if it lacked a hit. Onstage, Duane succeeded as a guitarist and bandleader. He failed in the latter, though, the first of several disappointments to gain success chasing hits.

Booking agencies in Atlanta and later Nashville ensured that the Allman Joys stayed active playing a relatively small circuit of southern clubs. The band also performed at regional colleges, including some gigs courtesy of Sylvan Wells, their former hometown rival who had quit playing music but was booking bands while attending Florida State University.[2]

Gregg recalled the Allman Joys' first out-of-state gig at the Stork Club in Mobile that summer. The engagement paid less than $11 per show: $444 for six forty-five-minute sets a night, seven nights a week. Gregg's first impression was memorable, to say the least. It was "a nasty fucking place. . . . The head of the club greeted us and told us to come back to his office. He unbuttoned his shirt and turned around and show us an Army .45. 'You listen up here, if you all got any knives or guns, or any shit planned for my club, just remember, I got bigger ones than this in here.'"[3]

Daytona Beach was violent as well. Musician Charles Atkins said it was common for someone to walk into George's Place "and start shooting." He bears a scar from a stray bullet fired in a lovers' quarrel at the VIP Room. South Carolinian Chuck McCorkle (brother of the Marshall Tucker Band's George McCorkle) witnessed a stabbing. The band "just kept playing. The police came and hauled everybody off." Robert Palmer shared a tale from rural Arkansas: "A rumpled old hillbilly approached, peered nervously over his shoulder and muttered low, 'Say, could you boys play me, oh *any* old Hank Williams tune? It sure would sound good to a man on the run. We played 'Your Cheating Heart.' Half an hour later, the state troopers arrived. A man had robbed a bank and they were hot on his trail; they felt sure he must have stopped here."[4]

Long hair added another complication. "It was hard to tell whom the rednecks hated more, African Americans because of their color, or white males who had long hair," musician and writer Marty Jourard recalls about Gainesville, home of the University of Florida and a regular stop for the Allman Joys. Some conflicts turned violent, which Duane and Gregg experienced in 1965 at Nashville's Anchor Motel near Vanderbilt. Gregg heaved a brick after "hostile exchanges, catcalls, insults" with a group of Shriners, who "burst into their room and worked Gregg over pretty good."[5]

As harrowing as touring was for white musicians, the situation was much worse for Black musicians. Despite the gains of the modern civil rights movement, Jim Crow made life challenging and dangerous for African American performers. Overt challenges of the color line could result in violence, even death. In 1951 a Black member of white bandleader Johnny Otis's band was brutally beaten at an Augusta, Georgia, concert for neglecting to say "sir" to a white man. In 1960 a bill of R&B stars refused to play a second show in Little Rock after belligerent whites disrupted the first, which was the city's first integrated concert. As gun-toting whites chased the Black performers out of town, singer Jesse Belvin lost control of his car. The wreck killed him and his wife, JoAnn. Local authorities never investigated reports that Belvin's car had been tampered with.[6]

Terry Johnson of the doo-wop group the Flamingos shared a story of pre-show threats in late-1950s Birmingham. As a phalanx of police officers escorted the band to their dressing room, they issued strict orders: "Do not, under any circumstances, make eye contact with whites in the audience." The request was as impossible as it was ludicrous. The Black audience was confined to the balcony. "It was a rule when we came in," Johnson recounted. "'I don't want to see any of you darkies looking at the white women out there. If you do, your ass is mine.' Cruel things like that."[7]

White musician Tommy Roe called his presence a matter of survival for his Black counterparts on a 1962 package tour with R&B stars Sam Cooke, Smokey Robinson, and Jerry Butler. Restricted from most eating establishments, they'd park the bus out of sight while Roe walked to the restaurant and picked up food to go.[8]

White Memphis native Bobby Whitlock recounted hassles when he played with the integrated Short Cuts. "We couldn't stay in hotels because one of us was Black. So we would park outside the hotel in the dark and someone would go in and get the room," he said. The South "got pretty heavy and hairy at times. If you were hanging out with Black folks in parts of the South you were discriminated against, too."[9]

As if racial discrimination wasn't enough, rhythm and blues touring was a particular grind. "Southern itineraries are very demanding," Landau observed. "The turnover rate is high, fights and violence not infrequent. The musicians often become dependent on drugs. The stars don't book for vast sums of money, but they work regularly. A good soul artist could earn $20,000 and $40,000 a month." Yet managers, promoters, and booking agents, typically white, and the Black stars themselves treated their musicians poorly. Landau said sidemen were paid "good money"—$175 per week. Jai Johanny Johanson called bullshit. "The stars did business old school. . . . We weren't paid jack shit."[10]

Shabby touring conditions were a fact of life for musicians of all colors, but touring earned income. It also built proficiency and confidence. Duane recalled, "I've been playing bars, nightclubs, lounges, and before that high school dances, little Y-Teen dances, and before that for anybody who would listen. Just learning things. It's kind of like studying to be a doctor. You start out with a frog and then you work up and dissect a dog and go on up to human beings, and you work your way up to saving folks' lives and stuff."[11]

The seediness, violence, and discrimination of the road was challenging, but in the pre-streaming era, playing live was where bands made names for themselves. After their stop at Mobile's Stork Club, the Allman Joys ventured east to the Sahara Club in Pensacola. Years later, Gregg recalled the impact of the performance. The band launched into "Paperback Writer" by the Beatles, he said, "and we mesmerized those people. For the first time, I believed it. I felt it. Pensacola was a real turning point in my life, because I realized that if we did things right, we could grab people with the first eight bars of a song, and we wouldn't have to worry about the rest of the night." Initially dubious of Duane's designs of stardom, the Sahara Club audience convinced Gregg otherwise.[12]

As they toured regionally, the Allmans encountered and inspired a wider network of southern musicians. Some gravitated into the brothers' musical circle, while others grew to fame and fortune separately. The impact of finding like-minded musicians was critical to the growth of the era's southern musical culture. Muscle Shoals was home to the 5 Men-Its, half of whom ended up playing with Duane and Gregg as Hour Glass in 1967 and 1968. In addition to Tom Petty, Gainesville boasted the Continentals, a band that featured, at various times, guitarists and Rock & Roll Hall of Famers Stephen Stills, Bernie Leadon, and Don Felder.[13]

The Allman Joys took to the road in summer 1965 and never looked back. Peers saw the brothers' early attempts to earn a living as musicians as inspirational. "The Allmans were professionals," Tommy Tucker of Daytona Beach remarked. "They were dedicated to doing this for the rest of their lives." They were, Alabama native and future bandmate Paul Hornsby said, "the first band I knew that played music and did nothing else. That was their thing."[14]

The Allmans' mastery of their material also set them apart. "They were that much better than everyone else," Lynyrd Skynyrd founding guitarist Gary Rossington said. Johnny Sandlin recalled, "Duane was very well-known throughout the South as *the* guitar player. Every band had seen him, guitar players all watched him. He influenced a lot of people."[15]

In addition to their musical chops, Duane and Gregg had the appropriate look. "We were still chubby little high school boys, baseball players," Rossington recalled, "and they were like rock stars, skinny guys with long blond hair." The brothers were the first long-haired musicians Sandlin ever encountered: "I mean long hair. Hanging way down past their shoulders." It was a dangerous look in Pensacola. "People just didn't cater to that in a Navy town," Sandlin said. "It was almost a cardinal sin to go around with long hair at that time, and I couldn't believe they hadn't gotten killed."[16]

"These guys were right on the cutting edge visually and audibly," Hornsby said. "Gregg was seventeen or eighteen and he already had that huge husky voice, that R&B voice. Duane was just playing like nobody I heard. Even though they were doing copy material, there was something about the way they were doing it that nobody else did." Sandlin called an Allman Joys' appearance at Pensacola's Spanish Village on July 22, 1966, "amazing, the best band I had ever heard. They were playing very different music from what we were: English stuff, Yardbirds, and Beatles' music. They were just incredible."[17]

A recording of the show Sandlin attended circulates online. The Allman Joys' repertoire included "Carol" by Chuck Berry, "On the Outside (Looking In)" by Little Anthony and the Imperials, and "Good Good Lovin'" by James Brown. Duane led the band through impeccable takes of the Righteous Brothers' "Old Man River," first made famous by Paul Robeson, and crooner Lenny Welch's "Are You Sincere." The British invasion rounded out the set, with "Help" by the Beatles, "Heart Full of Soul" by the Yardbirds, and "The Last Time" by the Rolling Stones.

The recording proves the Allman Joys adept musicians and imitators. Their presentation is tight, with the band playing instrumental passages behind Duane's introduction of the songs in the set. The lack of original material is evident. It has none.

Three months before the Spanish Village performance, the Allman Joys briefly joined forces with the Sandpipers, a teenage female vocal trio featuring sisters Charlyne (fourteen years old) and Debbie Kilpatrick (thirteen) and their friend Sally Hurst (fourteen). Though the combination might seem unusual at first glance, in 1966 Duane was the leader of a cover band. With the heavier blues sound of the Allman Brothers Band still several years in the future, the Sandpipers allowed the band to expand its set list with songs featuring female vocals.[18]

The partnership also resulted in Duane's first true audition. The Allman Joys had landed a summer gig well beyond their usual tour route, at Trude Heller's in New York City's Greenwich Village. Duane invited the Sandpipers and their parents to join them on the trip. A DJ at Pensacola's Sahara Club arranged an audition for them with producer Bob Johnston of Columbia Records, then producing Bob Dylan's *Blonde on Blonde*. Though Johnston passed, the Sandpipers landed a contract with Heller's label, Tru-Glo-Town.

After the failed auditions, Duane remained unbowed. Shepley said Duane returned from New York "very high about the music."[19]

The Allman Joys returned to the road. In summer 1966 they landed in Nashville at the Briar Patch, one of Music City's earliest rock clubs. It was there country songwriter and producer John D. Loudermilk used a trick he learned from Elvis Presley's manager, Tom Parker. "Turn around and watch the audience," Parker advised him. "You can see the emotion in their faces, and you can tell about how much they'll pay to continue having that emotion." As he watched Duane and Gregg, Loudermilk recalled, "The kids were going crazy." The Nashville veteran took the musicians under his wing. "They were quick to learn and they just listened to me. They listened very carefully and they learned real quickly."[20]

In August 1966, following a month living and working with Loudermilk, the Allman Joys entered Bradley's Barn studio in Lebanon, Tennessee. They recorded two blues covers—Howlin' Wolf's "Spoonful" (an arrangement copped directly from the Paul Butterfield Blues Band) and Robert Johnson's "Crossroads" (a cover of a short-lived, obscure project called Eric Clapton and the Powerhouse)—and three from the Yardbirds: "Shapes of Things," "Mister, You're a Better Man than I," and "Lost Woman." Only one, Gregg's "Gotta Get Away," was original.[21]

Buddy Killen's Dial Records eventually released "Spoonful." Although *Cashbox* awarded it a B+ for its "strong lead [and] instrumental backing, which features lots of timely far-out touches," it sold poorly. Duane later called it "a terrible psychedelic rendition." Killen was also unmoved by the band's prospects. "Nobody really understood what Duane and Gregg were about at the time," he admitted later. "Eventually I gave them their release." Duane remembered it differently. "We told [Killen] we wanted to be rock stars . . . and he said, 'No man, you cats better look for a day gig, you're never gonna make it—you're the worst band I ever heard.'" Several years later, when the Allman Brothers Band was in full swing, Killen called Phil Walden and offered to sell him his tapes of the Allman Joys. "I knew I should've spent more time with those boys," he told Walden. In 1973 Killen issued the Allman Joys' demos as an album called *Early Allman*.[22]

Though the first of Duane's studio efforts failed to attract attention, they would not be the last. "I tried to get all the guys I knew to go see them [live]," Loudermilk said of a group of friends that included producers Owen Bradley and Chet Atkins. No one in Nashville saw any promise in the Allman Joys. The rejection left Duane despondent. "You ain't going to get nothing done here," Loudermilk counseled. "I can tell you what to do—get your ass out of here and get to the coast." Loudermilk meant the West Coast, California. After failed auditions in New York City and Nashville, the music-industry veteran understood Duane had accomplished all he could in the South.[23]

After more than a year on the road, the Allman Joys had developed a reputation as an incendiary live act but had yet to create anything original beyond the stage. In the studio, even their covers were covers. Los Angeles was the epicenter of the rock music world. Home to the Beach Boys, the Los Angeles rock scene of 1966 and 1967 boasted a heavier rock sound from bands like the Doors, the Byrds, and Buffalo Springfield. L.A. had a robust network of studios, record labels, radio stations, and insiders.

Duane was unable to break through with the Allman Joys, but his stint with the band taught him important lessons. Foremost, success as a live performer drew attention, and from this point forward, Duane's bands would thrive in the live environment. The failure to earn a record contract taught him the importance of developing a more original sound. In California Duane also learned an important lesson about geography: it wasn't the South. And the South was important to his musical vision. He would struggle to fully express himself musically until he did.

CHAPTER 4

FRUSTRATION IN CALIFORNIA (1967-1968)

We had chops out the ass but didn't have the originality thing down yet.
Gregg Allman

The prospects seemed bleak for Duane to make the leap from success in a regional cover band to the professional world of Los Angeles
music making. Though discouraged after failures in in New York and
Nashville, Loudermilk's encouragement was validating. He was the
undisputed leader of the Allman Joys, but his creative input remained
limited to guitar and arrangements. Duane would eventually learn
that originality came in two forms, songwriting and arranging. It is in
this era he matured as an arranger, which helped him further develop
his artistic voice.

Though Duane never developed into a songwriter, Gregg internalized Loudermilk's lessons. The younger Allman had a hand in all
seven of the originals the Allman Joys recorded in its August 1966
sessions at Bradley's Barn. Duane wrote none. The pattern held for
the next two years, which Duane and Gregg spent in Hour Glass, a
record company–controlled effort that forced him to abandon his
southern sound and adopt a pose of pop-psychedelia in music and
image. Duane had no creative control, a view that dictated his terms
in all subsequent contracts.

With Hour Glass in Los Angeles in 1967 and 1968, Duane learned an
additional lesson: the South was vital to his artistic vision. Nashville
wasn't far enough, Loudermilk said; Duane had to leave the South to
make it. The guitarist realized his mistake soon after moving to Los

Angeles. He ultimately chose to starve playing music in the South rather than attempt what his record label defined as success.

The Bradley's Barn recordings coincided with an exodus of Allman Joys members weary of the grind of life on the road. Bassist Bob Keller quit first, rejoined, and then quit again. His replacement, Ralph Ballinger, also quit. Drummer Bill Connell had already replaced Maynard Portwood but then, to avoid the draft, joined the Navy.[1]

By early 1967, with his band in disarray, Duane turned to two musicians he had met the previous year, Paul Hornsby and Johnny Sandlin of the 5 Men-Its. Duane was in search of a new drummer and bass player; the Alabama-based musicians were looking for a singer and lead guitarist to replace Eddie Hinton, who'd quit to play sessions in Muscle Shoals.

The new group quickly coalesced around Duane's vision for one reason. Hornsby said, "When there was a Duane Allman in your band, there was only room for one leader." Joining forces with the Allmans brought things full circle for the Alabamans. "They had been trying to convince us we needed to go on the road, that life on the road was the next thing to heaven," Hornsby recalled. "And they were lying like a dog."[2]

The new band first carried on as the Allman Joys. They played "R&B covers and a lot of British covers—Yardbirds' stuff like 'Over Under Sideways Down,'" Hornsby said. He showed Duane the harmony parts for John Lee Hooker's "Dimples," which he'd learned from Eddie Hinton. More common in country music, particularly western swing and the Bakersfield sound of country hitmaker Buck Owens, "Dimples" was among the first uses of harmony in southern rhythm and blues. The technique would become an Allman Brothers Band trademark.[3]

The reconstituted Allman Joys leaned heavily on R&B and British blues. Hornsby called the band "a powerhouse." In reality, the effect was confusing. "They had several different styles that hadn't quite coalesced into one," John McEuen of the Nitty Gritty Dirt Band recalled. Author Tom Nolan dubbed their sound "contemporary adaptable," describing it this way: "One minute they were a go-go band, the next, a funkier Young Rascals with a strain of R&B evident throughout."[4]

In April 1967, Duane found his opening to head west. His band was playing a gig at Pepe's a Go Go in St. Louis's Gaslight Square, "the place to be for beats, preppies, well-dressed adults, street troubadours, and tourists," the *St. Louis Post-Dispatch* reported. It was a funky part of town that hosted concerts by Barbra Streisand, readings by Beat Generation poet Allen Ginsburg, and regular appearances by jazz trumpeter Miles Davis. While in St. Louis, bass player Mabron McKinney ran into California's Nitty Gritty Dirt Band at the airport. McKinney invited the group to hear the Allman Joys live. Sandlin recalled, "If you saw another person with long hair, you felt an instant kinship." The encounter changed everything.[5]

The Allman Joys astounded Bill McEuen, John's brother and the Dirt Band's manager. Their set was "like being drawn into a new musical form," he said. He called contacts in Los Angeles and declared, "I have just discovered the next Rolling Stones. I've found the greatest band in the world!" He urged the band to relocate to Los Angeles and sign with Liberty Records.[6]

Duane was eager to head west. His bandmates were less enthused. Gregg called it "a jive lick." Sandlin, too, was reticent. "I'd never been anywhere close to California," he said. "I wanted to do it and I *didn't* want to at the same time. It was one of those things where you were scared but knew if we were gonna get anywhere with the band, we had to go." Having already failed in New York and in Nashville the previous year, Duane understood this as well as anyone. "Duane bought into it," Gregg said. "So we went."[7]

In a move they all came to regret, the band signed an onerous contract with Liberty and relocated to Los Angeles. If Bill McEuen warned them that the agreement gave the record company complete creative control, that the band had no say-so in its records or in the management of its career, they didn't heed his advice. The detail would come to haunt them. But for now, Los Angeles offered an opportunity they didn't have in the South—a record contract. And they seized it.

Hour Glass joined a thriving musical community in L.A. when Duane and crew arrived in spring 1967. Buffalo Springfield, featuring Floridian Stephen Stills on guitar, and the Doors had just released debut albums; the Byrds had released their third. All three were part of a burgeoning West Coast rock scene that included San Francisco bands the Jefferson Airplane, the Grateful Dead, and Big Brother and Holding Company with Janis Joplin. These bands and others across the United States began replacing the more danceable forms of rock 'n' roll and R&B in pursuit of music as art. It was rock without the roll, more to be listened to than danced to. And once again, the transition also established a firm musical color line as the music industry marketed most Black artists who followed this trend not in the more lucrative rock market but as soul or rhythm and blues.[8]

Summer 1967 would forever be known as the Summer of Love. That June, fans and artists convened at the Monterey International Pop Music Festival. The event propelled the career of Janis Joplin and culminated in a landmark set by the then-unknown Jimi Hendrix. Monterey Pop was a statement that something significant was happening among American youth. Straight society didn't like what it saw.

In its July 7, 1967, cover story, *Time* traced the hippies' emergence as "a wholly new subculture" that rejected their parents' values, "a bizarre permutation of the middle-class American ethos from which it evolved." Hippies "preach altruism and mysticism, honesty, joy, and nonviolence. . . . Their professed aim is nothing less than the subversion of Western society by force of example." Unreality "permeates hippiedom, a cult whose mystique derives essentially from the influence of hallucinogenic drug, [for which] the hippies have popularized a new word, psychedelic."[9]

In September 1967, *Atlantic* writer Mark Harris used "psychedelic" to describe a bumper sticker he had seen in San Francisco. "The script was 'psychedelic.' That is to say, it was characterized by flourishes, spirals, and curlicues in camouflaged tones—blues against purples, pinks against reds—as if the hippie behind the message weren't really sure he wanted to say what he was saying."[10] American youth had started a movement. Music was one of its rallying points. And Duane Allman was in California, in the middle of it all.

The musicians, who all hailed from small southern towns, found Los Angeles disorienting. "Things seemed to be happening then which, I guess, were hip things to be happening, but they scared me to death. I didn't like them," Sandlin said. Hard drugs were prevalent, as was the decadence of big-city life. "Most of us felt awfully alienated," he said. "The entire experience drove the whole band crazy. Going out there was just strange, strange, strange."[11]

The band also experienced the caprices of the music business. They were hard lessons for the young, eager musicians to learn. Liberty Records assigned staff producer Dallas Smith to the band, and as was typical, Smith managed the entirety of the group's career, from its image to song selection to recording and arrangements. He changed the band's name to Hour Glass, minimizing the chance that audiences might associate the band with its two obvious stars, Duane and Gregg Allman. In an attempt to reach the hip market, Smith ordered the band to dress in psychedelic garb. It was a mishmash of historical outfits, with fashion elements from the medieval and Renaissance eras all the way through the nineteenth century, "the whole Hollywood trip," Sandlin said, "the clothes, everything." The band looked as out of place and uncomfortable in their costumes as they sounded on record.[12]

Smith's ideas about records and record making followed a pattern that emerged after the first wave of rock 'n' roll stars burst onto the American music scene in the mid-1950s. Rock 'n' roll's popularity caught the entertainment establishment by surprise. It reacted by searching out and recording teen idols—clean-cut, younger-looking males singing pop songs written by professional songwriters in the Tin Pan Alley tradition.

Ricky Nelson, star of the TV series *The Adventures of Ozzie and Harriet* featuring his family, ushered in the teen idol era in April 1957 with a TV performance and subsequent hit single of Fats Domino's "I'm Walkin.'" The music industry took note of Nelson's success with the emerging teen market, a new demographic with tremendous buying power that emerged in the post–World War II baby boom. In response, record labels and managers nurtured dozens of teen stars along with Nelson.[13]

The teen idols, Glenn C. Altschuler argues, sapped rock 'n' roll's vitality, making music "producer-induced" instead of "consumer-driven." The arrangement hurt artists the most. Duane was caught in the crossfire. "Record companies didn't know what they were doing," John McEuen of the Dirt Band recalled. "They don't make records, they distribute records, and quite often they think they actually 'make' records, so they find a group with a lot of energy, and they think they should dress one way or another, or should record one way or another." Such was Smith's approach with Hour Glass.[14]

Before assuming control over Hour Glass, Dallas Smith's greatest success had been with Bobby Vee, a teen idol who scored eight top-10 hits from 1961 to 1969. The producer sought a repeat of that success with Hour Glass. "We were happy just to be in L.A.," Hornsby recalled.

"We wanted to please the record company and do what they wanted us to do. We were glad to be doing anything."[15]

The arrangement frustrated Duane, who had always been in charge of deciding what, when, and how his bands played. Worse, Smith viewed Duane and the band as Gregg's backing group. "They wanted to cut Gregg out front and the band being inconsequential," Sandlin said. It was, Hornsby noted, "miles from what we were doing." Though the band disagreed with him, Smith had the final word. The producer spent the next year trying to mold the group into an act called Gregg Allman and Hour Glass.[16]

The band recorded its debut album in June 1967, and Liberty released it that October. The self-titled debut featured material by outside professional songwriters Smith approved. *Hour Glass* contained only one original, Gregg's "Got to Get Away," which the Allman Joys had recorded for Loudermilk the previous summer in Nashville.

Although a covers-heavy album was not out of the ordinary and Hour Glass was primarily a cover band, the material was an ill fit for the southern R&B and blues band. The record fell flat despite contributions from a wide array of excellent tune smiths, including Brill Building songsters Gerry Goffin and Carole King, soul musicians Curtis Mayfield and Jimmy Radcliffe, teen idol Del Shannon, and future folk-rock superstar Jackson Browne.[17]

Smith's heavy-handed style—"An absolute dictatorship," Hornsby said—grated on the band, particularly Duane. Smith's production amplified Gregg's vocals and buried the band deep in the mix under a sheen of sounds designed to reach the pop market. Duane's guitar was nearly inaudible as it competed for attention with robust horn and background vocal arrangements. "The music had no life," Gregg said.[18]

Worse, Smith and Liberty restricted Hour Glass from its bread and butter, playing live. It was an odd decision given the band's renown as a live act, but it was not atypical. A decade earlier, Colonel Tom Parker took Elvis off the road at the height of his career to generate more enthusiasm. Liberty took the same tack. Worried about overexposure, the label limited Hour Glass's live engagements, leaving the musicians in dire financial straits.

The band found a measure of salvation when they finally reached the stage. Rather than songs from their album, they played the music they knew best, southern blues and R&B. The repertoire remained mostly covers, including "Leaving Trunk" (Sleepy John Estes by way of Taj Mahal), "I'm Hanging Up My Heart For You" (Solomon Burke), and three Bobby Bland cuts, "Stormy Monday," "Feel So Bad," and "Turn on Your Love Light."[19]

Hour Glass's set lists presaged the Allman Brothers Band's own wide musical palate. They opened shows with an instrumental take on the Beatles' "Norwegian Wood" and closed with a current hit by country star Buck Owens. "They knew they were good," John McEuen said. "Anyone who heard them understood how good they were. Duane had total command and authority of the guitar and Gregg was just a great singer who could make anything his own." Yet the band hadn't found a firm footing and was still seeking an identity. By limiting live performances, Liberty Records stunted Hour Glass's ability to find that identity.[20]

When they did get to play, they frequented music halls that Gregg described as "somewhere between nightclubs and opera houses. . . . Basically they were roadhouses." They played at the Kaleidoscope, the Magic Mushroom, and the Whisky a Go Go in L.A. and the Avalon Ballroom and the Fillmore in San Francisco. Their too-rare live appearances commanded the attention of peers and audiences alike. "A lot of the Hollywood elite in the music world were there one night to see them just burn the stage," Johnny Townsend, a compadre from the southern touring circuit, recounted of one particularly well-received show at the Whisky. "Frightened people to death, really: 'What the hell is this? These guys are fucking killers!'" As he recalled gigs with Jefferson Airplane, Moby Grape, and the Animals, Hornsby said, "We were nobodies, but I'd have hated to be the headline act to follow the Hour Glass." Stephen Stills remarked to Gregg years later, "You sure were a tough act to follow."[21]

Duane was the band's focal point. "His playing was part of the song, he was part of the lick," Bill McEuen observed. "He was visually interpreting his music like when you watch John Lee Hooker or you got a chance to watch Hendrix. He was obviously totally glued and tuned in to those licks, and he knew that he wasn't just playing notes, that they were things that should communicate and when they did it was very exciting."[22]

Yet the live sound did not translate to the studio, at least not with

Dallas Smith behind the glass. Duane's experience recording Hour Glass's second album, *Power of Love*, in January and February 1968 was a rehash of the first. Smith again dictated the material and approach. Once again, he spurned Duane, whose inability to write or sing left him in the sideman's role. Duane actually quit mid-session and made haste for Daytona Beach before returning and completing the recording. Liberty released *Power of Love* in March 1968. Like its predecessor, it failed to chart.[23]

Power of Love demonstrated growth, most notably in Gregg's songwriting; he penned seven of the album's twelve tracks. None were particularly memorable and none reached the repertoires of his future bands, but Gregg's improvement was such that they made the final track list. Of the remaining five songs, fellow southerners wrote three: one by Spooner Oldham and Dan Penn and two more by Marlon Greene and Sandlin and Hornsby's former bandmate Eddie Hinton. Oldham, Penn, Greene, and Hinton all began their careers at a place that would loom large in Duane Allman's career, Rick Hall's FAME Studios in Muscle Shoals.

While in Los Angeles, the band bonded off stage with the music of their home region. Southern music offered comfort for the frustrated, homesick musicians. Pete Carr, a friend from Daytona who joined Hour Glass on bass for its second album, recalled playing the country ballad "The Long Black Veil," "I remember us harmonizing on it, and it really was a moment separated from everything else we were doing. It was like a close family thing."[24]

Though the recordings were a commercial failure, the Hour Glass experience inspired in Duane the desire to break free of the tight formats of the music business. "Duane and I would sit for hours in my front room playing guitar," Bill McEuen recalled. "We'd discuss the possibilities of getting that guitar up front, but we didn't know what kind of music to do it with because there weren't many guitar instrumentals that were making it, and Duane didn't sing very much."[25]

In September 1968, six months after *Power of Love* was released, Duane abandoned Los Angeles for good. After several years in cover bands, Duane had in mind a blues-heavy, guitar-based sound, one he'd captured playing live but had yet to harness in the studio. He demanded creative input, which was not possible under Smith's direction.

Hour Glass was a good band that lacked what all of Duane's bands until then lacked—a unique sound. "We had chops out the ass," Gregg said, "but didn't have the originality thing down yet." Duane knew originality was important, and he would never again cede creative control as he found his own voice.[26]

CHAPTER 5

DUANE RETURNS SOUTH FOR GOOD (APRIL-SEPTEMBER 1968)

Stick your papers and contracts up your ass. We're out of here.
Duane Allman

What precipitated Duane's departure from California happened during a spring 1968 tour in the East and Southeast. The band opened for Big Brother and the Holding Company in St. Louis, a mainstay on the Allman Joys' touring retinue. The tour took them as far north as Cleveland and as far south as Jacksonville. In April the band pooled its money and visited FAME Studio in Muscle Shoals. It was familiar turf for Hornsby and Sandlin. Eddie Hinton was on staff, and Sandlin had recorded at FAME before joining Hour Glass. By the end of the year, Duane secured a permanent position for himself at the studio as well.[1]

Hour Glass sessions in Muscle Shoals marked a turning point in Duane's career but not in the way he anticipated. Northwest Alabama was considerably quieter than Southern California, and FAME was far from the watchful eye of Dallas Smith. Elated with FAME's organic recording process and the music they recorded there, the sessions renewed Duane's spirits. They also reinforced how essential the South was his musical vision.

The band met Hinton at FAME on April 22, 1968. Jimmy Johnson engineered the recordings, which cost $500. Hour Glass recorded three tracks. The best was a medley of B. B. King songs, "Sweet Little Angel," "It's My Own Fault," and "How Blue Can You Get?" The arrangements mirrored King's 1964 *Live at the Regal* album; Hour Glass even played the tracks in the same order.[2]

At FAME, the band was fully in charge. "We had the freedom to dictate those sessions," Gregg said. Bassist Pete Carr explained, "We liked the sound at FAME better. None of us had been real comfortable with the sound we got in L.A., or with the overall approach to the recording process." The musicians were also comfortable at home. "It felt so good because we were back down South, on our turf," Gregg recalled. "Why did we ever leave?" Sandlin asked.[3]

After recording two albums that emphasized Gregg over the group, the Muscle Shoals recordings were *band* efforts. Smith had smothered Duane's guitar with layers of pop horns and background singing more reminiscent of the Fifth Dimension than Otis Redding. Hinton's production had Gregg as one-fourth of a band, with Duane, Hornsby, and Sandlin's instruments mixed prominently with, not behind, the vocals. It was the band Duane led when he signed with Liberty.

In Muscle Shoals Duane internalized a valuable lesson about the L.A. experience. While he was not a front man in the traditional sense, he was also far from a traditional sideman. Henceforth, Duane's projects would present the musicians as a singular unit.

Hour Glass returned to Los Angeles invigorated by the tour. They were ecstatic with the FAME sessions, which Liberty and Smith rejected with prejudice. "They didn't want to hear it," Gregg said. "The biggest bunch of trash they ever heard," Hornsby said. "Dallas was a pop producer," Carr explained, "and the tapes we cut at FAME were not pop hit-type songs."[4]

Smith had in mind a different sound for Hour Glass, one that was decidedly more urbane, less southern. "They didn't know what a southern rock band was supposed to sound like. It was Black, blues-based rock 'n' roll," Hornsby said. "He kept referring to us as a Motown band. We do Black-oriented music, but it's southern blues, southern Black blues. It's not Motown." Motown was the most successful Black music label at the time, but the famous "Motown sound" aimed at the white pop market reflected neither Hour Glass's sound nor its inspirations. To Dallas Smith and Liberty, Duane's ideas for Hour Glass had no sales potential whatsoever.[5]

Bill McEuen, a savvy music-industry veteran, understood the conflict. Smith was a formulaic producer who lacked an ear for good music, and Hour Glass was too inexperienced to usurp Smith's control. Why he never intervened is a mystery, though he acknowledged Hour Glass hadn't "developed enough, nor were they of the mindset where they could force control and say, 'Well, this is the way we're doing it.' It's their first record deal. They hadn't gotten to that stage yet where they could say, 'This is what we do.'" Hornsby reflected decades later, "I just can't believe they overlooked Duane."[6]

The truth lies somewhere in the middle. Yes, Duane was a tremendous guitarist. Yes, Smith's production buried his guitar in the mix. Yes, the producer focused on Gregg. But the songs and production on *Hour Glass* and *Power of Love* are a poor imitation of Buffalo Springfield and the Byrds rather than an exciting live southern R&B band.

To the members of Hour Glass, the Muscle Shoals demos represented their musical ideas far better than their output on Liberty. The FAME demos previewed what came less than a year later when Duane founded the Allman Brothers, most notably in the B. B. King medley featuring Duane's scorching lead guitar and Gregg's deep, bluesy vocals.

There has been much speculation that Hour Glass just wasn't the right combination of musicians for Duane's vision. If this was true, it certainly was not because the players lacked talent. Hour Glass comprised serious musicians, all of whom maintained long careers after the group disbanded. Carr eventually settled in Muscle Shoals, where he replaced Hinton on lead guitar for the Muscle Shoals Rhythm Section. Drummer Sandlin and keyboardist and guitarist Hornsby became staff producers for Capricorn Records. And, of course, Duane and Gregg went on to great renown in the Allman Brothers Band.

John McEuen said the band would have had success had the label just allowed Hour Glass to follow their own musical vision. "The group wasn't really ready," McEuen said. Though the label had signed Canned Heat, another electric blues band, around the same time as Hour Glass and distributed Johnny Winter's 1968 debut, *The Progressive Blues Experiment*, Liberty ignored Duane's ideas. Carr lamented, "It just wasn't ready to go yet, wasn't ready to happen yet."[7]

They clearly weren't ready. The Los Angeles–based music business was an ill fit. Duane had yet to find the right mix of musicians, and Gregg's songwriting was still emerging. The brothers, however, finally captured an original sound on the FAME demos. It was tightly arranged R&B. Gregg's vocals are prominent, but Duane's guitar stands out from the first two Hour Glass albums. "B. B. King Medley" highlights Duane's mastery of King's tone. On "Ain't No Good to Cry," his guitar answers Gregg's vocals throughout.

After Liberty's rejection of the Muscle Shoals demos, Duane quit Hour Glass for good. The band was under contract to a label uninterested in his ideas, a stalemate that weighed heavily on him. "I would have been happy to stay in L.A. and play forever," Hornsby said, "but Duane was sick of the label, and he wanted to come back to the South." Duane declared, "I just hate it out here. I need more respect than this."[8]

Duane reached his breaking point in a meeting with Liberty Records sometime in August 1968. "You, you, you, and you and Liberty Records can kiss my fucking ass," he announced. "Me and the guys are picking up and going the fuck back down South, or anywhere but here. Fuck this place, and all the tinsel, and all the other bullshit. Stick your papers and contracts up your ass. We're out of here."[9]

Out of options and with no bargaining power, Duane returned to Florida. The entire L.A. experience reinforced his belief in himself as a musician and bandleader. He would make his next move with full control over his music, live *and* in studio. He would never again be constrained in the pursuit of his musical passion.

September 1968 was a busy and pivotal month for Duane. In the span of a few weeks he quit Hour Glass, left California for Florida, recorded and played live with Butch Trucks's 31st of February, and played his first sessions as a sideman in Muscle Shoals.

Ever eager to start their next musical project, the brothers turned to Trucks upon arriving home from California. The brothers first met the drummer two years earlier after Trucks's band's failed audition at the Martinique in Daytona Beach because their folk-rock was undanceable. Butch and the Allmans crossed paths again when he filled in on drums for the Allman Joys at the Beachcomber in Jacksonville, a venue that catered to sailors from nearby naval bases who were less interested in dancing than drinking and meeting women. Butch's band, the Bitter Ind, soon took over the gig, their mellower folk-rock a better backdrop for the Beachcomber's clientele than the Allmans' R&B. The Bitter Ind eventually changed its name to the 31st of February after a dispute with the Greenwich Village folk club the Bitter End, and toured the same southern club circuit as the Allman Joys and 5 Men-Its.[10]

In June 1968, the 31st of February released its eponymous debut of eight original and four cover songs on Vanguard Records. When it failed to chart, the band sought to expand their sound. Trucks explained, "We were gonna try to get a little more into jamming because what we did was the Byrds, a lot of vocal stuff, and three-part harmony stuff with Scott Boyer just playing Fender twelve-string guitar and finger-picking. So we'd be a real full sound, but there wasn't really a lead guitar player." Duane solved their dilemma in September 1968 when he and Gregg signed on for a few gigs and to record demos at Tone Studios in Hialeah, near Miami.[11]

Though the true intention for the lineup remains in dispute, Butch long considered the "smoking-ass band" a full-fledged, long-term musical project. To Gregg, the 31st of February was a fantastic short-lived collaboration. "The right players weren't assembled for those sessions," Gregg said. "Butch and those guys had been playing . . . the whole folk rock thing. They sounded very, very good. . . . But that sound isn't what me and my brother were all about. . . . [We] were coming from a completely different direction," the blues.[12]

Geraldine Allman injected a third voice into the conversation. A letter to her niece dated September 25, 1968, shows keen understanding of her sons' musical careers and ambitions. "The band is practicing, and these boys are seasoned musicians," Geraldine wrote. "Scott [Boyer] sings and writes, David helps Duane with the emcee shit, and Butch is a terrific drummer. They are really a great bunch of young people." Her failure to mention Gregg could either be an oversight or indicate she knew Gregg's tenure in the band would be brief.[13]

Whatever the story, the 31st of February featuring Duane and Gregg recorded nine sides in Miami, demos intended to secure support from Vanguard Records to record a second album. Four were covers: "Nobody Knows When You're Down and Out" by Scrapper Blackwell; "Down in Texas," an Eddie Hinton/Marlon Greene collaboration; "Morning Dew," a folk song by Canadian Bonnie Dobson later made famous by the Grateful Dead; and "In The Morning When I'm Real" by Robert Pucetti. Gregg added three compositions: "God Rest His Soul," about the recently assassinated Martin Luther King Jr., "Well I Know Too Well," and "Melissa," which featured Duane's first recording on slide guitar. When Vanguard passed on the demos, the 31st of February disbanded.[14]

Containing half of the original Allman Brothers Band lineup, the 31st of February had potential. Like Hour Glass's "B. B. King Medley" recorded that spring, "Morning Dew" previewed the future Allman Brothers Band's sound. The 31st of February played an aggressive arrangement of Bonnie Dobson's original. Duane's guitar featured prominently throughout, including a blistering mid-song solo. Gregg's vocals added a blues tinge to Dobson's folk-pop. Yet the real difference maker wasn't Duane or Gregg; it was Butch Trucks. The drummer's playing was different than Sandlin's on Hour Glass's first two records. Butch hit the drums harder, providing a heavier rock foundation than Sandlin's rhythm and blues swing. Something else stands out: Butch and Duane are in lockstep. Butch seemed to anticipate Duane's moves, sometimes following him, sometimes goading him. The drummer propelled the song forward with a force that would later earn him the nickname "The Freight Train." Neither knew it at the time, but it was the beginning of the most significant musical collaboration of their lives. Six months later, Butch joined Duane in the Allman Brothers Band.

The 31st of February showed promise, but Duane and Gregg were both still under contract with Liberty. Gregg was eager to get back to California, where he had a producer sympathetic to his talents. By the end of September 1968, he sold three songs to producer Steve Alaimo and flew to L.A. Duane was furious when Gregg called with the news that Liberty would release Hour Glass and therefore Duane from its contract if Gregg recorded as a solo act. "He would've strangled Gregg if he could've gotten through the phone," Butch said. Hornsby contended that Gregg returned willingly: "I doubt they had to twist his arm very much. I think he really liked it. He liked the personal attention they were giving him. Can't blame him for that." Gregg surely felt pressure to fulfill Hour Glass's contract, but he also found California more enticing than Florida. Duane stayed in the South, still under contract to Liberty.[15]

The 31st of February was a fleeting but significant moment in Duane's career. In the span of a single month, September 1968, Duane quit Hour Glass, moved back to Florida, signed on with the 31st of February, and joined the band in the studio. The project didn't earn the band a record contract, but it did demonstrate Gregg's growth as a songwriter. "Melissa," featuring Duane on slide guitar, was the first of Gregg's songs the Allman Brothers Band would record. Equally significant was that the 31st of February was Duane's first recording with a future ABB member other than Gregg, drummer Butch Trucks. Most importantly, by late 1968 Duane had moved home to make music in the South. He would never move from the region again.

CHAPTER 6

DUANE IN MUSCLE SHOALS
(SEPTEMBER 1968-MARCH 1969)

I brought myself back to earth and came to life again.

Duane Allman

Duane entered fall 1968 with very few prospects. Without a band and without Gregg, Duane spent late 1968 and early 1969 in and around Muscle Shoals, where he regrouped after a chaotic eighteen months based in Los Angeles. The slower pace agreed with him, and it was the only time since he took the road in 1965 that he was not a touring musician. He quickly established a name for himself as a top-notch studio guitarist and earned the backing to start his next project. Stilted early attempts at a solo album reminded him how much he missed being a part of a band. The studio also reminded him how much he missed playing live. By March 1969 Duane left Muscle Shoals in search of bandmates who could play the sounds he had in his head.

Just before the 31st of February sessions in September 1968, Allman made his third trip to Muscle Shoals. He played guitar for the Bleus, a blue-eyed soul band from Gadsden, Alabama, in sessions at Memphis's Ardent Studios and at Bevis Studio, soon renamed Muscle Shoals Sound, in nearby Sheffield. While there, Duane sought out Rick Hall for a chance to record at FAME. Duane remained in the Shoals until the producer gave him an opportunity with Clarence Carter that September and October.[1]

Following the Carter sessions, Duane headed back to Jacksonville. He was eager to continue building his growing musical partnership with Berry Oakley, bassist for the Second Coming, a psychedelic blues-rock outfit with one of Florida's hottest lead guitar players, Dickey Betts. The Second Coming was the premier band among Jacksonville's thriving music scene. The group lived in a communal home in the city's Riverside neighborhood and hosted regular free jam sessions in nearby Willowbranch Park.[2]

While in Jacksonville, Duane received a telegram from Hall inviting him to Muscle Shoals for an upcoming session with one of Atlantic's top artists, the great Wilson Pickett. It was, as Duane said, "a trial session to get Pickett's recording business. He was getting musicians from all over to be on hand." The November 1968 session was career-changing for Duane.[3]

Why Hall finally relented and allowed Duane to play on the September Clarence Carter session at FAME in the first place is unclear. It probably had much to do with the guitarist's legendary persistence. Hall was captivated by Duane's guitar playing. He described it as "strange to my ear, so new it was unreal." He remembered Duane as "way-out" with "far-fetched" ideas, "brilliant, a great mind" and "the most dynamic man that I've ever had walk in the studio." Jon Landau reported, "He did not look like your ordinary Muscle Shoals regular," Shoals bassist David Hood declared, "He was a freak at that time." Guitarist Jimmy Johnson called Duane "the first free-spirited person I met, . . . [hair] down to his ass" and sporting red, white, and blue tennis shoes. Pickett described Duane as "a weirdo from the git-go. He came in with his long hair, and his weird pants on. I said to him, I think I'll call you Skyman." Eventually, Pickett's Skyman sobriquet merged with "Dog," a name from the Hour Glass days that the Shoals players had adopted because of Duane's shaggy hair and appearance. Duane carries the Skydog nickname to this day.[4]

Muscle Shoals comprises four northwestern Alabama cities—Muscle Shoals, Florence, Sheffield, and Tuscumbia—along the Tennessee River. It is an out-of-the-way place for a southern soul studio. In 1959 three white men, Rick Hall, Tom Stafford, and Billy Sherrill, founded FAME as Florence Alabama Music Enterprises. Hall assumed sole ownership the next year. Arthur Alexander's "You Better Move On" was Hall's first hit as producer, reaching number 24 on the Hot 100 in March 1962. The single drew the notice of the larger music industry, and FAME soon joined Memphis-based Stax, American, and Ardent, as studios that catered to southern soul artists, with their mostly white rhythm sections backing some of the more popular Black soul and R&B singers at the time, including Otis Redding, Wilson Pickett, and Aretha Franklin.

As was standard, Hall, as producer, and Jerry Wexler of Atlantic Records, Pickett's label, chose the songs for the November 1968 session. The musicians had little if any say in the material they played. "That was something you didn't mess with," Hood recalled. Duane either didn't know this or didn't care. He was an outsider, but he was not a wallflower. He asserted himself immediately by urging Pickett, a star with nearly two dozen Hot 100 hits since 1962, to cover the Beatles' "Hey Jude."[5]

Those who were there recall Duane's obstinace when Hall and Pickett rejected his suggestion. R&B artists regularly covered the Fab Four, but the producer and singer deemed it too unusual to cover a song currently rising on the charts. "Are you crazy?" Pickett asked. "The Beatles have released it. It'll be number 1 in two weeks." Duane replied, "That's the whole point. It shows we've got balls. We'll cover the Beatles, the biggest thing in the world. This is going to get the world's attention that you, as a Black act, have the guts to cut the same record which the Beatles have got out and that you think you can have a hit record with it." Duane's self-confidence astounded Hall, "an incredible attitude to have towards our business and our world."[6]

No one knows exactly how Duane convinced Pickett to record "Hey Jude" or what in particular inspired him to suggest the song, but everyone remembers the circumstances. When the session halted for a meal break, Duane and Pickett stayed behind rather than risk conflict because of Duane's long hair and Pickett's skin color. By the time the musicians returned to the studio, Pickett had acceded to Duane's idea. The band cut "Hey Jude" immediately.[7]

The cover they recorded was markedly different from the Beatles' own. Its arrangement focused on Pickett's vocals rather than the Beatles' ensemble performance. His singing carried the first two-thirds of the song, with horns and Duane's guitar flourishes replacing the Beatles' vocal harmonies. At 2:44, Duane served notice with a solo that launched his career. The band hit a vamp—a short sequence of chords repeated for an extended period—behind Duane's lead and Pickett's vocals. Duane dug in as the band transitioned to what Johnson called "an incredible, intense ending. We didn't want to stop playing." Duane "stood right in front of me as though he was playing every note I was singing," Pickett said. "He was watching me as I sang, and as I screamed, he was screaming with his guitar." Hall mixed the vocals and guitar at nearly equal volume.[8]

Sure he'd just recorded a hit, Hall immediately phoned Wexler in New York and played him the track. "An absolute stroke of genius," Wexler responded. "The vocal was fabulous," Wexler recalled, "but it was the guitar solo, a running obbligato over and under Wilson's impassioned cries, that held the whole thing together." Hall agreed. Duane's improvised solo "glued the song and the groove together and made the record sing, sing, sing." Wexler heard something unique. "I knew all the session guitarists, but not this guy. Who is he?" he asked Hall. "He's got hair down below his butt. He's a hippie," Hall replied. "I'll be damned if he didn't talk Pickett into singing the song. Wilson said a Beatles' tune didn't fit him and the hippie said, 'What's wrong, you don't got the balls to sing it?'"[9]

"Hey Jude" catapulted Duane into the next phase of his career, one that saw him reach the heights he'd long been striving for. "Duane's whole career spun off that Pickett session," Jimmy Johnson said. "It's amazing how one incident, one session, can change a person's life." Duane's changing fortunes inexorably changed the trajectory of southern music. After several fits and starts and a disastrous stint in Los Angeles, Duane finally found acclaim. It was at FAME, in the South, the region he called home.[10]

Hall signed Duane to a recording and management contract and invited him to relocate to Muscle Shoals. "Go home and get your gear and move up here," Hall told him. "You can play anything that comes through the door and make gobs of money." The arrangement freed Duane to explore his artistic vision, and he knew he had earned a tremendous opportunity. "There's a good chance I'll be able to cut an album of my own soon," he wrote to Donna Roosman, his then girlfriend, later his wife and the mother of their daughter, Galadrielle.[11]

Duane moved to a cabin with windows overlooking a lake. He was far from the chaos and noise of Los Angeles and its officious music industry. "I just sat there and played to myself," he told Tony Glover. "I brought myself back to earth and came to life again."[12]

Recording for Hall at FAME differed from Smith in L.A. The producer and record labels still dictated song choice, but FAME's sessions were less grueling, a combination of the South's more laid-back atmosphere and the wishes of the artists who recorded there. "We did mostly R&B stuff and those cats were real loose," Duane said. Hall "just wanted everybody on the session to play their ass off; never told you what to play." Long stifled creatively, he valued how the atmosphere of "play whatever the hell you felt" produced "organic music."[13]

Duane worked as a regular session musician for less than seven months. He arrived in Muscle Shoals in September 1968, relocated there in January 1969, and departed for good in late February or early March. During this relatively brief interlude, Duane recorded with luminaries Aretha Franklin, Arthur Conley, Clarence Carter, King Curtis, Laura Lee, and Spencer Wiggins. In Muscle Shoals, he also built his reputation on slide guitar, which represented the majority of his session work in this era. Duane's slide first appeared on Clarence Carter's "The Road of Love." His slide set a swampy groove on Aretha Franklin's cover of the Band's "The Weight," and his blistering solo anchoring a track that reached number 24 in March 1969.

Whether playing slide or traditional fretted guitar, Duane earned respect in Muscle Shoals. Hall remarked that Duane "could eat up a guitar like no one I had ever heard in my life. He had absolute faith in his abilities. He believed that he was the most unique and gifted guitar player in the world." Allman's infectious personality and intense focus on music left Hall smitten. "He always had a positive attitude and a smile from ear to ear. I never heard him say a bad word about anybody—not ever. He was so wrapped up in his music that he didn't have time for jealousy or gossip. He was always totally focused on his music and totally wrapped up in the moment." Hall concluded, "Duane brought tomorrow into my studio and into my life. . . . 'Dog' and I weren't writing the same book, but I was totally into his free spirit, never-say-die attitude, and the mind-boggling things he could do with his guitar. Duane's music and his way of thinking were much more influential on me than I ever was on him."[14]

What the producer and guitarist did not agree on was Duane's direction as a solo artist. Hall supported Duane and gave him the freedom to play guitar as he wanted to, but he was unable to unlock Duane's talent. Hall recalled that Duane "wanted to record all the old 1950s stuff. He kept telling me, 'Rick, that's the big thing, man. Kids today are digging on all that old blues stuff—bottleneck [slide] guitars, harmonicas, and that Mississippi Delta back porch sound.' I said, 'Dog, you're ten years behind the times. I'm not interested in any of that old garbage.'" Duane would soon prove Hall wrong.[15]

Hall saw limited potential in Duane's ideas for his solo career. Duane was a leader, yes, but it was clear he would never thrive as a solo artist. But Hall misjudged Duane's creative instincts. The guitarist knew audiences were ready for an updated southern sound steeped in the blues, and he was determined to form a band that provided their soundtrack. He would need backing from someone other than Hall, who had grown disenchanted with his firebrand guitarist.

Duane found his patron in Phil Walden. Walden had been managing artists and booking concerts in the rhythm and blues music since the early 1960s. His first client was fellow Macon native Otis Redding, whom he managed until Redding's death in a plane crash in December 1967. Well acquainted with the world of southern and African American music, Walden initially became affiliated with Atlantic Records when the label distributed "Love Twist," a single by Johnny Jenkins, another Maconite he represented.[16]

Walden first heard Duane on "Hey Jude." "That's not your guitar player," he remarked. "Who the hell is this guy? He's great!" So enamored was Walden of Duane's sound that he offered to buy Duane's contract on the spot. "I'm going down there to sign him up and put a group together," he exclaimed. To fund his investment in Duane, Walden joined forces with Atlantic's Jerry Wexler. They paid $10,000 to Hall for Duane's contract. It was a hefty sum for a musician who was neither a singer nor a songwriter or at that point a bandleader. "Rick thought the heavens had opened," Wexler recalled.[17]

The heavens had opened for Duane, who knew his fortunes had finally changed for good. "I just signed a personal management contract with Phil Walden," he wrote to Donna. "He used to manage Otis Redding, and he still manages Arthur Conley, Clarence Carter, Aretha Franklin, and a bunch of other people." In a diary entry from January 6, 1969, Duane expressed similar enthusiasm about Atlantic: "I met Jerry Wexler. What a good cat. Saw Tom Dowd and met Arif Mardin and all the Atlantic folks. A damn good organization."[18]

Atlantic was one of the most successful independent record labels in the country. It was home to stars such as Pickett, Carter, and Franklin, all of whom Duane had backed in sessions. A network of relationships with subsidiary labels across the United States such as Buddy Killen's Dial, Rick Hall's FAME, Stax in Memphis, and later Capricorn provided the label with a steady stream of hits. Though based in New York, Atlantic artists recorded in a variety of settings, some of their own choosing, some the label's. Atlantic had nurtured the careers Ray Charles, Otis Redding, and Aretha Franklin and had recently gained a foothold in the rock market with artists such as Buffalo Springfield (Hour Glass's L.A. contemporaries) as well as Cream and Led Zeppelin from England.

Duane joined forces with Walden just as his solo sessions with Hall began to fall apart. Part of it was a lack of connection between the men. "Hall was very dark, very intense, very old-school, very straight," Jon Landau remarked. Duane was intense, but that was where the comparisons ended. On January 5, 1969, he shared his frustrations in his diary: "First part of session terrible. Couldn't get Rick to accept new idea for guitar parts. . . . What a drag."[19]

Hoping to re-create some of their past magic, Duane invited his former Hour Glass bandmates to join him in Muscle Shoals. "These people at Atlantic like what I'm doing and want me to cut some demos." he said to Hornsby. Hornsby played keyboards on sessions featuring Duane, Hour Glass drummer Johnny Sandlin, and Duane's new friend and collaborator, bassist Berry Oakley. Gregg, still in L.A., did not participate. It was Duane's show. "Finally," Hornsby recalled thinking, "he gets to step out."[20]

The solo sessions featured an amalgam of tracks, none of them particularly distinctive except that they were the first recordings to include Duane Allman and Berry Oakley together. Jaimoe was there, but he was unfamiliar with studio work and sat out the sessions altogether. Only one of the songs was an original, "Happily Married Man," Duane's tongue-in-cheek homage to absence in a marriage. Howlin' Wolf's "Goin' Down Slow" was another step closer to the Allman Brothers Band sound, a blues standard with urgent, stinging electric guitar. The vocals are another story altogether. While poignant, Duane's singing seems strained, particularly when compared to his brother's. None of the songs made the Allman Brothers Band's repertoire.[21]

Neither Hornsby nor Sandlin saw any future in Duane's latest project. "In the past it had always been the Gregg show. But here was

Duane. We'd just spent two years in Hour Glass and those were the stepping stones," Hornsby recalled. "I'd done stepped on that stone, and I was just trying to move on." Sandlin took the same course. "I don't think there had ever been a rock band that had broken out of the South," he said. "Anybody from the South that made it had to go to L.A. or New York, and I definitely didn't want to go that route. We'd just been through it, and I was just burned out from it."[22]

Six months after quitting Hour Glass in August 1968, Duane gave up on his solo project for good. The result of the Muscle Shoals sessions wasn't a record. It was a reminder to Duane of "the desire to get back into the group thing." Duane knew he was most fulfilled playing music in tandem with others, and he was determined to find the right mix of players.[23]

His time at FAME, particularly his success on "Hey Jude," validated Duane's ambition. He believed in his ability, but to that point had been unable to get anyone interested enough in him to support him as he developed a band and a style. "Hey Jude" unleased Duane's talent and opened the door to support from Phil Walden with help from Jerry Wexler and Atlantic Records.

The Los Angeles and Muscle Shoals experiences also clarified for Duane that he had to pursue music without the interference of non-musicians. While FAME followed a more organic recording process than Liberty, the studio environment remained constraining. The stars who recorded in the Shoals had their own careers and did not want to be upstaged by their guitar player.

In northwest Alabama, Duane came to understand that the things he valued most in music, particularly creating it in the moment with simpatico players, required a full band. He also accepted he was not cut out to be a traditional front man. "Duane just wasn't a singer," Hornsby remarked. "He could have been but I think it bored him. He wanted to play guitar." Besides, Duane already had a singer in mind: Gregg, who was still in Los Angeles.[24]

The six months Duane spent in the Shoals was the only time in his adult life he didn't spend regularly performing live. And he missed it. "I wanted to get to playing in joints again, which is what I did before I did anything else. Play for people," he said. Duane was too antsy for full-time session work. "Those cats in Muscle Shoals couldn't understand why I didn't just lay back on my ass and collect five bills a week," he said. "I'm just not the laying-back-on-your-ass sort of person." He wrote Donna in December 1968, before he even started his solo sessions with Hall, "I'm going to start getting my gigging band together. I can hardly wait. I love working in the studio, and it is a very valuable experience, but I know I was born to play for a crowd, and I'm really itching to get started."[25]

Bored with studio life and eager to play in front of audiences again, Duane left Muscle Shoals and returned to Jacksonville in early March 1969 to play with a collective of musicians who had begun coalescing around the Second Coming, featuring Oakley and Betts. The previous summer, Duane and Berry had formed an intense bond from their first meeting at an Hour Glass gig at Jacksonville's Comic Book club. The two discussed forming "the best group we could possibly get together," Duane recalled. By the following spring, Duane was ready to pursue the ideas he and Berry had discussed. "I told Rick the studio thing was stringing me out and I wanted to go back to Florida and work in a little more creative capacity." Duane would build his next musical project around Oakley.[26]

"I'm just looking," Walden recalled Duane saying of his quest for musical collaborators. "I'm just gonna ride around to various southern cities and just sort of sit in with the music scene and see what's going on. See if I can put together something that I have in my head." The South was home, where Duane felt most comfortable and knew the most people. It was also where he knew the he'd find musicians who shared his same musical roots and a similar spirit for how to combine those influences into a cohesive musical statement.[27]

"Duane would call from time to time from this place or that," Walden said, "and I'd send him a little money." Sometime after March 26, 1969, he called Walden from Jacksonville. "I've got it. I've got the band," he announced.[28]

The band comprised six musicians. All were southerners: Berry Oakley of Jacksonville by way of Chicago, on bass; Jai Johanny Johanson of Ocean Springs, Mississippi, on drums; Dickey Betts of West Palm Beach, Florida, on lead guitar; and Butch Trucks of Jacksonville, on drums. Duane would play lead guitar, and brother Gregg joined on organ and vocals.

The musicians' influences reflected the breadth of American popular music. Duane, Gregg, and Jaimoe were seasoned rhythm and blues players. Jaimoe was steeped in jazz. Oakley, Betts, and the Allmans were heavily influenced by the blues. Betts was intimately familiar with country music, especially string music, bluegrass, and western swing, and he and Oakley used psychedelic rock as an improvisational guidepost. Butch loved classical music, and his previous bands had a decidedly folk and folk-rock bent. Gregg, too, had a folkie side, having drawn influence from writers such as Tim Buckley and Jackson Browne in California. All six had grown up playing rock 'n' roll and were road-hardened veterans of the touring circuit.

While it would take a little more than two years to achieve success, Duane had finally found the collective through which he could best express his musical values, the Allman Brothers Band.

CHAPTER 7

THE BIRTH OF THE ALLMAN BROTHERS BAND, JACKSONVILLE (MARCH 1969)

The band was so good we thought we'd never make it.
Dickey Betts

Duane had a particular sound in his head for his next musical project, and it was only a matter of weeks after leaving Muscle Shoals before he found it. After first visiting Donna in St. Louis, Duane arrived in Jacksonville sometime during the first week of March 1969. He brought with him a new bandmate, drummer Jaimoe, with whom he'd been living and jamming in Muscle Shoals. Within three weeks, Duane identified and recruited the musicians to join his next, most important musical project: the Allman Brothers Band, whose members, individually and collectively, unlocked Duane's originality.

By early 1969 Duane lost interest in his solo career and fled the comfort of his full-time Muscle Shoals gig altogether. He had the talent and personality to front a power trio like Hendrix and Clapton had done, as was Rick Hall's idea for Duane. But, Betts said, "Duane was too warm and personal for that. He needed a lot of other guys to get that full sound he wanted." As Duane assembled the band in early 1969, he sought others who would push him creatively, bandmates he, in turn, could also push.[1]

In Jacksonville in March 1969, Duane finally assembled players with skills and spirit to match his own, virtuosos who fused their individual influences into an original sound built on live improvisation

81

and musical conversation. Betts described the band as developing like a Polaroid photograph, with various elements slowly coming into focus. What quickly became clear was that playing together brought something special out of each musician. "We knew what we now had," Betts said of their sound. Jaimoe called it "less copying. We brought our own thing to it." The environment fueled Duane's fire.[2]

Duane came of age as a bandleader in the era of the blues-rock guitar hero. His American contemporaries included Mike Bloomfield, Jimi Hendrix, and fellow white southerner Johnny Winter. British guitar gods included Eric Clapton, Jeff Beck, and Jimmy Page, the Yardbirds' triumvirate who, Robert Palmer writes, "were among the first to define themselves primarily as instrumental virtuosos and refuse to settle for the subservient sideman's role."[3]

Duane's influences evolved from the same source his peers, the blues, particularly slide guitarists Robert Johnson and Elmore James. He revered Jesse Ed Davis, whose slide on "Statesboro Blues" led Duane to take up the technique. "He plays so pretty," Duane said of Davis. "You've got Jeff Beck and Jimmy Page ringing all the tension and hard loud violent sounding stuff, then Davis comes along and it's like somebody came in and opened the window in the cool air came in when he's playing. Man that's the kind of stuff I like."[4]

Cream, featuring Eric Clapton, provided a template for Duane. The British power trio played an amalgam of hard rock and electric blues, much heavier than Clapton's work in the Yardbirds and John Mayall's Bluesbreakers. Clapton formed Cream in 1966 with Jack Bruce on bass and Ginger Baker on drums. Bruce and Baker proved adventurous musical foils with jazz chops to match; they transformed Cream into something far more than the blues band Clapton imagined. "We had no control over it whatsoever," Clapton remarked. "We were just scrambling for the forefront." Playing live provided additional inspiration. "The real feedback we got was when we played in front of an audience," he said, "we realized that they actually wanted to go off somewhere. And we had power to take them there."[5]

Though Cream imploded in 1968, the group left a model for bands to follow: virtuosos performing originals and blues covers with a dose of jazz-inspired improvisation. Doing so live made audiences an important part of the music. Duane sought to create similar experiences, but first he had to form a band.

African American drummer Jaimoe—born Johnny Lee Johnson, stage name Jai Johanny Johanson—from Ocean Springs, Mississippi, was Duane's initial recruit. "Was I in the original band?" Jaimoe remarked. "Shit, I was with the band when it wasn't no band." Jaimoe had played drums professionally for five years when he met Duane in 1969. "I didn't choose music—music chose me." He first caught the bug when he saw jazz pianist Arthur Rubinstein on television in the late 1950s. "I'm going to play Carnegie Hall," Johanson declared to his mother, Helen Johnson. "Baby, mother would be proud if you do," she replied. It was beyond far-fetched to imagine her young Black son would grace the stage of one of America's most storied music halls.[6]

Jaimoe found playing drums in marching band liberating, and drums have consumed his life ever since. "All of that stuff that I had really dug before, I didn't want to be bothered with it anymore," he explained. Lessons were infrequent, and he learned mostly from other drummers. He became adept at rudiments, the building blocks of drumming. "In my school, I was the rudiment champion," he said.[7]

Jai Johanny's love of drums coincided with his lifelong love affair with jazz. "Jazz just slapped me in the face," he said. "It knocked the sense right out of me." He found divine intervention in an unlikely place: his high school library. "God sent *DownBeat* magazine to 33rd Avenue High School for me," he said. "I read that magazine from front to back, everything in it." He ignored the popular music of the day for jazz. "If it wasn't Miles Davis or John Coltrane," the drummer remarked, "I didn't want to hear nothing about it," and he tuned into stations from as far away as Cuba and Europe on short-wave radio. From the conga and timbale players in the big bands of Dizzy Gillespie and Stan Kenton, "I got my introduction to basic percussions," he said.[8]

His first professional gigs were in 1964 on drums for a local band called the Sounds of Soul featuring future ABB bassist Lamar Williams. A year later Jaimoe toured with R&B singer Ted Taylor. In 1966 he joined Otis Redding's band. His jazz inclinations fit poorly with Redding's rhythm and blues. "I wasn't ready yet," Jaimoe recalled. "I could play my drums and all that stuff, but my timing wasn't all that good." Because jazz is improvised, players need to be adept at staying in the moment while simultaneously anticipating where the music is headed. Jaimoe had yet to integrate the two poles. "My timing was terrible because I was always so into the future," he said. "I wasn't into what was happening now."[9]

Jaimoe excelled at improvisation and Redding's sound depended on a precise rhythm and blues backbeat. Jaimoe preferred instead to play less-predictable patterns like jazz drummers Elvin Jones and Jimmy Cobb did. "Otis was into that rock 'n' roll type thing," he recalled. "I'm talking about energy. I didn't have the experience playing like that." As one of two drummers in Redding's band, Jaimoe backed the lower-billed stars on the tour: Sam and Dave, Percy Sledge, Patti LaBelle, and James Carr. "That gave me the chance for variety. I'd rather play for three hours behind them rather than play for an hour behind Otis."[10]

After a few months on the road, Jaimoe realized Redding's band was not the right gig for him. "It was way too loud. And I couldn't play rock 'n' roll like I can now." He left Redding in December 1966 and joined Percy Sledge's band, where he met Twiggs Lyndon, Sledge's tour manager. The drummer and Lyndon maintained a regular correspondence for the next two years, leading to Jaimoe's relocation to Macon in late 1968.[11]

While his jazz rhythms were an awkward fit for Redding's rhythm and blues review, Jaimoe's time on the road honed in him a keen understanding of how to best support his bandmates and propel the music forward. In this construct, drums do more than just provide a rhythmic foundation; the drummer helps stitch the music together. "When I started off I wanted to be the greatest drummer in the world," he recalled. "On the road I learned that making the music sound good was more important than my personal gains."[12]

By 1968 Jaimoe had grown weary of the R&B touring circuit. "I was done with that whole scene where the people who became stars treated their musicians just like they were treated—like dogs," he said. "They made all the money, we got all the crumbs." Even worse, he said, the artists favored stardom over music: "They were so knocked out by what's going on, they forget what the hell is going on."[13]

Life as a backing musician was drudgery. Touring itineraries were demanding. Racism was omnipresent. Pay was abysmal. Things came to a head for Jaimoe in winter 1968 when Clarence Carter's manager docked him $25 for "driving costs." When he learned the poorly paying gig didn't even cover his transportation, Jaimoe left R&B touring for good.[14]

Jai Johanny had joined Carter's touring band from Macon. He had relocated there at Twiggs Lyndon's invitation to play in a studio band Phil Walden was assembling. Jaimoe had even offered to pay his own way to the audition. "Dig man about that studio gig," he wrote Lyndon in April 1968, "I am very grateful for your consideration toward me but as I told you on the phone, I've surpassed what I was doing and to prove it I will gladly pay back anybody who wants me to audition for them."[15]

Jaimoe was the first and as it turns out, the only musician to sign on with Walden's new rhythm section. Broke and with no discernible prospects ahead of him, Jai resolved to leave the South for New York in pursuit of jazz. "I figured if I was going to starve to death, it might as well be doing something I love," he said. Then an invitation to join Duane Allman changed his life.

Jaimoe's motivation to meet Duane was purely financial. "Plain and simple, I went down to Muscle Shoals to make money," he said. He remembered advice from his mentor, drummer Charles "Honey-boy" Otis: "If you want to make some money, go play with them white boys."[16]

The drummer and guitarist found immediate connection. Money no longer motivated Jaimoe. From the first note, his partnership with Duane centered on one thing, the music. It was, he said, "the greatest music I ever played and I knew this was it. I wasn't going anywhere without him. Two days after meeting Duane, all of my dreams came true. We didn't have a nickel but we were all just as happy as could be, doing exactly what we wanted to do."[17]

Duane's playing, spirit, and vision matched Jaimoe's own. "I had been preparing to play in this band without really knowing *what* I was preparing for," Johanson recalled. "It was from playing with all those other musicians that I got all that fiery stuff that people hear in my playing."[18]

Most drummers on the southern R&B circuit tended to stick pretty closely to 4/4 rhythms with a heavily accented backbeat, the precision allowing the stars of the show to shine the brightest. But Jaimoe was different. Bruce Hampton recalled "a richness in his playing" that echoed influence of John Coltrane's drummer Elvin Jones and drummer Zigaboo Modeliste. "He plays so weird nobody knows if he's any good or not," Phil Walden said to Duane. "You're kidding" was Duane's response. "This cat's burnin!"[19]

What made Jaimoe special was not only that he approached the instrument as a jazz drummer but how great he and Duane sounded *together*. While backing R&B stars, the drummer said, he played "bebop stuff on my bass drum, rather than playing a steady pattern that kind of floats along with what the bass player is doing. If you listen to jazz players, they don't necessarily play the bass drum along with the bass player. They just punctuate here and there, and just do different things with it." Jaimoe's technique translated brilliantly with Duane, who found his first official bandmate. "After we started rehearsing, things just sounded so good and loud," Johanson recalled. "I forgot all about the star trip."[20]

Improvisation was important to their musical communication, and it came naturally to Jaimoe, as it is a foundation of African American musical tradition. For musician and Wheaton College professor Delvyn Case, improvision is "the raising of individual creativity/expression to the highest place within the aesthetic world of a song."[21] Wesley Morris writes that without improvisation, "a listener is seduced into the composition of the song itself and not the distorting or deviating elements that noise creates. Particular to Black American music is the architecture to create a means by which singers and musicians can be completely free, free in the only way that would have been possible on a plantation: through art, through music—music no one 'composed' (because enslaved people were denied literacy), music born of feeling, of play, of exhaustion, of hope." Improvisation is "a miracle of sound, an experience that can really happen only once." More than "just music," improvisation affects "the mood or inspiration from which those moments arise."[22]

Already firmly grounded in the blues, Duane's ease with Jaimoe's improvisational aesthetic added new possibilities. His next move was to firm up the rhythm section. "Wait till you hear this bass player," he told Jaimoe. "This cat's bad, man. We're going to have a hell of a band." Though Berry Oakley remained committed to his own band, the Second Coming, Duane was confident he would eventually relent and join the new band.[23]

When Oakley briefly joined the duo for sessions in Muscle Shoals in mid-January 1969, the virtuosity of the two white musicians surprised and impressed Jaimoe. "At that time, there were only a few white people I thought could play music: guys like Stan Getz and Buddy Rich." White musicians tried too hard to mimic Black music "instead of letting themselves come out." Duane and Berry played a louder, heavier sound than he was used to but within a music that allowed him the freedom he sought on the drums.[24]

In a still somewhat unique arrangement for the time, Black and white southerners sharing lodging in the small-town South, Jaimoe moved in with Duane in Muscle Shoals. While Duane played sessions, Johanson rehearsed in FAME's unused studio. During breaks, Allman rolled his amp from one studio to the other to play with Jaimoe. Their music baffled and intimidated FAME's other musicians, all first-call session players. "They'd just come in, sit around the wall and look at us," Jaimoe remembered. "You'd try to get them to jam and they'd say, 'No, not with you.'" The duo "scared the hell out of people," he said. "Nobody would touch a goddamned instrument."[25]

Twiggs Lyndon had a particularly memorable impression: "They jammed for what was probably ten or fifteen minutes, but it seemed longer. I had been in the music business for five years and I'd heard some fine music. I'd heard Jimi Hendrix playing with Little Richard, and Hendrix was almost as good then as he was later." He had one thought as he listened to Duane, Jaimoe, and Berry play together:

> If all the headaches and all the problems I had to go through as a road manager with all those bands for five years were the dues I had to pay to bring me into that studio for that moment in time, to hear this fellow Duane Allman play guitar for this one jam, it would have been worth it. And that if Phil Walden walked in right then, as a spokesman for Fate, and said, "Okay Twiggs, back on the road for another five years with Percy Sledge and Little Richard, and after that I'll let you come back and you can hear him play again," I would have gone right out that studio and done another five years. That was the thought that went through my mind.[26]

The trio was great, but Duane had a larger band in mind. Duane's ideal lineup had two lead guitarists and two drummers from the beginning, ideas virtually unheard of in rock. The Grateful Dead were the only rock band of note with two drummers, though some bands, most notably Santana, employed a drummer on a full trap set and another on percussion, usually congas, bongos, cymbals, and hand-held rhythm instruments. "It's been said that Duane was at first going to put together a power trio like Jimi Hendrix or Cream," Jaimoe noted, "but I would never have been the right guy for that—I was never a power drummer, that's not what Duane was thinking." To Duane, drums were a linchpin that integrated the sounds of a soloist to that of his bandmates. He "wanted the bass, keyboards, and second guitar to form patterns behind the solo The band "comped" as the soloist soloed, improvising their accompaniment along with, rather than behind, him. To Duane, the arrangement required two drummers.[27]

Not yet officially signed on to Duane's new project, Oakley was Duane's next target. The bassist first came into Allman's orbit in July 1968 when Linda Oakley brought her husband to see Hour Glass at the Comic Book club in in Jacksonville. Following the show, Duane and Berry engaged in deep discussions into the wee hours of the morning about their shared musical influences and vision. The meeting sparked an intense, fruitful musical partnership. "You have got to come to the park and see my band play," Berry told Duane. "You will not believe the crowds. All those kids were just hungry for some decent music, and we are giving it to them. They show up by the hundreds and we just play whatever we feel."[28]

A native of Park Forest, Illinois, near Chicago, Oakley took up guitar in 1962, at age fourteen. He soon began leading bands, first the Vibratones, then the Shaynes. Sister Candace Oakley recalled, "[Berry] did all the organizing himself, finding places to play, being the roadie, and playing lead guitar." The Shaynes became part of the youth music scene in the Chicago suburbs, playing Park Forest's teen club and winning a talent show at St. Lawrence O'Toole Catholic Church in nearby Matteson.

Like Duane, Berry was driven to success at a young age, and his talent won him acclaim. At seventeen he was playing guitar on Rush Street, the center of Chicago nightlife. "It was the beginning of his senior year in high school," Candace said, "and he was playing in the city at night and getting home at the crack of dawn."[29]

Sometime in 1965 the Shaynes opened for Tommy Roe and the Ro-emans. Roe was an Atlanta native who had scored several hit singles, with "Sheila" reaching number 1 in 1962. He worked as a solo art-ist until a 1963 tour of England with the Beatles convinced him to find a steady backing band. He found them in the Roemans, a group based in Tampa that played a similar Florida circuit as had the Allman Joys—teen clubs, National Guard armories, and ballrooms.[30]

In fall 1965 Oakley got his break. The Roemans' bass player was drafted, and though Berry didn't play the instrument, he volunteered for the gig. He'd grown bored in Chicago and was eager to move on.

Candace remembered her brother as "very fiery, aggressive. He said, 'Hell, I'll play bass,' and he got a bass and he learned how to play it." His skill and experience on lead guitar made him an especially intuitive bass player, particularly in complement to the guitars. The bass, which Oakley played with a thumb pick, was to remain his pri-mary instrument for the rest of his life.[31]

Berry dropped out of high school at seventeen and relocated to Roe's home base of Atlanta. Though he left the Roemans after a few months, he remained in the region. From that moment forward, the Chicago native was officially a southerner. "I've been down South ever since and I really dig it," he said.[32]

By 1967 Oakley had migrated to southwest Florida and joined the Bittersweet where he met guitarist Dickey Betts. They were the only men in town with long hair. "People would throw shit at us," Dickey Betts recalled. Betts and Oakley formed an immediate musical bond.[33]

Music was a long-standing family tradition for Dickey Betts. "I was probably five years old when I first joined in the weekly family musical gatherings, during which the combined sounds of fiddles and guitars would fill the household," he said. The family played "country- and bluegrass-style music on acoustic instruments." The music's "natural beauty left a deep, lasting impression." His love of country music and admiration for country stars Lefty Frizell and Hank Williams inspired his first goal: "I'm gonna play on the Grand Ol' Opry."[34]

Dickey played ukulele, mandolin, and banjo before moving to gui-tar. He built his guitar chops playing Chuck Berry solos he'd memo-rized to Jerry Lee Lewis's "Whole Lotta Shakin' Goin' On." "I had all these leads that I'd learned. Then I started cutting them in half and piecing them together and then, before I knew it, I was making up stuff of my own and adding to my repertoire." A friend introduced him to bluesmen John Lee Hooker and Muddy Waters, and that led him to Robert Johnson, Blind Willie McTell, and the three Kings: Albert, B. B., and Freddie.[35]

In 1960 Dickey began playing professionally, touring with the Bradenton, Florida-based Swinging Saints. The group played multiple sets a day on the midway of the World of Mirth traveling circus. "We made $125 a week, twenty to thirty shows a day from 10 a.m. through midnight," Betts said. "Road schooling," he noted, "taught me that music has everything to do with what's in your heart."[36]

Betts returned from the World of Mirth gig more determined than ever to play music for a living. He quit high school and went on the road, promising his mother he would eventually finish high school. He never did.[37]

In 1968 Betts joined forces with Oakley, whose commitment to original music inspired him. When they met, Dickey fronted the Sarasota-based Soul Children, a band that included his wife, Dale. The group had some local success playing top-40 covers and scattered originals. They were making good money, $300 a week, but playing covers was a musical dead end. Oakley showed Betts the way forward. "Berry was pretty hip," Dickey remembered. "He knew how to get out of clubs, which was to quit playing Top 40 shit. Berry was trying to get me into playing all originals, quit the club scene and do concerts— even if it had to be free concerts. He had all these great ideas to make us poor!"[38]

In 1968 Oakley finally convinced Betts to pursue original music with the Blues Messengers, a group with Oakley on bass, Dickey and Larry Reinhardt on guitar, Dale Betts on keyboards and vocals, and John Meeks on drums. Though the effort was less successful financially for Betts than Soul Children had been, the guitarist saw in Oakley something many also saw in Duane: the bassist had insight and wisdom that belied his youth. Oakley was convinced there was an audience for the improvisational, blues-based music they played, and he was determined to serve it. "He was the real visionary," Betts said.[39]

Tampa, about sixty miles north of Sarasota, became home base for the Blues Messengers, who scored a regular gig at Dino's blues club. The owners of The Scene, a new club in Jacksonville, recruited the band to play six nights a week. Seeing the long-haired, bearded Oakley's resemblance to popular images of Jesus, they asked the group to change its name to the Second Coming.[40]

The Second Coming didn't play originals as much as they developed exciting arrangements of electric blues and rock. Betts said the group "really sounded a lot like the Allman Brothers. The bass—two guitar players playing lead—real absurd time changes." Its repertoire leaned heavily on the blues. Betts sang Paul Butterfield Blues Band's "Born in Chicago" and Albert King's "Born under a Bad Sign." Oakley handled vocals on Albert King's "Oh Pretty Woman" and on Muddy Waters's "Hoochie Coochie Man," a heavier and more up-tempo arrangement than the original. Reinhardt took the lead on Hendrix's "Fire" and "Manic Depression." Dale Betts sang Grace Slick's parts on Jefferson Airplane songs.[41]

The band found success in Jacksonville. "We were like no other band at the time," drummer Meeks recalled. "We knew it and the people knew it." The band's musicianship "far exceeded anything that anyone else was doing except for the superstars like Cream, the Doors, Jimi Hendrix, Led Zeppelin," he said. Ever the gracious host, Berry invited Stephen Stills and Neil Young to jam after a Buffalo Springfield show in Jacksonville. Stills, one of the era's top guitarists, didn't stay long. As Meeks remembered it, "Dickey was playing at such a higher level that they just couldn't keep up."[42]

In 1968 the Second Coming recorded their lone single, a cover of Cream's "I Feel Free" and Jefferson Airplane's "She Has Funny Cars." Though the arrangements were nearly identical to the originals, the guitar solos are more than mere interludes; they are an integral part of the song's construct. The style would become an Allman Brothers trademark.

Oakley's bass provided the foundation for these explorations. His playing was firmly rooted in blues and rock, but he approached the bass more melodically than rhythmically. He was an endlessly inventive player. Betts said, "We inspired each other's improvisational creativity." Just as he would with the Allman Brothers, Oakley gave the Second Coming three lead instruments, Betts and Reinhardt on guitar and Berry on bass.[43]

The bassist drew particular inspiration from the Grateful Dead and the Jefferson Airplane, two flagship San Francisco bands. Oakley's playing carried from and was of equal measure to their groundbreaking bassists Phil Lesh of the Dead and Jack Casady of the Airplane. The critic Mikal Gilmore calls Oakley "a singular bassist [with] a profound melodic sense that combined fluency with a pulsing percussive touch." Like Lesh and Casady, Oakley "knew how to get under a band's action and lift and push its motion." Joe Dan Petty observed, "Berry played a lot like a guitar player. He played a lot of notes, but he was always very precise, extremely surefooted, extremely tasteful. He had probably the best imagination I've heard in a bass player. He could really step out with those guitar players—and not stomp them, not walk all over what they were doing, but just ride underneath them. He was an extremely aware musician." More lead guitar than rhythm instrument, Berry's thundering, inventive playing took the bass in new directions. "We have one big guitar and two little ones. All we need now is a bass player!" Betts joked.[44]

The Gray House in Jacksonville's Riverside neighborhood served as the Second Coming's headquarters. Under Oakley's direction, a robust music scene developed around the band. "Berry was real socially and politically minded, knew how to make things happen. I was more reclusive, singing and writing was it for me," Dickey recalled. "We were the first people in town to have long hair," he continued. "Berry wanted to bring all of the people together and show the people in Jacksonville that there were a lot of us that thought a certain way." Oakley and the band hosted regular jam sessions at Jacksonville's Willowbranch Park, a few blocks from the Gray House; other times, the players convened at the Forest Inn in the Lake Shore district.[45]

For Berry, Duane's new band remained strictly part time. He remained committed to the Second Coming, particularly in his loyalty to and affinity for Betts, whose guitar work had long garnered notice. Richard Price of the Jacksonville band the Load called Betts "one of the hottest guitar players in Florida." As Michael Ray FitzGerald remembered it, "Betts's guitar playing was our drug," and he recalled his disappointment when he first saw Duane with the Second Coming. "Betts stood by as most of the solos were taken by a diffident young man who looked like the Cowardly Lion and spent most of the show staring down at his Fender guitar." FitzGerald was outraged that "Betts let this guy hog the solos." He was unaware he had witnessed the very beginnings of a remarkable guitar collaboration between Dickey Betts and Duane Allman.[46]

Dickey and Duane were not strangers when they crossed paths in Jacksonville in March 1969. A Floridian, Betts was born in West Palm Beach and moved to the Sarasota area in seventh grade. He and Duane met in the mid-1960s before either had found his distinct voice as a musician or bandleader. The meeting was less than cordial. "They didn't take to one another just right," Joe Dan Petty said. Betts recounted, "I respected Duane a lot from the very first because of his guitar playing, but he was a bit standoffish."[47]

As he courted Oakley, Duane joined the jam sessions in Jacksonville. Berry kept telling Duane that "magic was happening when Betts was around jamming." Simply put, Duane and Dickey sounded fantastic in tandem. "Duane's melody came more from jazz and urban blues," Betts said, "and my melodies came more from country blues with a strong element of string-music fiddle tunes. We were almost totally opposite except we both knew the importance of phrasing. We didn't just ramble about." Improvisation was key. "When we started improvising, things fit, and we didn't analyze it," Betts said. "It fit together beautifully."[48]

Part of that magic was in Duane's ability to improvise harmony guitar underneath Dickey. Betts recounted how "Duane started picking up on things I played and offering a harmony, and we built whole jams off of that." Betts loved the sound. "As we started jamming," he recalled, "we all realized that Duane and I playing harmony guitars together was something that we weren't expecting to hear." Second Coming keyboardist Reese Wynans said, "Dickey's whole thing from the first time I met him was the harmonies. He would come up with these great melodies, and he wanted to get harmonies going for them."[49]

Dickey's love of harmony dated to hearing western swing on country radio. Western swing evolved in the late 1920s in Texas and the Southwest. Its roots and influences were in country and western music, but the form included elements of pop and the folk music traditions of white and black southerners, including jazz and blues. Its most notable performer was Texan Bob Wills, whose Texas Playboys included saxophones, trumpets, clarinets, piano, steel guitar, and drums in addition to the traditional country accompaniment of fiddle, pedal steel, guitar, banjo, and stand-up bass. Western swing also moved the guitar to a prominent position in the music, just as Duane and Dickey would do in southern rock.[50]

Once Dickey joined Duane's ensemble, Oakley officially signed on as well. Duane's band was now a quartet. Though he had some preconceived notions about the final alignment, he remained open to ideas—as long as the players were good and the music was original. "It just formed naturally," Betts said. "If someone fit, they stayed." The collaboration was exciting. "We had discovered the very thing we had been looking for, even if we didn't know it beforehand. We all knew that something very, very good was happening," Betts said. "Berry had a band and a big house and everything. We stayed there and we got it all together. Butch would come over every day so we'd jam. We just all said, 'Well, sounds pretty good, let's try it out on somebody.'"[51]

Butch Trucks became the band's second drummer. "Jaimoe was a real good drummer," Betts recalled, "but the sound was bigger and he wasn't really able to handle the power. It just wasn't his style." Butch, he said, "had that drive and strength." Richard Price also observed, "Butch was well known as a strong-in-the-pocket player, while Jaimoe was more of an embellisher."[52]

A few months shy of his twenty-second birthday, Trucks was the only original Allman Brother with more than cursory formal musical training. He sang in his church choir, took up piano at age twelve, migrated to drums in marching band by eighth grade, and played tympani with the Jacksonville symphony. "I didn't listen to rock 'n' roll that much," he recalled. "I did listen to rhythm and blues on WLAC, but when I listened to music it was mainly classical." Butch brought this influence to the ABB. "As far as people other than drummers influencing my music," he explained, "I'd have to say that Beethoven, Dvorak, Ravel, Debussy, and Gershwin would come long before guitar players. I grew up listening to this music and my approach to music is derived from them and the music I learned in church."[53]

In addition to the symphony, Butch joined his high school's concert and marching bands before making the migration to rock music. He learned from diverse sources: Dave Brubeck's drummer Joe Morello; the Byrds' Mike Clarke; "Wipe Out" by the Surfaris for its bass drum syncopation; and Cream's Ginger Baker. His parents, scions of the

North Jacksonville Baptist Church, did not initially endorse his interest in rock music, but they finally relented and bought him a drum set, he said, "as long as I promised never to play in a place where they served liquor."[54]

In 1964 Butch joined his first band, the Vikings, and by 1965 he was with the Echoes, a Beatles-inspired cover band. While attending Florida State University in 1966, he teamed with fellow Jacksonville natives David Brown and Scott Boyer to form the Bitter Ind, a folk-rock band they later dubbed the 31st of February. In 1968 Vanguard Records released their self-titled debut to little acclaim. The band broke up that September when the label rejected its follow-up, a short-lived collaboration with Duane and Gregg Allman.

Following the dissolution of the 31st of February, Trucks returned to Jacksonville and eventually gravitated to Oakley's jam sessions. His playing added a rock-solid foundation to the music and pushed the band forward. His classical music influence encouraged the explorations. Butch not only was used to groups of musicians turning complex, individual pieces of music into a larger, more cohesive sound; he preferred it.

With Butch's arrival, Duane's new band truly coalesced. "Things started happening with Jaimoe and Butch as soon as they played together," Price recalled. "They formed this strange symbiotic thing and melded into a terrific unit. Over a series of nights you could see something very substantial developing." The band knew the combination of players and the attitude of exploration was extraordinary. "We were all smart enough to say 'this guy's special' about one another," Betts said. The new ensemble offered something different, something they valued. "The whole thing was just about playing music—no agenda, no egos," Betts reflected, "and it was good."[55]

The two guitarists were the band's central focus, and Dickey and Duane's chemistry was undeniable. "They were both willing to take chances rather than returning to parts they knew they could nail," Wynans recalled. "Everything they tried worked."[56]

The rhythm section was also key. As Duane put it, the band needed two drummers "because we knew we was going to be playing loud, and both cats can play everything they need to play if there's two of them instead of one cat having to flog his ass off the whole night." Each drummer's ability, attitude, and affinity for the other made the arrangement work instantaneously. "It happened the first day and it's been happening ever since," Butch said. "It's spontaneous. It's a natural feeling we have for each other."[57]

Two drummers was and is rare in rock music, which is why the concept seems out of the ordinary. But nearly every drummer, including Butch and Jaimoe, first learned to play drums with others in marching band. Yet marching band drummers play carefully choreographed parts, something Trucks and Johanson never did. The two ABB drummers instead meshed their vastly different styles into a drum sound that was bigger than the two of them. Most importantly, Trucks said, "we both listen. Jaimoe listens to what's going on in the band and so do I." Oakey rounded out the rhythm section, his lead bass playing simultaneously holding the rhythm section together while providing a melodic counter to the band's guitarists.[58]

It was a stellar lineup with players who could and would solo at any point in a song. The music was rooted in the blues but veered beyond the standard blues form. This inspiration initially came from Oakley, whose knowledge of and skill on blues guitar and fondness for extended improvisations glued together the various musical elements. "Berry was very dedicated to jamming and deeply into the Dead and the Airplane and the psychedelic approaches and always playing that music for us," Wynans recalled. "It was pretty exotic stuff to our ears, because there were no similar bands in the area. Dickey was a great blues player with the rock edge. And then Duane arrived and he was just on another planet. The power of all combined was immediately obvious."[59]

The music was a southern version of psychedelic rock, a sound that emerged from the San Francisco Bay Area in the mid-1960s. Psychedelic rock, Grateful Dead historian Dennis McNally observes, "is music seeking transcendence through improvisation and an extremely broad understanding of what is music, including things like dissonance and feedback." That this same definition could apply to jazz is not coincidental. In many ways, the jazz impulse inspired the genre. The bands that played psychedelic rock, particularly those that influenced the Allman Brothers Band, played music with the jazzlike ideal of improvisation and individual and group expression. Like jazz, it was music made in and for a particular time and place, the moment.[60]

The difference between jazz and psychedelic rock was the musicians' state of consciousness. Rock musicians added psychedelic drugs such as LSD, psilocybin, and mescaline to the typical regimen of alcohol, marijuana, and pills. The drugs caused disorienting experiences that some players used to push themselves beyond traditional musical boundaries. Psychedelics also further blurred the lines between musician and audience. Because bands and audiences often took the same substances, music became more than mere entertainment; it gave audiences and musicians a feeling of connection.

Duane's new band would meld together all of these styles and inspiration. Like Duane, Oakley and Betts were devoted students of the blues. Unlike Duane, they took an innovative approach to the form. "We would try to take a blues tune," Betts said, "and instead of respecting the sacredness of it, we would go sideways with it." They did so with their amped-up arrangement of Muddy Waters's "Hoochie Coochie Man" or Spencer Davis Group's "Don't Want You No More," an obscure B-side from 1967. Despite exciting arrangements, the Second Coming "was always missing a certain foundation," Dickey said, "while Duane and Gregg didn't quite have the adventurous kind of thing Berry and I brought. When we all came together, we gave each other a new foundation."[61]

On March 23, 1969, after several months playing in jams around Jacksonville, Duane, Jaimoe, Berry, Dickey, and Butch, with Reese Wynans on keyboards, convened to play in an impromptu session that birthed that the Allman Brothers Band. The band set up at Oakley's house at 2844 Riverside Avenue. "We whipped into a little jam," Duane said. "And the jam lasted two and a half hours. When we finally quit, nobody even said a word, man, everybody was speechless." Jaimoe said, "The spirits met and that was it." Butch agreed: "It was like being born again, a revival meeting. I had felt that before playing symphonic music, but this was the first time I'd ever really felt it playing a set of drums, playing rock 'n' roll."[62]

Duane knew this lineup was remarkable. "It really frightened the shit out of everybody," he said. "Right then I *knew*, I said 'Man, here it is, here it is!'" Butch said, "It was pretty obvious what was working. It was this particular group of people who all had the same philosophy. Different musical backgrounds, but what we were looking for at that time was that note." The band created music spontaneously, complementing the soloists on their improvisational forays. It was also made to be played live. The ensemble lacked one crucial element: vocals. "We knew that the band was something special," Dickey said, "but nobody really sang as good as the band could play."[63]

Help soon came from Duane's original collaborator, Gregg. Though the brothers were somewhat estranged following Gregg's return to L.A. after the 31st of February sessions the previous September, Duane intended to enlist Gregg in his new project. Linda Oakley remembered Duane looking out for his younger brother when he first arrived in Jacksonville that March. "We've got to get my brother here, out of that bad situation [in L.A.]. He's a great singer and songwriter and he's the guy who can finish this thing," Duane told her. Jaimoe said, "There was never a doubt that Gregg would be the singer."[64]

After the jam session on March 23, Duane called Gregg in California. "We got it shaking down here and all we need is you," Duane said. "The cats love to play. They're all really into their instruments, they sing a little bit but there's not a whole lot of writing going on so I need you to come and sing and write and round it all up and send it in some sort of direction." Gregg long called it "the finest compliment I ever had."[65]

Since he returned to California to fulfill Hour Glass's contractual obligations, Gregg had recorded and released just one single for Liberty, a cover of Tammy Wynette's "D-I-V-O-R-C-E" released as "Greg Allman & The Hour Glass." Billboard found "a solid blues feel via [a] soulful and dynamic treatment. Much pop and R&B appeal." Gregg called it "sellout bullshit." Unhappy in L.A., Gregg immediately left for Florida.[66]

In addition to playing keyboards, Gregg provided the final two ingredients missing from Duane's new band: vocals and songwriting. The former was a well-known weapon in Gregg's arsenal. "Duane could see Gregg's talent long before he saw it in himself," their mother, Geraldine Allman, reflected. Though he would never develop into a songwriter, Duane knew his brother would. "His stuff don't need much improvement," he said of Gregg. "From the start, his stuff's pretty goddamn good."[67]

Gregg brought to the mix the vocal influences of R&B stars such as Bobby Bland, Ray Charles, Muddy Waters, and his favorite, James

"Little Milton" Campbell. Gregg's ability to channel these gifted vocalists impressed Jaimoe immediately. "I played with Otis Redding and Percy Sledge and saw Ray Charles and B.B. King and every other great and I'll tell you this: there's not anybody I ever heard who sang with more truth and passion than Gregory. He was at the very top. And that shit about him being one of the great 'white blues singers' is straight bullshit. He's a great blues singer. A great singer, period."[68]

In Los Angeles without Duane, Gregg had sharpened his songwriting talents. John McEuen described a demo recording of Gregg's "It's Not My Cross to Bear" as "the sound of Gregg really finding himself." Gregg explained, "I didn't want to be a jukebox anymore, so I kept writing. . . . I was sick of learning parts and making sure they were right." Singer-songwriters Tim Buckley, Stephen Stills, and Jackson Browne offered additional possibilities. "All I had known was R&B and blues," Gregg said. "These guys turned me on to a more folk-oriented approach." Jaimoe appreciated the results. "Gregory's music and singing were based on rhythm and blues and blues he said, but his songwriting was so influenced by people like Bob Dylan and Jackson Browne and other people who wrote poem songs. What made him so unique is the way he combined those things."[69]

Gregg arrived into a pressure-packed situation in Jacksonville. It was a band of top-flight musicians. "You had no choice but to be very good at what you were doing," Jaimoe noted, "because it was a reflection of what you were hearing and everyone around us was so good." On March 26, 1969, Gregg stepped into his first band rehearsal. "Jesus Christ, what a band!" he said. "It just knocked me out." He fit right in as band revved up its cover of Muddy Waters's "Trouble No More." "His voice and his lyrics were like two more instruments," Jaimoe recalled." Gregg was the final piece of the puzzle, just as Duane planned.[70]

Gregg's arrival completed the lineup, and Duane had finally found the creative outlet and originality he'd long sought. It made a believer out of Jaimoe, who until he joined forces with the Allman Brothers believed white musicians merely mimicked great Black musicians. "They never allowed themselves to come through," he said. In Jacksonville with the Allman Brothers, Jaimoe learned otherwise. "Gregg sounded great," the drummer said, "but he sounded like himself. He had that right from the first day I met him." Black musicians chastised

Jaimoe for playing with the ABB. "Jai Johanny, what are you doing with these white boys? Why are you in a rock 'n' roll band?" they would ask. "Those motherfuckers can play!" he responded.[71]

Gregg brought the picture into sharp focus. "In the beginning it was so amazing I don't even know how to put it into words," said Betts. "We all knew we were on to something special because we'd been putting bands together for years at that point." Duane's former bandmate Paul Hornsby noticed the difference. "I don't know how it could have been any better or anybody else they could have chosen that could've done a better job," he said. "You had six people that were just out there just slaying it. Duane is part of it and it's a unit. It's not just a lead guitar player out front, it's not just a lead singer. This whole thing was just one big glob of power." For Duane and his mates, the band was the fulfillment of a long quest. "When the six of us got together," Jaimoe recalled, "we became what we were looking for and who we were looking for and it was clear as a bell. It was just a great bunch of guys playing and it was just so natural. We never talked about what we were doing or told each other what to do. Everyone just played." The new band played a mélange of southern musical flavors with a contemporary rock music flair. It was what Jaimoe called "American music."[72]

Live audiences responded affirmatively from the very beginning. Gregg recounted the band's first appearance at a Second Coming show in Jacksonville: "Toward the end of the gig, Oakley said, 'We got a little surprise for you,' and my brother and I join them on stage. The place went berserk. . . . Those people were howling—that night changed them." The response changed the band as well. "It was clear," Gregg concluded, "this was fucking working. . . . On the drive back home, all we did was talk about this or that, and this part right here going over there—it was just lined up. . . . We could see our destiny, and we set out to get it."[73]

After several failed attempts at grabbing the brass ring, Duane Allman and his bandmates created an original sound and musical construct. . The band would be a live ensemble, and the players understood the endeavor as decidedly uncommercial. If the music industry was not interested in their music, so be it. "Before we start anything," Duane said, "let's just say to hell with it, man! Let's don't get that same shit started up." The band "did everything possible against being commercial. Luckily, we got away with it." Duane's recording deal with Atlantic allowed him to put together something that "would just sound like us, instead of something that they would just try to get to sell," Duane said. It was "the best thing that ever happened to any of us." Betts said, "The band was so good, we thought we'd never make it."[74]

They got away with it because of the patronage of Atlantic Records and its partnership with Phil Walden. "All of us were playing in good little bands," Betts noted, "but Duane was the guy who had Phil Walden. And Duane was hip enough to say, 'Hey Phil, instead of a three-piece, I have a six piece, and we need $100,000 for equipment.' And Phil was hip enough to have faith in this guy. If there was no Phil Walden and no Duane Allman there would have been no Allman Brothers Band."[75]

With the formation of the Allman Brothers Band, Duane Allman had earned a hard-fought victory to pursue his musical vision. He had graduated from the leader of cover bands playing in small-town nightclubs and bars, to failed attempts in Nashville and Los Angeles, to life as an A-list session musician, to leading his own band. Most importantly, the band would play original music and play live as often as possible.

A HOME IN MACON
(SPRING AND SUMMER 1969)

We're doing what we want to do more than anything else, and if we can make a living at it too, that's just beautiful.

Berry Oakley

Within a few weeks of Gregg's arrival from L.A., the band left Jacksonville for Macon, home of Duane's manager Phil Walden. Given his experience with Dallas Smith and Liberty Records, it might seem curious that Duane agreed to live again under the watchful eye of the music business. But Duane trusted Walden, and the band trusted Duane. Besides, Macon wasn't the big city; at around 120,000 residents it was about one-fifth the size of Jacksonville.

In Macon, the Allman Brothers Band forged their brotherhood as players and as people. The atmosphere offered the band a laid-back environment in which to grow its sound. In the relative calm of Macon, the ABB grew ever more determined to present themselves not as rock stars but as a band of everyday people.

Twenty-nine-year-old Phil Walden founded Phil Walden Artists & Promotions while he was still in high school. His first client was Otis Redding, whose career was tragically cut short in a plane crash in December 1967. Redding's death devastated Walden. His star was on the rise after a blistering set at the Monterey Pop Festival that June, and the two had been building a studio together in Macon. Walden vowed to never again get close to an artist, a pledge he broke with Duane.[1]

Talent notwithstanding, one other factor influenced Walden's interest in Duane: his race. Walden signed Duane after attending the

1968 conference of the National Association of Television and Radio Announcers (NATRA), a trade association for African American DJs. As is true in most matters regarding money, there was friction between the predominantly white label and radio station owners who were doing the least and making the most, and the Black artists and DJs, who provided the labor. Things came to a boil at the 1968 NATRA conference in Miami when Walden, Wexler, and a number of white music-industry professionals were threatened with violence over the issue. Walden chose to shift focus. "I decided to go into white rock 'n' roll," he said.[2]

Walden and Duane first came in contact in early 1969, a little more than a year after Redding's death. "Phil was a very charismatic guy who just had it," FAME's Rick Hall said. "He wanted to be big in the pop rock world, and he saw Duane as the means to do that." When Walden heard Duane on Pickett's "Hey Jude," he said to himself, "That's the guy I want." With a loan from Jerry Wexler, Walden purchased Duane's contract from Hall.[3]

Walden had an unshakeable belief in Duane. "This guy is going to be a superstar," he said. In the early, lean years, Duane appreciated Walden's support. "Without Phil Walden, there'd be no Allman Brothers," Duane said. "He believed in us and helped us in every possible way."[4]

The band that relocated to Macon was young. Betts, at twenty-five, was the senior member of the group, followed by Jaimoe (twenty-four), Trucks and Duane (twenty-two), and twenty-one-year-olds Gregg and Oakley. They were young but not callow. "For such young cats that band was really mature," Betts recalled. "We weren't a garage band. We were a nightclub band. We had brought ourselves up in the professional world by actually playing in bars, and that really gives you a lot more depth. We all had a lot of miles under our wheels when we first met, despite our ages." Their music was road-hardened. "Each man in the group has been a musician for years, working in bar bands, country and jazz groups, the whole route," Oakley said. "Our music just sort of evolved out of that mixture. It was a sound that was truly unique to the band."[5]

Once in Macon, the ten-member band and crew moved into Twiggs Lyndon's two-room apartment at 309 College Street, which they dubbed "the Hippie Crash Pad." The group maintained an intense regimen of rehearsals, developing a repertoire that included Gregg's originals and new arrangements of blues songs. The environment encouraged each player to explore his own sound and influences as they created a cohesive sound. "The music was so important to us," Gregg said. "The only thing we wanted to do was get our sound tighter and tighter, get it better and better. We played for each other, we played to each other, and we played off each other."[6]

This unity of purpose was important to Duane's creative ideal. "These six guys have always worked for one sound, one direction," Duane said. "But everyone plays like he wants to play. He just keeps that goal in mind. If you know what you can do and you're satisfied in your heart that you're doing it, you ain't gonna have no problems." "We're doing what we want to do more than anything else," Oakley said, "and if we can make a living at it too, that's just beautiful."[7]

Atlantic Records executive Wexler recalled, "They were concerned only with music, and not with the promulgation of a rock 'n' roll appearance, or the projection of a rock lifestyle. It was just music." Hour Glass taught Duane how little visual presentation mattered. "He found those appurtenances laughable and absurd," Wexler said, "all these attempts to fortify the music with some sort of visual act." Music was enough entertainment in itself. "If the music didn't entertain us," Wexler remarked, "there was nothing else we were interested in."[8]

It is easy to take a cynical view of the musicians' rejection of the commercial aspects of the music industry. Wexler's and Walden's support did give the band some financial stability while they developed their sound. Similarly, later successes surely color their memories. Nevertheless, from the beginning it was clear that the band sought more than just financial and chart success. "Music became something other than a career," Butch recalled. "We were all out to be rock stars, that's what everybody wanted to do, but once we played that music together, then music became something else. It was more of a religion than it was a way to make money." Duane explained, "We're just working our way up, trying to perfect what we think is right. We're studying our particular method of communication and trying to iron it out to where there can be no doubt in anybody's mind as to what we're trying to do. To portray our lives and main success through music."[9]

As the band settled in Macon, a new element entered its milieu: psychedelic mushrooms. The drug was particularly conducive to the band's developing sense of improvisation. "There's no question that taking psilocybin helped create so many spontaneous pieces of music," Gregg said. The band would get up, eat breakfast, and each eat half a pill of psilocybin extract. "Our shit would be set up, somebody would name a key, and we start jamming, and that really spurred on our creative process," he said. Gregg described the jams as otherworldly, "so powerful that we wouldn't talk for a long time afterwards—no one would say shit. We kept doing that, learning how each other played, learning where each guy was coming from. Our musical puzzle was coming together and mushrooms certainly enhanced that whole creative experience."[10]

A mushroom soon became the band's official symbol. It was the product of two artists from Atlanta's Wonder Graphics firm, W. David Powell and James Flournoy Holmes. Powell said the band didn't request a mushroom logo, but "it didn't require much of a fight to land on the subject. Drug culture was pervasive throughout the music industry and the hippie movement." And while psychedelic mushrooms were very much part of the band's culture, Gregg debunked the notion that the band intended its logo to be as an advertisement for drug use. "That mushroom logo wasn't screaming, 'Hey, people, go take psilocybin.' It was screaming, 'Listen to the fucking Allman Brothers,'" he said. Eventually, every member of the Allman Brothers Band and its road crew got a tattoo of the logo on his right calf, a trend the band carried on with new members until its final year in 2014.[11]

The mushrooms aided in the band's improvisation, an aesthetic of a composition in-the-moment that became the foundation of the band's sound. Eric Clapton and Cream again provided inspiration. "They were the first rock band to really get into improvisation," Butch said. "They were an absolute necessity to what came later. Without them, you don't get us." Jaimoe introduced his bandmates to another vital piece of the improv puzzle, jazz, from John Coltrane, Miles Davis, Charlie Parker, and Cannonball Adderley, among others.[12]

The Allman Brothers amalgamated a variety of musical sources, but how the group manifested its jazz influence sets them apart. The band exemplifies what writer Ralph Ellison called "the jazz impulse, . . . a constant process of redefinition" as artists present themselves simultaneously as individuals, members of communities, and carriers of tradition and culture. With jazz, scholar Craig Werner asserts, "who you are, the people you live with and for, the culture you bear, everything remains open to question, probing, reevaluation." A primarily instrumental medium, jazz manifested in a wide repertory of pop, folk, and religious standards and minstrelsy, ragtime, and blues. The form offered musicians an unfettered opportunity for individual and collective musical expression.[13]

John Coltrane's version of Rodgers and Hammerstein's "My Favorite Things" from *The Sound of Music* is one example of the jazz impulse. The studio version from Coltrane's 1961 album of the same name is among Duane's most cited influences. In it, Coltrane expands the Rodgers and Hammerstein show tune to thirteen-plus minutes, with the saxophonist and pianist McCoy Tyner improvising solos over a two-chord vamp. Each begins with an interpretation of the melody, providing a familiar frame for listeners. After soloing for several measures, the saxophonist and pianist return to the melody, signaling a transition to the next section of the song for bandmates while also offering a change of pace for the listener. At the end of Coltrane's second solo, he plays the melody one last time, the coda completing the passages Coltrane began nearly twelve minutes earlier. With "My Favorite Things," Coltrane completely changed a two-minute show tune into one of the best-known jazz tracks in history.

From Coltrane and Miles Davis, whose album *Kind of Blue* featured Coltrane and set a template for modal jazz, Duane and his band learned ways to incorporate improvisational concepts and ideas into their own music. Like Coltrane and Davis, solos would be extemporaneous, with bandmates providing support with their own improvised chords, rhythms, and countermelodies. Also like Coltrane and Davis, soloists would adhere to song format and structure, however loosely.

Spontaneity was essential. "The whole sound evolved and developed out of that spontaneous jamming," Trucks stated. From jams and improvisations the band developed songs and arrangements. "Gregg would have a song with chords," Betts said. "We'd forget about the song and just play off two or three chords, and just let things kind of happen. Berry would start a riff, and everybody would go to that and try to build on it. And if it didn't happen, we'd go on to something else. As vague as it sounds, that's why it sounded so natural; that whole thing was a real natural process."[14]

The extended jams became both a means for the band to satisfy itself musically and yet another way to turn its back on the music business. "We didn't want to just play three minutes and it be over," Gregg recalled. "We definitely didn't want to play nobody else's songs like we had to do in California. We were going to do our own tunes, which at first meant mine, or else we're going to take old blue songs like 'Trouble No More' and totally refurbish them to our tastes."[15]

"Trouble No More" by Muddy Waters was the first song the six band members played together with Gregg when he arrived in Jacksonville. A demo recording the band made in Macon in April 1969 features an arrangement close to Waters's 1955 original. But it is an original arrangement, considerably faster and a full minute longer, and it more heavily stresses the backbeat. "Trouble No More" carries long instrumental passages and guitar solos by Dickey and Duane, the latter on slide guitar. The dual-lead guitar arrangement represented a new dimension for blues rock. It was Duane's second major stamp on American popular music.

The demo session included an instrumental version of the Spencer Davis Group's "Don't Want You No More" that segued into Gregg's "It's Not My Cross to Bear," a tune he brought with him from Los Angeles. The Allmans adopted the Second Coming's basic arrangement of the former but shortened it from nine minutes on a bootleg recording marked as March 1969 from Jacksonville to 2:24 on their debut album. Unlike the Second Coming's vocal arrangement, the ABB recorded "Don't Want You No More" with Dickey and Duane harmonizing the vocal melody lines on guitar, which became an Allman Brothers hallmark.[16]

Harmony guitar is a somewhat exacting technique, as it requires musicians to play different notes in a scale at the same time, called intervals. For this reason, most musicians work out harmonies in advance, as Duane and Dickey did with "Don't Want You No More." But that wasn't always the case. Because neither Betts nor Allman had any appreciable formal musical training and the band thrived on improvisation, the guitarists instead worked out harmony arrangements by ear in rehearsals and jam sessions. "We didn't study the structure of the scales or spend time figuring out on paper what should work," Betts explained. "We approached harmonizing guitar parts in the same way we approached vocal harmonies: we would try a few different ideas, and go with the one that sounded the best to our ears."[17]

Macon found Gregg in the midst of the most prolific writing period of his career. Of the two dozen songs he brought with him from Los Angeles, only two, "It's Not My Cross to Bear" and "Dreams," made the repertoire. Inspired in the new environment, he quickly composed "Whipping Post" and "Black Hearted Woman." The band worked tirelessly on his songs, changing arrangements, varying time signatures and tempos, adding their own flavor to the mix. Rehearsals developed the band's musical vocabulary. "We liked playing together so much, and someone would always come up with a new idea and keep a song alive," Gregg wrote. "Some songs were regular length, but some were real, real long." Jaimoe said they'd practice the songs "four or five times to get the arrangement down, and then play them." The band would then road-test the songs. "After we played them on a couple of gigs," Jaimoe explained, "Duane would say, 'On this part here, let's do this or that instead.'"[18]

This is how "Whipping Post," one of the band's most famous songs, developed. Gregg originally brought the band what Dickey called a "melancholy, slow minor blues." Oakley reworked the ballad into a driving blues tour de force, beginning with an emphatic repeating bass line that changed the song's introduction from the more traditional 4/4 time signature to 11/8. The change sped the song up, giving it an urgency that adapted well to the live environment.[19]

Oakley's arrangement on "Whipping Post" is yet another example of his importance to the band. "As much as Duane," Trucks said, "Berry was responsible for what this band became." His approach to his instrument provided texture as well as a solid foundation. As bassist, Oakley was the glue that held the rhythm section together. But the bass is also a melodic instrument, and this is where Oakley excelled in the musical structure of the Allman Brothers Band. "Oakley was a very instinctive bass player," Gregg said. "He knew when to just sink into the repetition of a song, so the bottom was there for the rest of the band." Jaimoe shared how the bassist's approach impacted his playing. "Berry was the first cat who allowed me to relax and enjoy his playing," he said. Perhaps most importantly, Berry's playing fit Duane's vision, Gregg said. Oakley was "the bass player my brother had always been looking for. They were so tight—spiritually, musically, brotherly. . . . They really had a thing going."[20]

Oakley's lead bass became a major element of the band's developing sound. Berry's off-the-cuff melodies sparked the band's improvisation. "There were times when Berry would be playing a line or phrase and Duane would catch it, then jump on it and start playing harmony," Betts recalled. "Then maybe I'd lock into the melodic line that Duane was playing, and we would all three be off. Berry would take over and give us the melody."[21]

While Duane didn't model the Allman Brothers Band on the Grateful Dead, the San Francisco band was the Allman Brothers' closest corollary, and from their earliest days, people compared the bands. Formed near San Francisco in 1965, the Grateful Dead were among the first and most notable American rock bands. Unlike the ABB, their oeuvre was rooted in folk, not blues, but both bands excelled at R&B and blues covers. Each group had its share of instrumental virtuosos, though even hard-core Deadheads acknowledge the Dead's lineup lacked the across-the-board virtuosity of the ABB.

The Dead were among the bands that ushered in the rock era in America. The Allman Brothers Band followed in their wake. Rock was an evolution of popular music that transformed rock 'n' roll from dance music to music experienced live. Rock shows were an individual and collective cultural experience that blurred the lines between musician and audience. "[Rock] spoke exclusively to youth," historians Bill Malone and David Stricklin observe. "[It] reflected a nonconformist, anti-establishment youth culture . . . whose traits became virtually worldwide: long hair, unconventional dress, illicit drug use, sexual freedom, and hostility toward or disinterest in politics or civic and religious authority figures."[22]

The transition from rock 'n' roll to rock changed live music into a full-fledged musical event. Concerts became participatory art. "The live setup," critic Richard Meltzer notes, "adds *visual* accompaniment to mere music and a space for it to fill and bounce around at least metaphorically." Concerts provided the backdrop for cultural expression in tandem with audiences.[23]

This mindset was especially true for the Grateful Dead, whose music and live shows quenched the "desire for meaningful ritual," the

Dead's Jerry Garcia argued. Psychedelic drugs played a huge role in the events as the musicians grew less inhibited onstage. "Playing high instilled in us a love for the completely unexpected." Listeners were an active part of the performance. "Each person deals with the experience individually," Garcia noted. "But when people come together, this singular experience is ritualized."[24]

Where the Dead and Allman Brothers most closely intersect is in the styles of their bass guitarists, Phil Lesh and Berry Oakley. One only needs to listen to "Dark Star," the Grateful Dead's psychedelic masterpiece from their 1968 album *Live/Dead*, to hear the Dead's influence on the ABB. The twenty-three-minute track is primarily instrumental; the band is in constant communication throughout multiple movements, tempos, and sounds. On "Dark Star," Lesh plays lead bass throughout, never losing the rhythm while having an intense musical conversation with his bandmates, holding the music together while playing along with and encouraging Garcia's lingering leads. The jam revolves around Lesh, as every Allman Brothers Band jam would revolve around Oakley.

Though the bands had similar musical aesthetics and audience-first philosophies, the Allman Brothers Band and the Grateful Dead approached their music differently. The Dead began as an electric jug band; the Allmans remained firmly rooted in the blues. The Dead's extended jams, particularly on *Live/Dead,* were unconventional musical adventures, less tethered to song structure and formula and more like psychedelic explorations. The Allmans had elements of this in their sound but did not follow the Dead's unbridled, free-form style. The ABB hewed more closely to arrangements. The bands sounded similar because they approached music from the improvisational perspective first. The Dead's success and influence in this manner validated the ABB's own pursuit of music that focused first on composition in the moment and live performance.

Another example of the Dead's influence on the Allman Brothers Band is on "Mountain Jam." The jam derived from "There Is a Mountain," a 1967 single by British folk artist Donovan. Given Oakley's interest in the Dead, the Allmans also might have picked up the idea from Jerry Garcia, who quoted the melody in "Alligator" on the Dead's 1968's *Anthem of the Sun.* "It was literally a jam that turned into a song," Betts recalled. Gregg said, "We just started playing it one day, a happy little melody and it makes for a really nice jam." The earliest recording of the 100 percent improvised instrumental that became "Mountain Jam" is a twelve-minute snippet from a bootleg recording from Macon's Central City Park on May 4, 1969. In less than a year, the band would stretch out the song beyond thirty minutes, including multiple movements and solos from all six members.[25]

Donovan's simple pop song provided a platform for the band's explorations and influences. Jaimoe recalled Duane quoting "Shortnin' Bread," a nineteenth-century Black folk song, which prompted "Dickey's melody that answered and made statements in response to Duane's melody." In a nod to the band's southern musical roots, Duane would often lead the band in the Carter Family standard "Will the Circle Be Unbroken" as the song wound down.[26]

Only three audio sources survive from 1969 to give a sense of the band's developing music: studio demos from April, a partial recording of a May live set from Macon's Central City Park, and *The Allman Brothers Band*, the group's debut album, recorded in August and released in November. The band recorded four demos at Capricorn Studios soon after arriving in Macon in April 1969. The tracks present a band in the earliest stages of its development, and it is hardly surprising that the sound is somewhat tentative at times. The group had been together for less than a month, and only Duane, Gregg, and Butch had any appreciable studio experience. Of the four songs, only "Dreams" emerged markedly different on the band's debut album, with Dickey forgoing the wah-wah pedal and Duane adding a slide solo. Duane played slide with swagger on "Trouble No More." An instrumental "Don't Want You No More" clocked in at a tight two minutes. Gregg's "It's Not My Cross to Bear" sounds more contemplative than the bolder version they recorded later in the year.

The Macon Central City Park show on May 4 is the only circulating live Allman Brothers recording from 1969. It includes Gregg's "Black Hearted Woman" and two blues covers, "Outskirts of Town," a standard of the era the band borrowed from Ray Charles, and John Lee Hooker's "Dimples," both of which Duane and Gregg had played in Hour Glass. By August 1969, when the band began to record its first album, it added at least three more songs to its repertoire: Gregg's "Every Hungry Woman" and "Whipping Post" and one cover, "Statesboro Blues," the song that inspired Duane to pick up slide.[27]

The songs and ideas sprang from a deep well of musical influences the new bandmates introduced to each other. "We all dug this different stuff," Gregg said. "Everybody had their records that they listened to and we just shared them," Jaimoe said. "I had no idea who the Grateful Dead or the Rolling Stones were, though I had heard some of their songs on the jukebox. Butch turned me on to all that stuff. Dickey was into country and Chuck Berry. Duane, Gregory, Berry, and myself were the rhythm and bluesers." B. B. King remained on the turntable, as did Albert King, Junior Wells, Elmore James, Lightnin' Hopkins, Blind Willie McTell, and Robert Johnson and stalwarts such as Ray Charles and Eric Clapton. "What came out was a mixture of all of it," Gregg said.[28]

Jazz set the bar for the band's musical aspirations, and Miles Davis's *Kind of Blue* and John Coltrane's *My Favorite Things* were in regular rotation. Duane said, "[Jazz] cats catch the flow, so it's on a level man that—like if you can ever achieve, you'll never be satisfied with nothing else." Jazz added color to the palette. Betts said, "The blues background was right in there, and then Roland Kirk, Pharoah Sanders, and John Coltrane gave my music that far-out effect, and then adding that blues thing makes it a little more soulful."[29]

As they developed their sound, Duane and his mates kept one thing in mind: the importance of a live audience. They played music that moved them, and they pursued audiences who responded to it. It was a symbiotic relationship, one Duane sought with intentionality. It was the prime motivator for him to leave his cushy session job in Muscle Shoals in the first place.

The band-audience dynamic began with the musicians first playing for each other. "We're up there playing for ourselves first and foremost," Butch said. "If I'm not getting myself off, how can I expect anyone else to get off on it? I start with myself then move out to the guys in the band, and then we start communicating. We kick it into overdrive and go into places that we can't go by ourselves."[30]

This was the essence of "hittin' the note," the band's musical philosophy and ultimate goal. To hit the note was to play music free of pretense, the band's best musical expression, what Betts called "getting down past all the bullshit, all the put-on, all the acting that goes along with just being human. Getting right down to the roots, the source, the truth of the music. Letting it happen, letting that feeling come out." To Jaimoe, hittin' the note described spiritual transcendence, "times when I was so at peace with what I was playing, that my spirit left my body, right on stage."[31]

The ABB's new sound quickly attracted a following. Producer Tom Dowd said the band "had a very strong groove, with jazz permutations and elements of blues, and then they could rock. And the audience was ready for it." Betts said, "The audience was taken by what we were playing—getting way into it, and telling us they hadn't heard anything like what we were playing." Listeners, the guitarist recalled, "wanted to hear the improvisation and the individual expression of each different band member."[32]

The Allman Brothers Band hit at the right historical moment for a band to present itself as regular people expressing individuality through music. American culture was skewing younger, and by 1970, more than 40 percent of Americans were under age twenty-five. Individual expression was their gold standard, shifting American culture and shaping its music. The Allman Brothers Band reaped the dividends. "We just try to make the audience be consumed by what we're doing and if we can make that magical kind of music happen," Betts explained. "They don't know what's happening exactly, except they know that we're really focused on what we're doing and it sounds good, and the energy is good. What they will do is forget about this and forget about that and have fun, just simply have fun for two or three hours." Duane agreed. "Music is fun," he said. "It's not supposed to be any heavy deep intense thing."[33]

From their home base in Macon, the Allman Brothers developed a reputation as a band that represented everyday people, projecting an image that they were no different from their audience. They were the same age, wore the same clothes, and spoke the same language. "We weren't any different from the people we played for except we were a band," Betts said. The band represented the audience onstage, and audiences valued this. "There was a bond between us," he said. It was music for working people, "common people, like me." It was a simple formula: "No star shit, or any kind of intellectual shit." The Allman Brothers Band members saw themselves as workaday musicians and people. Within two years, this idea would manifest in the band's promotions as the "People's Band."[34]

THE JOURNEY BEGINS
(MAY-DECEMBER 1969)

You don't, can't, "listen" to the Allman Brothers, you *feel it, hear it, move with it, absorb it.*

Miller Francis Jr.

That the Allman Brothers' music translated poorly in the studio and therefore in the marketplace remained a frustration for the band, its label, and fans—until *At Fillmore East* broke the band into the mainstream in 1971. Until then, the ABB trod a more traditional path, of studio albums and relentless touring. The group spent the first nine months of that journey sharpening their sound and building a reputation as a "don't miss" live act. In August 1969 they recorded their debut album, *The Allman Brothers Band*. It failed to dent the charts.

The Allman Brothers Band's official live debut was May 2, 1969, at Macon's College Discotheque, advertised as an "Experimental Blues Rock Music Feast" with an "underground blues-rock group from Florida . . . the most inventive experimental blues rock group in existence today." Duane—"formerly a member of a San Francisco rock group THE HOUR GLASS"—received top billing. "Nicknamed 'Skyman' by Wilson Pickett for his unusual style as he played guitar on 'Hey Jude.' When Atlantic Records heard his performance on 'Hey Jude' he was immediately requested to do recording sessions for some of their other artists. Included in his credits are 'The Weight' by Aretha Franklin, 'Ob-La-Di, Ob-La-Da' by Arthur Conley, and 'The Road of Love' by Clarence Carter."[1]

Given Duane's discomfort with being singled out from his mates, the flyer highlighting him as the group's star was surely Walden's idea.

In marketing Hour Glass as a San Francisco band, Walden hoped to connect the ABB with the well-known Bay Area music scene in the minds of fans. The flyer's language sent an additional signal to express the band's connection with youth culture. The concert was more than a performance; it was an event. "Prepare your mind to be musically educated as you experience the Allman Brothers," it advised. A radio promotion added a special invitation to hip youth: "Heads welcome." Despite the efforts, the hometown audience was unmoved; the show drew less than forty paying attendees.[2]

One week later, May 11, 1969, the band journeyed ninety miles north to play a free show at Atlanta's Piedmont Park. The event made a lasting impression on the band and audience, a bond that built as the group played the park regularly for the next eighteen months. The Piedmont Park shows bolstered the band's confidence in its new sound. The free concerts were also an extension of the jams Berry Oakley organized in Jacksonville.[3]

"Pure as hell" is how Bruce Hampton of the Atlanta-based Hampton Grease Band remembered the ABB's performance that day. "You could feel the purity in the fire in the intensity: nobody was playing checkers or talking business. This was music for music's sake. The chemistry of putting all those guys together took them to a different level." Promoter Alex Cooley said the musicians were "so in tune with each other that when they are playing together so perfectly, they all knew what each of the others were doing."[4]

The Allman Brothers' appearance at Piedmont Park on May 11 earned it a cover story in the following week's issue of the *Great Speckled Bird*, Atlanta's alternative newspaper. Attendees told of a band that created exciting, cohesive music with a spirit of improvisation and freedom. "They set up about 2 o'clock," an anonymous "friend and reader" wrote, "and proceeded to blow everybody's mind within eye and ear range for the next several hours. The general opinion going through the crowd was that these guys could stand up against the best—Hendrix, Cream, etc." Steve Wise called it "incredible music [that] shows how irrelevant, silly most verbiage is. Including this." Philip Lane recalled the concert as "a physical and spiritual experience, six guys all playing as one giant organism."[5]

"You don't, can't, 'listen' to the Allman Brothers," began Miller Francis Jr.'s *Great Speckled Bird* May 19 cover story on the ABB's first

Piedmont Park appearance. "You *feel it, hear it, move with it, absorb it* and enter into an experience through which you are changed." The Allman Brothers were "fantastically together," he wrote, authentic interpreters of Black music drawing "as heavily from the blues as the experience of young white tribesmen can without exploiting its source." The musicians, he remarked, "play a form of what some might want to call 'hard blues' but that term says nothing of their real achievements. What informs their creation is not Black music but the experience of young white tribesmen in experiencing Black music. Thus Black music can be approached creatively by our musicians if the jumping off place is our experience of that music rather than the music itself." The Allman Brothers Band, Francis concluded, "know all this, and a lot more."[6]

Working from Macon, the Allman Brothers Band began a relentless touring schedule that kept them on the road for nearly three hundred days a year for the next two and a half years. On May 30–31, 1969, they made their first trip north to play a music industry showcase at Don Law's Boston Tea Party. The Allman Brothers opened for the Velvet Underground, whose gritty urban rock was a poor match with the Allmans' bluesy, improvisational approach.

The band made a tepid impression. "Most of the agents didn't really understand what the band was trying to do," Walden recalled. Consensus was that the Allman Brothers needed to emphasize entertainment over their workaday stage presence and improvisation. "Everyone present had all manner of suggestions," Jon Landau reported. "One individual suggested that 'the good looking boy' [Gregg] get out from behind the organ and do the lead singer thing. I agreed, and also suggested that they needed more of a stage act. Someone else chimed in with the thought that they should turn down the volume."[7]

Someone advised Walden, "Dress up those guys a bit." Duane's response was curt: "If you wanna go to a fashion show I suggest you go to the garment district. But if you want to hear rock 'n' roll music, you shouldn't be too concerned about what we're wearing." Duane had already learned this lesson. He gave little credence to music-industry critiques, particularly those that suggested how to present his music. With Walden's support, he did things his own way.[8]

The showcase's host, promoter Don Law, found the ABB "exciting and exhilarating and magical," and he booked them for a return engagement opening for Dr. John on June 19–21. Unable to afford the round trip to Macon, the band squatted in an abandoned building in Boston, setting up and playing a free show for the locals just as they had in Jacksonville, Macon, and Atlanta. "We were elated with our sound," Betts said, "so we just started to travel around the country playing for free." It was, Capricorn's Bunky Odum explained, "the secret of their success: working. This band played in almost every town that had a hall. They'd play anywhere, and if they were passing through a town on a Sunday, their day off, they'd play in a park if they could get electricity."[9]

The free shows were Oakley's idea, an expression of his values and those of his generation. It was an expansion of the jams he had hosted in Jacksonville that led to the creation of the Allman Brothers Band. The success of the concept shows another aspect of Oakley's leadership of the ABB. He was more than just Duane's ideal bass partner; he was also his chief accomplice. "Berry was as much the leader of this band as Duane was," Jaimoe remarked, "the brains behind the Allman Brothers Band." Dickey remembered the bassist's "sharp sense of the big picture." Dickey said Berry "knew enough about how to do business, and he knew how to deal with people. He was the social dynamics guy. He wanted our band to relate to the people honestly. He was always making sure that the merchandise was worth what they were charging, and he was always going in and arguing about not letting the ticket prices get too high, so that our people can still afford to come see us."[10]

Free shows demonstrated the band's kinship with and commitment to audience. The shows broke down barriers between the artist and listeners. And they were Oakley's brainchild from the beginning. "Berry had a sense that it was more than music," Betts said. "He wanted to bring everybody together." Gregg said Berry "was a real motivated guy. If there wasn't some stuff happening, he'd start it."[11]

As far as the audience was concerned, the band's willingness to play for free meant more than just free music. The musicians were giving something away, sure, but their playing inspired listeners' own desire for individual expression. In this environment, music took on a deeper meaning. After the ABB's first Piedmont Park gig Francis reflected, "There are times when it's easy to think that the rock and roll musician is the most militant, subversive, effective, whole, together, powerful force for radical change on this planet, other times you know it's true." Music, E. Bommba Jr. declared, "is the greatest radicalizing force in our culture." Music drew the youth counterculture to Piedmont Park, especially, Bill Mankin said, "the newest and most groundbreaking music, which was the most fluid, subversive and powerfully influential catalyst helping the counterculture to spread and coalesce. It alone seemed to have the power to act as a common, galvanizing thread, weaving together disparate individuals, groups, interests, and intentions."[12]

From the band's perspective, Betts said, "Our music was always about playing, getting to know the audience to the point that we're communicating. With us, it was our whole thing, identifying with the people that came to see us. And in doing so much roadwork, we did exactly that. We found out who they were, and we found out who we were."[13]

Once again, the Grateful Dead served as exemplars. The hippies who emerged from the Summer of Love in 1967 were at the forefront of a cultural movement of youth rebellion against authority with everything from sexual mores to drugs to civil rights and the Vietnam War. The post–World War II baby boom had exploded the American youth population whose sheer numbers changed American culture. Rock music was a catalyst, the Grateful Dead were among the movement's flagship bands. Young people rallied around the Dead not because they carried an expressly political message but because they connected with audiences culturally as peers.[14]

By late 1968 the hippie subculture had infiltrated the conservative South as southern youth grew out their hair and began to more openly push against the economic, social, and political culture of the region. As they did, they sought their own distinct music. Just as the Grateful Dead were in San Francisco, the Allman Brothers were at the forefront of the South's countercultural movement. The group's connection to its home was its cultural touchstone for the region, its people, and its music. And Berry Oakley and Duane Allman led the charge musically.

No one kept track of how many free shows the Allman Brothers Band played in its early years, but they were myriad. Several moments stand out. The ABB frequented Piedmont Park through at least September 1970. Photographs and a partial recording exist of a show on

January 26, 1970, at University of California–Riverside, where the band spent an afternoon "playing soulful rock on the grassy knoll near the bell tower." Bruce Harvie recalled that the band set up its gear and "proceed[ed] to blow for 3 hours or so" for a small, appreciative audience. The *New Orleans Express* published photographs of a free concert on August 23, 1970, at a regular Sunday gathering of youth in the city's Audubon Park.[15]

Free shows offered the group opportunities to rehearse and to build ABB's live reputation. "Back then we weren't as polished as we are now," Gregg said, "we weren't as good as we are now, we weren't as tight as we are now, and we didn't have the songs that we have now. But, by God, we were there, and we were doing it for free. We were doing it for the people, and we were doing it for us, because we loved to play."[16]

While playing for free was important to the Allman Brothers' aesthetic, paying gigs kept them solvent. Early engagements were at venues familiar to Hour Glass and the Second Coming. Money was tight, road manager Twiggs Lyndon recalled: "Berry and I would sit down and call these people up, ask to work for 50, 80 percent of the door, no guarantees. We worked a job in Cocoa Beach, Florida; we had a 60/40 deal, and our 60 percent of the door was $52.50." Promoter Alex Cooley booked the band in "real small places like Statesboro and gymnasiums in Valdosta [Georgia]. They used to play Florida, just any wide spot in the road: tent shows in Memphis, Chattanooga, Jacksonville. I remember playing Daytona Beach at an armory." Conditions were less than inspiring. "It was depressing," said Cooley.[17]

Despite the challenges, band members fondly recalled those early days, their memories less focused on hardship than musical accomplishment. "We were having too much fun for it to be hard," Trucks said. "We did a lot of playing; we worked our butts off. We didn't want to be nowhere else. It was the only place to be. It didn't matter whether or not people liked it; we liked it. That's all we wanted to do."[18]

The ABB built an audience slowly and methodically, playing a relentless schedule of dates at smaller clubs and at colleges in the South. "The road proved indispensable in gradually building a following," Capricorn Records' Odum said. "It all comes back to going out there, having the will to do it, and going forward. Playing for the American public. A real, true people's band." They carried themselves not as rock stars but as normal, everyday people. Those qualities held particular appeal for their audience.[19]

Duane and his bandmates had nothing to lose in following that path. "Not one of us in the band really thought we would be that ultra-successful," Betts said. "We were purposely trying not to be commercial; we were just saying, 'We're gonna play music, and we're gonna play for our people here, that we can look in the face and see, and we're not gonna play for record executives and people that sell things.'"[20]

One groundbreaking early live appearance happened in Gainesville, Florida, on Labor Day weekend 1969 at the Southeast Pop Music Contest. Buster Lipham, a local music store owner, hosted the battle of the bands. Ineligible to compete because they had a record contract in hand, the ABB likely played the gig as a favor to Lipham. He had advanced the band more than $10,000 in equipment, which they were paying back in weekly installments of several hundred dollars.[21]

The Allman Brothers Band was an altogether different animal than the brothers' previous groups that had played Gainesville, and Duane's new band floored the audience. Gainesville musician Marty Jourard recalled the "power, precision, and unity of their overall sound." The ABB, he declared, "set a local standard for musical excellence. . . . [It was a] *band* in the best sense of the word, working together to create their own sonic universe. The Allman Brothers Band showed us that the elusive 'next level' . . . was there for the taking." After an August 1969 show in Tampa, Rory O'Connor reported, "Everyone was being mowed over." The Allman Brothers "brought the audience up off the floor onto their feet, clapping and shouting for encores in a frenzy."[22]

In 1969 the band toured heavily along the eastern seaboard. The ABB played multiple shows in its home turf of Florida and Georgia, with scattered gigs in South Carolina and Alabama. Don Law continued to book them at his Boston Tea Party, and in August the ABB made its first New York City appearance, at Ungano's.

In December they performed two shows at what Betts called "one of our favorite roadhouse gigs," Cincinnati's Ludlow Garage. A combination rock club and youth community center, Ludlow Garage founder Jim Tarbell was devoted to the underground rock scene and artists ignored on AM radio such as Dr. John, Taj Mahal, and the Allmans'

Atlanta friends the Hampton Grease Band. The band was still breaking out of the underground when they first played Ludlow Garage. No secret to music lovers who had seen them live, Betts said the ABB had "a private, almost cult-like following."[23]

Amid the touring, on August 3, 1969, the Allman Brothers Band began recording its debut album at Atlantic Studios in New York City. The record included seven songs—two covers and five Gregg Allman originals. The ten-day recording experience proved tense. Though the band recorded the entire album live—"solos and that sort of thing was done right when the track was being played," Duane said—it was away from its natural element: the stage. "We play live," Duane said, "and making records, you can just do it over and over and over if somebody makes a mistake." He found the environment disorienting. "The pressure of the machines and stuff in the studio makes you kind of nervous." This was particularly true for Betts, who called the studio "a padded cell" and carried contempt for studios for years thereafter. Dickey called studios "a prostitution of music. You been out playing in bars, then you go into concerts, and it's always the raw communication between people. But here you are in this tin can with a bunch of machines all round you, and you're expected to produce." Gregg was never satisfied with the debut album. "We didn't spend enough time on it, we didn't refine it enough. We were better than that."[24]

Atlantic released *The Allman Brothers Band* on November 4, 1969. Reviews were muted but generally favorable. Most described the music in generic terms. *Billboard*'s Ed Ochs called it "the meanest, hardest traveling music." John Wren described it as "heavy, hard blues-rock, dynamic and raunchy." *Creem*'s Ben Edmonds found it "tight and well disciplined, flashy but solid."[25]

Most compared the Allmans to more popular bands. Dan Vining found the band "new and fresh and original, heavy but with more restraint, more tightness and control" than Led Zeppelin. Roy Eure called the ABB's mélange "almost impossible to classify or categorize. It is blues, but it is also Latin and jazz flavored." He compared the band favorably to the Grateful Dead, particularly the way the Allmans used "original material as a jumping off place for a jam that can go into many musical idioms and back to the original form, and still fit together."[26]

The band's instrumental focus, Edmonds argued, demonstrated

how the ABB functioned "as a high-powered unit rather than individual talents," resulting in "an especially full sound." He found the approach baffling.

> The problem that arises out of the hard unit approach of the Allman Brothers Band is that, while the band as a whole functions very tightly, the individual identities of the band members are hidden. Even in the case of the guitars, which are most often at the forefront, we have no clear picture of who the musician is, as both Duane and Dickey Betts are listed as playing lead guitar. I suspect that Duane handles the yeoman's share, but who can be sure? Perhaps with a wider range of material, the identities of the band members will emerge, but on this we'll have to wait for the next Allman Brothers album.

In fact, outside of "Dreams," which featured Duane exclusively, Betts and Allman split guitar duties on the record.[27]

Critic Lester Bangs was emphatic in his praise of the album and became among the ABB's earliest converts outside of the South. In his February 21, 1970, *Rolling Stone* review he declared the Allman Brothers the real deal. "For all the white blooze bands proliferating today," he wrote of the bands that had sprung up in the wake of the British invasion, "it's still inspiring when the real article comes along, a white group who've transcended their schooling to produce a volatile blues-rock sound of pure energy, inspiration, and love." Bangs heard intentionality in the music.

> The Allmans know what they're doing, and feel it deeply as well, and they communicate immediately. One of the virtues of a simple, standardized form like the blues is that when played right it's such a comfortable place to return to. The whole album is like that. You've been here a thousand times before, and it feels like home instead of mind-numbing banality because the Allmans have mastered the form with rare subtlety, and also because their blues keep you vibrating from one brilliant hard rock interpolation to the next.[28]

"Dreams," the penultimate track, is the record's standout. Bangs called it "the album's pinnacle." An unnamed reviewer called it "one of the most beautiful songs in the world." Edmonds wrote of "Dreams" that it "breaks the pattern. Gregg's organ playing is heavy and shroud-like, illustrating the title very well. The guitars, up until now the front instruments, tone themselves down to fit the mood nicely."[29]

Among the first of Gregg's originals to make the band's repertoire, the track is also the album's most clearly jazz-influenced. "'Dreams' is the effect that good jazz has had on us," Duane remarked. The song's world-weary lyrics belie Gregg's youth and call to mind Malone and Stricklin's observation of the South as "a source of images and symbols, both positive and negative, which have fueled the imaginations of musicians and songwriters."[30]

The band loosely based its arrangement of "Dreams" on Miles Davis's "All Blues." Like "All Blues," from which Jaimoe derived his drum part, "Dreams" carries a gentle 6/8 waltz-time rhythm. Duane's mid-song solo is his best on the album, among the finest of his entire studio career. Duane's solo answers the desperation of the first verse Gregg sings: "The whole world was falling, right down in front of me. / Lord, help me babe, this will surely be the end of me." The band settles into a tranquil groove as Duane begins to play. Halfway through, he moves to slide and plays a solo that simultaneously feels urgent and restrained, building the energy back to the second verse, when Gregg's lyrics seem to find some redemption: "Pull myself together, put on a new face. Climb down off the hilltop, get back in the race." For Bangs, the lyrics tell "a familiar story, but the way it's written and delivered by the Allmans makes it poignantly realistic and universal."[31]

"Whipping Post" closes the album. Like "Dreams," "Whipping Post" is a remarkable song with evocative lyrics and shifting time signatures that conjure a variety of moods. The song conveys a "high energy level," Jim Gillespie observed, "building in intensity until one is left completely drained." The arrangement features fiery solos from both Duane and Dickey and strong vocals. But something is missing. The studio version doesn't capture much of the tune's spirit and power at all. The band and soloists all seem constrained by the brevity of the track, which at 5:17 is at least two-thirds shorter than the versions they played live.[32]

The Allman Brothers Band was a strong debut, indicative of the band's evolving sound. But ultimately, as Rory O'Connor remarked, "If you have heard the band live, the album may be just a slight disappointment. On stage, the band is pure power and energy. The album captures the feeling, but not the intensity of the band. But it's not fair to compare the album with the live thing."[33]

Phil Walden was sure *The Allman Brothers Band* would break through. "He just thought that this music was so good that everybody would immediately figure that out and it was just going to go through the roof," Butch recalled. The album sold fewer than 40,000 copies, barely grazing the charts at #188 before dropping off altogether. The dismal sales led Wexler to recommend a new location. "Nothing was ever going to emerge from the South," he told Walden. But Walden and the band believed otherwise.[34]

Why was Wexler so adamant about the band leaving the South? The issue wasn't musical. Rock music had evolved from rock 'n' roll, which itself evolved from southern musical traditions. More than likely it was Wexler's perception of the public's bias against the region in the immediate aftermath of the South's campaign of massive resistance against the modern civil rights movement.

The band ignored Wexler's entreaty to leave the South; they returned to the road. If they weren't going to break through with a studio record, they could at least make a living playing live. Word of mouth became the band's most valuable promotion. "That was true of everyone," Law recalled, "but especially for a band as strong as the Allman Brothers. It was obvious to anyone who saw them that they were fantastic." They were, O'Connor commented, "the kind of band that has to be heard live to really be believed." But concerts had limited reach. The band needed radio airplay to drive album sales. *The Allman Brothers Band* gave them neither.[35]

CHAPTER 10

THE ABB BUILDS ITS REPUTATION (DECEMBER 1969– SEPTEMBER 1970)

They were their own best advertisement. Each gig added a few more destroyed heads to their following.

Ben Edmonds

In the months following the release of their debut album, the band met promoter Bill Graham, whose support and belief in Duane and the Allman Brothers Band became legendary. Graham ran two of the most famous venues in rock, San Francisco's Fillmore West and Fillmore East in New York's East Village. Though the ABB continued to play smaller bars, nightclubs, and school gymnasiums throughout 1971, Graham helped the band break into the next tier of stardom. The promoter's ability to sell tickets to Allman Brothers shows on both coasts proved the band's value as a live act.

The Allman Brothers Band spent 1970 on the road and recording their sophomore album, *Idlewild South*. Audiences left shows ecstatic; record buyers were less enthused. Backstage at the Warehouse in New Orleans on New Year's Eve 1970, Duane hinted at what the band planned for 1971. Its third album would be live. He didn't yet announce the venue for the sessions—Fillmore East.

Graham was a somewhat unlikely tastemaker for rock music. "From the very beginning," he wrote, "I accepted the fact that I had no real personal knowledge of the rock scene of that era." He did not listen to radio. "I didn't really know what was going on." Graham didn't impose himself as an arbiter of talent. He watched what his crowds responded to and served them more of the same. Grateful Dead guitarist Jerry Garcia said, "I don't think Bill noticed our music much. . . . He always loves it when the crowd gets off even if he doesn't personally understand or personally dig the music."[1]

The musicians around Graham exposed him to Black performers such as the Staple Singers, Bobby Bland, James Brown, Chuck Berry, and Otis Redding, "the *ultimate* musician everyone wanted to see," he said. It was a coup for Graham to secure Redding to perform in San Francisco in December 1966. The star had yet to truly break through to the white market, and the touring business remained segregated. "Otis had worked to white audiences but at white colleges in the South because it was a tradition," Phil Walden recalled. "Black people *always* entertained white people down there." Redding was, Graham recalled, "*by far* the single most extraordinary talent I had ever seen. There was no comparison."[2]

Eric Clapton first played Graham's original Fillmore Auditorium in 1967 while touring with Cream. "The first time I went to San Francisco," he stated, "I experienced the kind of more introverted or serious or introspective attitude toward our music." Clapton noticed that Graham's "deep-seated feelings for what was right in the music" created an atmosphere of risk-taking that encouraged musical exploration. Joshua White, who ran the light show at Fillmore East, observed, "Bill never thought he was the music. Bill was always the scene. He never stopped loving the artists."[3]

One of the groups Graham grew to love was the Allman Brothers Band. "I played them because I thought they were really good and I thought the public would think so as well. I wanted to build them into a headliner, and I thought they should have turned the corner sooner," Graham said. "I used the Allman Brothers as much as I could." The band, he said, "made me feel good in a particularly physical way. You may not move, but it affects your body as well as your emotions. Less than ten bands, in all of rock, have that potential, for me, to get out there and make me feel really good; to put out the good spirit within you. The Allman Brothers have that ability."[4]

The ABB made their Fillmore East debut on December 29, 1969. Expectations were low, the venue's staff put off by the gatefold image in their first album: a photo of the band naked in a stream. The image brought to mind stereotypes, "a bunch of redneck yo-yos," Allan Arkush remembered thinking. The band also arrived late, which was a cardinal sin. "This van pulled up, and they piled out of it," Arkush continued. "These rednecks with their crummy, beat-up Marshall amps. We were going, 'These guys are going to be something else. Hope they don't get naked.'" As the band sound checked, "everyone stopped working and just sort of stood there and went, '*Oh*. These guys are for real.'" The band made an even bigger impression when the lights were on. "We thought they were fabulous," said Arkush.[5]

The Fillmore East audience that night, there to see Blood, Sweat, and Tears, disagreed. "Their music was very different from ours," Gregg recalled of the headliner, whose sound was more Tom Jones than Cream. "Some of the people there weren't ready for blues like we played." Fillmore East manager Kip Cohen agreed. After the show, Cohen apologized to road manager Twiggs Lyndon for the pairing and asked what bands the Allmans would pay to see. "B. B. King, the Grateful Dead, Roland Kirk in that order," Lyndon replied.[6]

Within two weeks, Graham booked the band to open for King and bluesman Buddy Guy at the Fillmore West. The band trekked from Philadelphia to San Francisco and opened for the bluesmen from January 15 through 18, 1970. "I love your band," Graham told Lyndon. "How did they enjoy playing here?" Playing with King, the road manager answered, "was heaven." Graham asked, "He was you're first choice, wasn't he? I felt so bad, having put you on that bill [with Blood, Sweat, and Tears] in New York, I wanted to make it up to you. You've got two weeks to get back to the Fillmore East because I've got you booked in there with the Dead."[7]

With the Allman Brothers Band, Duane finally found originality. In Walden, he found record industry support. In Graham, he found a powerful promoter who appreciated the approach. Graham encouraged artists who played original music, and he understood the ABB's music wasn't inaccessible so much as it needed presentation in tandem with similar sounds. King and Guy were much more simpatico than Blood, Sweat, and Tears. It was, Gregg wrote, "exactly what we needed."[8]

Two weeks after the San Francisco shows, the Allman Brothers opened for the Grateful Dead at Fillmore East on February 11, 13, and 14, 1970. Dead soundman Owsley Stanley recorded the Allmans that weekend, portions of which the Allmans first released officially in 1997. Duane played slide on three set-list staples from the band's first days: "Trouble No More," "Statesboro Blues," and "Mountain Jam." They also played "Outskirts of Town" and "Hoochie Coochie Man," the latter with Oakley, and only two songs from their debut album, "Trouble No More" and "Whipping Post." At 8:11, "Whipping Post" had already expanded to three minutes longer than the original. By the end of the year, live versions of the song would top the twenty-minute mark.

About nine minutes in length, Dickey Betts's instrumental "In Memory of Elizabeth Reed" began the set. "Elizabeth Reed" demon-strated Betts's talent as a composer and marked a completely new avenue for the band: instrumentals. "Dickey wasn't secure enough about what he was doing," Jaimoe reflected, "which worked to his advantage, because he'd have something almost perfect before he'd bring it in."[9]

"In Memory of Elizabeth Reed" reflects the influence of Miles Da-vis and John Coltrane on Betts and the entire band. The song's ar-rangement in February 1970 is similar to the studio version recorded later that year and most famously on *At Fillmore East*. It features mul-tiple movements and tempo changes as well as solos by all but Oakley, who plays lead bass throughout. Though instrumentals were not new to the band's repertoire, "In Memory of Elizabeth Reed" was its first original, fully formed instrumental. It remained in the band's set list for the next forty years.

Betts called the tune a pure expression of his spiritual commitment to music: "When I write something that I'm proud of, like 'Elizabeth Reed,' where does that melody come from? That melody is *given* to me because I've dedicated myself so much to that guitar." Betts's use of religious terminology conveys his (and the band's) belief that music is a spiritual and communal experience. ABB audiences understood and appreciated this connection. Though secular, young people also ascribed spiritual language in talking about rock music.[10]

Audiences were not, however, attracted to the band's lone single, "Black Hearted Woman" backed with "Every Hungry Woman," or with *The Allman Brothers Band*. This left the band frustrated but undaunted. In response, the ABB built its audience the hard way, gig by gig. Gregg recalled, "It started dawning on me that the more we got around and got seen, it was worth ten times anything else we could do. The key was not to worry about the record sales, and trust that shit will take care of itself. . . . What we had to do was keep getting out there and letting people know that we're there." ABB roadie "Red Dog" Campbell said, "Every time we played someplace, when we came back, there was a bigger crowd, just from word of mouth; the band sold itself."[11]

A spring 1970 run included some of their earliest documented appearances on college campuses outside the South: the University of Massachusetts–Amherst, Sullivan County (New York) Community College, State University of New York (SUNY) at Stony Brook and at New Paltz, and Swarthmore College in Pennsylvania. On March 13, 1970, the band opened for bluesman Albert King, its first of many appearances at the famed Warehouse in New Orleans.

Touring was an intense experience. The Allman Brothers Band and its touring retinue represented the counterculture, and touring as hippies had complications. "It was a different world," Bruce Hampton recalled. "It was life or death. You'd stop at a gas station and you'd wonder if you were going to die. That's no joke. If you had long hair, you were a target." Indeed, long hair regularly caused problems. "Somebody starts calling you some kind of faggot or something about your long hair," Betts said. "We were shocking in those days, and some of those damn cowboys are pretty quick to show their feelings."[12]

Things did turn violent. Thom Doucette revealed an incident in an Ohio airport. "These guys were messing with us, making fun of our long hair and flipping Dickey's hair," he said. When their harassment turned to Jaimoe, Doucette recounted, "Dickey just puts his fork down and goes, 'Come on.' [Soon] the guy's on the floor bleeding and Dickey's sitting back down. When the police arrived and harassed the band, the restaurant owner defended them, saying, 'This is his party—the guy laying on the ground bleeding. You know him. He tried to push these boys around and they pushed back. Boys, your bill's on me.'"[13]

The Allman Brothers had other encounters with the law while on the road. The worst was on April 29, 1970, following the band's first of at least five appearances at SUNY–Stony Brook. The band played Aliotta's Lounge in Buffalo, New York. The next morning, ABB road manager Twiggs Lyndon stabbed owner Angelo Aliotta to death over his refusal to pay the band. Authorities arrested Lyndon and the band continued touring, playing shows in Cleveland, Philadelphia, and New Paltz, New York, over the next three days. Lyndon's friend Willie Perkins soon took over duties as road manager. A New York judge would later find Lyndon not guilty by reason of insanity, essentially ruling that life on the road with the Allman Brothers had driven him temporarily crazy.

A second harrowing incident occurred on March 22, 1971, in Jackson, Alabama. The band and crew were arrested following an incident at Ray and Tom's Restaurant, where the band found themselves after missing a turn on the highway. The group was tired, hungover, drug sick, and, perhaps most damning, traveling with a Black man. "A dirty, scroungy-looking bunch," local judge Fred L. Huggins remarked. "It looked like they had been sleeping in the cars for days [with] beards, long hair." Authorities arrested everyone for possession of marijuana, PCP, and heroin and placed the entire crew of nine whites and one African American in the Black section of the segregated jail. Road manager Perkins coordinated the band's release on bond the following day, March 23. It was the second anniversary of the band's first jam together. The group eventually forfeited their bonds and never again set foot in Clarke County.[14]

Segregation had long been a problem for Black and white musicians touring the South. Though few bands were integrated, the earliest rock 'n' roll tours of the late 1950s and early 1960s had racially mixed rosters, and problems regularly occurred. White artists routinely skipped the southern leg of these package tours as a result of those problems, such as a 1957 tour that included white singer Bill Haley and Black performers the Flamingos, the Platters, Frankie Lymon, and Clyde McPhatter. Haley played the May 20 date in Birmingham as scheduled but skipped the rest of the southern leg of the tour after threats from the Ku Klux Klan. Two years later the University of Georgia cancelled a Dave Brubeck show because his band had a Black bassist, Eugene Wright. Tulane University cancelled a 1961 show by the Black bandleader and trumpeter Dizzy Gillespie because school officials considered his Argentinian pianist, Lalo Schiffren, white.[15]

The Beatles had a no-segregation clause in their contracts since their first North American tour in 1964, and by the mid-1960s the British Musicians Union was advising its members not to play segregated venues or accept any bookings with racially discriminatory terms and conditions. Such considerations were not necessarily the case in the United States, where the American Federation of Musicians was the second-most racially segregated national union in the country in 1960. The federation's segregation policy continued for years, often with the complicity of Black musicians, who were, Brian Ward argues, concerned that "Black demands would go unheeded in integrated locals where there were simply more white members."[16]

For the Allman Brothers, touring with Jaimoe added challenges, and while he has not spoken of the indignities he experienced on the road, his bandmates have. "There were places we'd get turned away from eating, 'What're you guys doing' with a n——r in the band?'" Gregg recalled. "We were always a little on guard for someone to mess with him," roadie Red Dog said. "We got messed with a lot." Betts recounted his reaction to the harassment: "[They] stick out in my mind. I was horrified at that kind of thing."[17]

One clash happened in June 1969 at a Merritt Island, Florida, venue. "You guys can play, but the n——r can't," the promoter announced when he saw Jaimoe. "If he ain't playing, we ain't playing," members responded. The promoter relented but not without complaining about parents objecting to their daughters being in the same room as a Black man.[18]

By mid-1970 the band added language to its contract prohibiting such exclusion: "Employer agrees that admission to the engagement shall be open to all, regardless of race, color, or creed and that there shall be no segregated seating facilities based on race, color, or creed. . . . Artists shall be free to engage the services of supporting musicians of their choice without regard to race, color, or creed. Noncompliance by the employer with the provisions of this paragraph shall give artist the right to cancel." The band never had occasion to enforce the clause.[19]

While the five white musicians in the band may not have overtly campaigned for civil rights, their support and inclusion of their African American bandmate is significant. Gregg described "perennial redneck questions: 'Who them hippie boys and who's the n——r in the band?' We dealt with that second question quite a bit. Keep in mind, this was the 1960s, we were in the deep South, so having a black guy in the group came up a lot. But Jaimoe was one of us and we weren't going to change that for nobody."[20]

Being an integrated band was a way bigger deal than the principals remember. "Macon was just barely integrated [in 1969]," said "Mama" Louise Hudson, proprietor of the H&H, a Macon soul-food restaurant. "We didn't really have any white customers. And nobody around here had seen guys who looked like them. I had not. A lot of white folk around here did not approve of them long-haired boys, or of them always having a black guy with them." Lyndon's brother A. J. recalled visiting the band's communal home at 309 College Street: "I remember seeing a little blonde head on Jaimoe's chest and thinking, 'Well, this is different.'"[21]

The arrangement was indeed different, but Macon seemed to accept the band with few hassles. "We were a little apprehensive about going to a real small Southern town. We were some pretty off-the-wall characters," Betts said. Yet the band kept its focus on music and earned a "pass" from the Macon community for being southern longhairs in a band that included a black man. "People realized we were there for the music," Betts said.[22]

Despite his pathbreaking role as a Black musician playing in a rock band from the South, Jaimoe eschewed the activist label. "I never really considered myself some kind of civil rights crusader or anything, people were already doing that before me," he said.[23]

Yet the drummer understated how truly significant the integrated Allman Brothers Band was. With Jaimoe, the ABB flouted racial conventions. In doing so, the band not only broke down barriers in the South but also challenged stereotypes about white southerners that existed in other parts of the country. Dismantling racial boundaries was not a political act. Instead, the group sent a more subliminal message. Its musical and cultural roots included Black music and a kinship with southerners of both races.

The shared experiences of joy on stage and the intense struggles off of it made the sound ever more cohesive. Songs began to expand as the players discovered new ways to approach the tunes individually as soloists and collectively as a band. As the Allman Brothers made preparations to record the second album, concerts served as rehearsals. Other bands of the era were beginning to spend months in studio crafting albums. The ABB would do this work in front of audiences.

In February 1970 the band returned to Macon to record demos for its second album, *Idlewild South*. They began with "Hoochie Coochie

Man" and "Statesboro Blues," songs in rotation from the group's inception, and a new original from Gregg, "Midnight Rider."[24]

Atlantic producer Tom Dowd, in Macon on other business, caught the rehearsals. "I heard this music coming out, and it was swinging," he said. "They were blues, they were hard driving, they were everything, all in one." He implored Walden, "Send them to me as quickly as you can. They're ready now. Just the way they are."[25]

Dowd had served Atlantic as an engineer and producer since 1949, working with rhythm and blues stars such as the Coasters, LaVern Baker, and Ray Charles and jazz artists such as John Coltrane. He had recently moved into rock with Cream's *Disraeli Gears* and *Wheels of Fire*. Dowd would produce the ABB's second album.

In March 1970 the Allman Brothers gathered at Atlantic's Criteria Studios in Miami to record *Idlewild South*. In addition to the tracks they worked on in Macon, the band recorded two more Gregg originals, a slide guitar blues "Don't Keep Me Wonderin'" and "Leave My Blues at Home," whose twin-guitar attack and syncopated groove favored "Black Hearted Woman" and "Every Hungry Woman" from the debut album. The group recorded Gregg's ballad "Please Call Home" at a later session in New York City.[26]

Idlewild South also included two Dickey Betts originals, "In Memory of Elizabeth Reed" and "Revival," his first for the band. "Revival" began as an instrumental. "We would refer to that first instrumental section of the song as 'The Gypsy Dance,'" Betts explained. "When I wrote it, I had the image of gypsies dancing around a fire in my mind, and I tried to conjure that spirit in the music." The tune kicks off the album with Duane on acoustic guitar followed by harmonized guitar lines. Jaimoe plays congas, giving the song a Latin feel similar to Santana. Dickey saw "Revival" as a counterpoint to Gregg's deep blues. "I was in a band with Gregg Allman, who is basically a melancholy kind of writer," Betts reflected. "I'm thinking how do you balance this out? I don't want to write a song that makes you want to go hang yourself in the bathroom. So, I would really make an effort to write more up songs, to balance the band out." Though Betts wrote the song, Gregg sang it.[27]

"Revival" is the only song Duane Allman recorded with the Allman Brothers Band whose lyrics overtly address youth culture. The music is pure Allman Brothers, featuring harmony guitars, driving percussion, and powerful vocals. Betts's lyrics evoke the musical gatherings in Jacksonville, at Piedmont Park, and at free shows the band held while on tour in 1969 and 1970. The song borrows imagery from the Youngbloods' 1967 hit "Get Together" and identifies the band with the counterculture:

> People can you feel it?
> Love is everywhere
> People can you hear it?
> The song is in the air
> We're in a revolution
> Don't you know we're right
> Everyone is singing, yeah
> There'll be no one to fight.[28]

Though the last lines probably referred to the general social and cultural tumult in America at the time, they also apply to the country's involvement in Southeast Asia. The Vietnam War loomed large throughout this era for the band's generation. Lyndon was a veteran and served in the Marine Corps in Vietnam, but every band member avoided the draft. Butch attended Florida State University where he majored in "staying out of Vietnam," he joked. Gregg and Duane took separate tacks. Duane wore women's lingerie and pretended to be gay at his 1965 induction ceremony. The ruse failed, but he was not drafted; his mother, Geraldine, a widow of an Army veteran, successfully argued that Duane was needed at home. A year later, Gregg took a more painful route, intentionally shooting himself in the foot the day before his induction, earning him 4-F draft status: "Not qualified for military service."[29]

"Revival" came as close to a public political statement as the band made during Duane's lifetime. "We were aware of what was going on," Gregg said, "and we cared about what was happening with the war in Vietnam and what happened at Kent State [but in] truth, though, we were sheltered by the music and the traveling." Duane made his convictions clear as a member of the youth culture. "When people realize that there is a young vote they're going to have to appeal to it to get their votes," he told an interviewer. "Young people will start getting their way. If you want to start talking about politics, that's the only way. I watch it and I like to see things right. It makes it a lot easier on everyone if someone with some sense is in a position to make laws and set things up for a change."[30]

In spring and summer 1970, the ABB performed some of their better-known gigs. They played Ludlow Garage on April 4 and 5, 1970, a gig that was released as an album in 1990. The show is in many ways a precursor to *At Fillmore East*, recorded eleven months later. The set spans nearly two hours over nine tracks, only three of which appeared on the band's debut album: "Dreams," "Trouble No More," and "Every Hungry Woman." Three songs were live rehearsals for tunes the band was trying to record for *Idlewild South*—"Statesboro Blues," "Hoochie Coochie Man," and "In Memory of Elizabeth Reed." Two others, "Outskirts of Town" and "Mountain Jam," were set-list staples. Duane sang John Lee Hooker's "Dimples" in what would be his only ABB vocal. "We don't do this song very much, but I feel like singing," he announced before the band ripped into a song he had been playing since the Hour Glass days. "Statesboro Blues" offers an interesting comparison to what was to come. The Ludlow Garage version has a more relaxed pace than later arrangements and features an extended outro that expanded the song to twice the length of the versions from the *At Fillmore East* sessions the following March.

On July 4 weekend 1970, the ABB played promoter Alex Cooley's Second Annual Atlanta International Pop Festival. Held in Byron, less than twenty miles from Macon, it was a triumphant hometown gig. The band opened and closed the event and played the festival's free stage at least once. The estimated crowd of 200,000–500,000 was the largest audience Duane would ever play for.[31]

Two weeks later, the Allman Brothers headlined a similar festival in Love Valley, North Carolina, July 17 through 19. Called "That Love Valley Thing," the event was the brainchild of Andy Barker, who founded Love Valley in 1954 as an ersatz western "cowboy" town. Barker staged the festival for his daughter Tonda, who he said was too young to attend Woodstock the previous summer. Though attendance estimates range for Love Valley range from 75,000 to 200,000, Barker collected money for only 25,000 tickets at $5 each. Like Woodstock and nearly every other rock festival of 1969 and 1970, a majority of attendees crashed the gates. Love Valley was the second large festival audience the Allman Brothers Band had entertained in one month, and the band recorded its set for a possible live album. It is also one of only four times the Allman Brothers Band was filmed during Duane's lifetime.[32]

Set lists from the two festival shows include two songs the ABB had recorded for *Idlewild South*, "In Memory of Elizabeth Reed" and "Don't Keep Me Wonderin.'" "Stormy Monday"—at nine minutes, more than twice the length of Bobby Bland's original on which it was based—replaced "Outskirts of Town" as the set list's slow blues; "Mountain Jam," "Dreams," and "Hoochie Coochie Man" remained. The closing set at Atlanta Pop included "Whipping Post," which one account noted "was a mean heavy rush, driving wall of sound that left the crowd ecstatic." Clocking in at more than fourteen minutes, it is nearly three times the length of the studio version. The expanded version displayed the band's comfort with its ability to create and compose in the moment.[33]

Live performance remained central to the band's approach in recording *Idlewild South*. "They didn't record in one sitting," Dowd recalled. "They would record maybe five songs. Then they might say, 'I don't think that song was good enough,' or, 'I don't think that song was ready to record.'" They'd play songs into shape on the road. Betts also used the live environment to compose new melodies.[34]

Betts's instrumental "In Memory of Elizabeth Reed" entered the ABB's set list in 1970 and remained on the list for the next four decades. The band also played "Statesboro Blues" at every show for which recordings exist, though they tinkered with the arrangement throughout the year. In February 1970 the band played tight, four-minute versions of the song in their studio demo and recordings from Fillmore East. By April at Ludlow Garage and SUNY–Stony Brook, May at Swarthmore College, and June at Tampa's Hillsborough Junior College, the group had tacked on an extended instrumental outro. By July at Atlanta Pop, the band dropped the outro and reverted to the tighter arrangement from earlier in the year. After all the tinkering, "Statesboro Blues" did not even end up on *Idlewild South*. It would instead kick off *At Fillmore East*.

Capricorn Records released *Idlewild South* on September 23, 1970. Like its predecessor, the album is more song- than jam-oriented. *Idlewild South* is lighter in tone than the debut album, reflecting the desire to make a record with more widespread appeal to the marketplace. "From the first four bars," Allman biographer Tom Nolan writes, "we hear a crisper recorded sound, a surer attack, and a tighter band. The music is more textured; sections of delicate picking fit logically into a strong blues-rock framework."[35]

Critics heralded the changes. A *Kentucky Kernel* reviewer heard in *Idlewild South* a "synthesis of American music: the blues, jazz, and country western traditions." *Rolling Stone*'s Ed Leimbacher praised the album's "briefer, tighter, less 'heavy' numbers." The record, Stuart Stevens wrote, presented "a new direction, a break from their previous hard-driving blues sound." Rory O'Connor considered the release an important transition: "Looking above and behind the Led Zeppelinish appeal of the Allman Brothers first album, it was pretty apparent that something very mellow, soothing, almost ethereal was going on." *Idlewild South*, O'Connor contended, "brings this quality to the very front of the Brothers' music, without ever, for a moment, losing the basic rock 'n' roll/blues feel. It is about ten times as funky and swinging as the first album. But a gliding, flowing motion drifts in and around the funk and swing."[36]

Acclaim was not universal. A reviewer in the Guilford College *Guilfordian* called *Idlewild South* "basic rock & roll." Reviewer Dick Hartsook described the ABB as "a former R&B band gone heavy with a wide array of instruments jammed into a blues orientation." Leimbacher called "Please Call Home" and "Leave My Blues at Home" unoriginal, "a Buddy Miles parody and an Allman Brothers first album reject." Butch Ochsenreiter wrote, "The Allman Brothers' second is a disappointment. Somewhere they lost something, and this one just does not match their first."[37]

The *Great Speckled Bird*'s Miller Francis Jr., the band's first major proponent in print, enjoyed *Idlewild South* as "a fine presentation of Allman Brothers music [with] every achievement of the first album and some new elements." Francis took issue with one of the latter: Dickey's instrumental "In Memory of Elizabeth Reed." The studio recording, which Francis had heard several times in person in 1970, left him cold. He considered the song "a lovely, Santana-ish blues ballad that escalates into a strong, but belabored explication of 'white blues' riff on top of riff on top of riff. As usual, the solos are good, but they don't really catch on fire. It's almost exasperating to hear musicians like the Allman Brothers lavish such expertise on musical ideas that they themselves have already exhausted."[38]

It seems odd that Francis found "In Memory of Elizabeth Reed" derivative, as it is among the most beloved songs in the ABB canon. Two thoughts emerge in considering why. First, the seven-minute instrumental was too long for Francis's tastes, especially on *Idlewild South*. Francis preferred the album's song craft as in "Midnight Rider," calling it "maybe the best thing the Allman Brothers Band has ever done." Second, while "Elizabeth Reed" was distinctive, its studio version lacked spark. Though Dowd and the band sought to re-create the live experience in studio, the environment paled in comparison to the excitement of creating improvisational music in front of others. For Francis, *Idlewild South*'s "In Memory of Elizabeth Reed" did not carry this energy.[39]

Idlewild South performed better than its predecessor but was not a breakout hit. That December, the record peaked at number 38 on the *Billboard* albums chart.[40] By January the record fell to number 81. And although "Revival" was the band's first single to make the charts, it made even less of an impact, topping out at number 92 on the Hot 100.[41]

The failure of *Idlewild South* to place higher on the charts frustrated everyone. "I doubted myself," Walden recalled. "It seemed like I had just been wrong and that they were never going to catch on. People just didn't grasp what the Allmans were all about—musically or any other way."[42]

While *Idlewild South* didn't sell well, Leimbacher predicted that it would "augur well for the Allmans' future." Francis wanted more of the same. He intoned, "Let's hope they give us more 'Midnight Riders.'" They didn't. Gregg and Betts would each continue to write ballads, but none appeared on *At Fillmore East*, the band's next record.[43]

Idlewild South revealed "the subtle side of the ABB much as their debut record laid out their powerhouse force," Nolan observed. The album demonstrated the band's expanding musical identity and garnered attention. Edmonds noted, "They weren't yet rolling in royalties or fan mail, but everybody seemed to agree that they were on the verge of becoming something big." *Idlewild South* was in rotation on college stations beyond the South, and the album did make the charts. Duane recognized that this meant the band's hard work was starting to pay off. He said, "Our record nationally did like up in the thirties . . . so somebody bought it somewhere, you just can't do that in one town."[44]

The band nurtured its devoted grassroots audience. "They kept touring, establishing themselves city by city as the best live band around and building a base," Walden said. Edmonds wrote, "They were their own best advertisement. Each gig added a few more destroyed heads to their following."[45]

The Allman Brothers Band spent an estimated three hundred days on the road in 1970. As they further honed their sound, they headlined the 1970 Atlanta Pop Festival, with its enormous audiences. Duane continued to chase success with studio recordings, and success would continue to elude him. Though *Idlewild South* was well received critically, it was less indicative of the band's live dynamic than it was of the more ethereal side of the Allman Brothers Band. Once again, middling sales left the band and its record label displeased. That would change with the band's third album.

CHAPTER **11**

PHIL WALDEN AND CAPRICORN RECORDS (1969-1971)

I mortgaged everything for this thing. I believed in it that much.
Phil Walden

Phil Walden was as important to the success of *At Fillmore East* as any nonmusician involved in the project. The album was payoff for his belief in and support of Duane's artistic vision. He built Capricorn Records around Duane and most importantly, fought his partner Jerry Wexler's efforts to move the Allman Brothers Band from the South to break them nationally. Duane and the group wanted to remain in the South in order to do their best work, and Walden supported Duane's vision.

One of a cadre of white southerners deeply involved in the southern African American music business, Walden was well familiar with Wexler and Atlantic Records when they co-founded Capricorn in 1969. Otis Redding was signed to Stax, an Atlantic subsidiary out of Memphis; Redding's protégé Arthur Conley was signed directly to Atlantic. The ABB fit well on Atlantic's burgeoning rock roster, including heavyweights Buffalo Springfield, Cream, and Led Zeppelin as well as Springfield offshoot Crosby, Stills, Nash, and Young.

Brothers Ahmet and Nesuhi Ertegun founded Atlantic in 1947. The label operated as an independent, unattached to America's major labels of the time: Columbia, RCA Victor, Decca, Capitol, and Mercury. When the majors ignored Black audiences, historian Michael T. Bertrand writes, independents like Atlantic "were left virtually alone to advance and exploit the tastes of commonly disregarded segments of the population. They furnished the infrastructure from which rock 'n' roll would emerge." Atlantic acquired smaller labels and made distribution arrangements with others and thus, Robert Gordon argues, "became an indie that functioned on a national scale."[1]

By 1969 Phil Walden was still a relatively small part of this equation. He had bet big on Redding, whose death in 1967 devastated him financially and personally. Walden forged ahead with plans to open a studio in Macon, and he began to recruit a rhythm section—the heart of the southern soul recording industry—to back the stars he would recruit to record there.

When Wexler suggested he found a record label to release Duane's music, Walden demurred. He didn't make records; he produced and promoted artists. "I was unsure I could afford or was willing to make a commitment to make albums for people," Walden said. He had a change of heart when Wexler offered to front him the money in exchange for label co-ownership. In a nod to the times, the pair dubbed the venture Capricorn Records after their shared astrological sign.[2]

Duane was the focal point of the Capricorn partnership from the beginning. "I was betting on Phil Walden," Wexler acknowledged. "But I had an absolute solid belief in Duane Allman." Walden, too, heard something special in Duane. Jaimoe recalled, "Phil had real good insight. He was looking for what we got into and eventually became."[3]

Walden built his business around the Allman Brothers Band. Among his most significant hires was Frank Fenter, then running Atlantic operations in Europe, to run the label. Walden continued in artist management. Together, Walden and Fenter built an empire of southern music.[4]

Fenter is an unsung hero of the Allman Brothers Band story. "A brilliant record man," Capricorn executive Dick Wooley said. Before joining Capricorn in 1969, the South African native had secured for Atlantic two premier British rock bands: Cream and Led Zeppelin. "Phil needed somebody who really understood the record business, and that's Frank Fenter," Ahmet Ertegun said. "Phil was the one who had the relationship with the artists, and Frank was the one who knew the day-to-day business. Whatever success they gained, they gained because of the efforts that each put in."[5]

Like Duane's insistence on artistic independence for the Allman Brothers Band, Capricorn's independence from Atlantic was equally important. "We want to be autonomous from the standpoint that we create, produce, and figure the exploitation [promotion and marketing] of our own records," Walden said. "We want Capricorn to be a company, not just a label." Under Fenter and Walden, Capricorn would do more than produce and sell records. "You can be a record label and produce one type of music," Fenter recalled, "but you can't be a record *company*. We've always anticipated being a thoroughly involved *company*." Their model included business subsidiaries, all operating under the Capricorn banner: label, artist management, booking agency, music publishing, and later, merchandise.[6]

While all was calm on the surface, obvious conflicts of interest arose, particularly as the band and label grew more successful. Wexler was an Atlantic Records executive and co-owner of the Atlantic subsidiary Capricorn. Walden was the ABB's manager, co-owned Capricorn, its record label, and controlled its publishing. Wexler might make decisions that were best for Atlantic but not for Capricorn; Walden could choose something that was best for Capricorn but not the ABB. Their relationship held together until 1972, when Walden and Wexler parted acrimoniously after Walden exercised an option to move Capricorn from Atlantic to Warner Brothers Records. Walden had learned the move from Wexler, who pulled a similar stunt on Jim Stewart at Stax in 1967.

The financial issues between Walden and the Allman Brothers Band first came to a head in the late 1970s, after Dickey Betts successfully sued Walden for back royalties. It was but the first of many legal cases between the band and Walden. By 1979 Capricorn declared bankruptcy, leaving its debts to the Allman Brothers Band unpaid and shuttering a company that had produced nine platinum and seventeen gold albums and five gold singles. Its greatest legacy, however, wasn't in record sales. It was impact. Capricorn moved southern music to the forefront in American music by launching the career of the Allman Brothers and helped invent the Southern rock genre.

The arrangement with Walden proved fruitful while Duane was alive. Duane, the ABB, the label, and the fans benefited from the partnership. As an independent label Atlantic took chances—and absorbed losses—with developing artists, the Allman Brothers among them. Capricorn, as a subsidiary of Atlantic, shared in the risk. The arrangement gave the band time to mature, which was important to Duane. When asked about his first major break in the music business, he did not mention "Hey Jude." He cited his label. "Getting with Atlantic," he answered. Duane called Wexler "the solidest cat with the clearest eye," an executive who left the creative decisions up to the artists. "They dig our music, man," Duane said. "And Ahmet, the president, he loves to listen to good sides."[7]

Most importantly, Duane felt Ertegun and Wexler saw more than money in music. "They know what [music] means and they know what it's worth," he said. Ultimately, Duane concluded, Atlantic was "satisfying everybody that they got. . . . [I]f you want to make a lot of bread, they'll make you a fucking fortune. Want to be a rock 'n' roll star? They'll make you a rock 'n' roll star. Want to play music? They'll make sure people hear your music." It was a refreshing attitude from his label after Duane's experience with Liberty, and he expressed his gratitude in a postcard to Wexler in January 1970: "Thanks for your help, guidance, confidence but most of all your friendship. Love to you and yours always."[8]

While Atlantic was supportive of the Allman Brothers Band as artists, Wexler was less enthused with the group's commercial prospects. After eighteen months and two albums, the group had failed to achieve any commercial success. The ABB were "a notch or two higher than the standard rock 'n' roll band," Walden said. "We had some concern that this band was possibly too musical to fit into the current scene." Wexler was unhappy, Walden undeterred. "I believe in these guys," the southerner told his partner. The band was gaining momentum. "As we traveled around," Betts recalled, "everybody else started getting it except the record company." Years later Walden said, "I mortgaged everything for this thing, I believed in it that much."[9]

With the Allman Brothers Band, the economics of artist development didn't work in Walden's favor. Capricorn's Odum explained,

We had a lot of money sunk into the band. When you're in the management business, you're in it to develop, and that's what we were doing. When you have a band making $1,000 to $2,000 a night, you can't reach out and take a 15 percent commission, but you can put it on the books and that's what we did. A lot of the money invested was just keeping them alive and on the road. In the course of a year, $100 here and $300 there adds up with the band and crew.[10]

Walden's largesse was only part of the equation. He also continually fought attempts to move the band to more music business–friendly environs in New York or Los Angeles. "We held fast and we didn't want to leave our roots and where we felt comfortable," Betts said. "We fought tooth and nail to prevent Atlantic from moving us out of the South, when they said we'd never make it living in Macon, Georgia, and playing that type of music. They insisted we should go to New York or L.A. and they'd break us out of there." Betts later said, "Thank God we, along with Phil Walden were smart enough to know that that would ruin the band."[11]

In early 1970, band headquarters in Macon became "the Big House," a 6,000-square-foot, three-story, Tudor-style home built in 1900. The home entered the Allman Brothers Band story in late 1969, when Linda Oakley answered a home-for-rent advertisement for her, Berry, and their daughter, Brittany; Duane, Donna, and their daughter, Galadrielle; and Gregg and Candace, Berry's sister, then in a short-lived relationship.

With three couples sharing the house, the $225 monthly rent was more than feasible. In December 1969 Linda put on a "little homemaker with child persona" and signed the lease. When Macon's Day Realty learned more than one couple shared the house, they increased rent by $10. The band made a permanent home there, at 2321 Vineville Avenue; it today houses the Allman Brothers Band Museum at the Big House.[12]

The importance of the Big House to the Allman Brothers Band's ethos and development is significant. Home is why they didn't want to leave the South, and the Big House was the band's home. Berry Oakley insisted it be so. "It was important to him to maintain some semblance of normal family life when they were not on the road," Berry's sister Candace said. At the Big House, the women of the home played an important, often unsung role in the band's life and work. Thom Doucette acknowledged that "Candy Oakley, Linda Oakley, and Donna Allman made a huge, unbelievable difference in the band's life. We came back to the Big House [from tour], it was truly a home, which contained all the heart, feeling, and togetherness of the band. I had played in a lot of bands that had hangouts, but this was a different deal, made possible by those three women, and I was taken away by it and greatly admired it." Willie Perkins said, "What had been built as a prim-and-proper residence for Southern elite had been transformed into an informal, comfortable, warm, and loving home for several young families and a headquarters for an up-and-coming rock 'n' roll band."[13]

With Walden's blessing, the band made Macon home base. "Phil Walden had complete faith in us," Butch said. "He was close to bankruptcy a lot of the time and Atlantic kept telling him we didn't have a chance. But during that first three years, Phil never once tried to change us." Capricorn producer and former Hour Glass bandmate Johnny Sandlin likewise recognized Walden's faith in the ABB: "Phil went out on a limb for them. Atlantic Records didn't think they could sell this band. And Phil pushed it through." The subsidiary relationship between Capricorn and Atlantic allowed the ABB freedom to continue to chart its own course. "We stuck with it," Betts said.[14]

In Macon, the band benefited from Walden's intuitive sense to leave the musicians alone to create their art. He enjoyed their music and knew others did too. "They sounded spectacular," Walden said. "They weren't trendy, there was never any attempt by the Allmans to be a show band. They played music. On occasion, when they were allowed to, for hours." If the band members believed they needed to stay in the South to make their best music, Walden was supportive.[15]

Not everyone trusted Walden. Jaimoe initially refused to sign a management contract with Walden because of the preference he had seen him give R&B stars over sidemen like himself. Walden had expected the Allman Brothers Band to function similarly, something Gregg noticed in the band's first meeting with their manager after moving to Macon. "He only looked at Duane," Gregg recalled. "He was used to dealing with people like Percy Sledge, and then they dealt with their bands—and I can see his point in doing it that way, because he had signed Duane not the band. That didn't last, though, because Duane went in there and told him, 'Hold it. My little brother is in this goddamn organization, you will treat us all the same or you won't treat us at all.'"[16]

Duane's trust in Walden won out. "My brother trusted Phil," Gregg said, "and when I started asking questions about my publishing, he would just poke me and say, 'Hey man, be fucking thankful that we got enough to eat. Just sign the fucking agreement so we can get going.' . . . So that's how I signed all my publishing rights away" to Walden's No Exit Music. Gregg's reluctance proved prophetic. As Gregg was the band's chief songwriter, Duane's lack of concern for matters of money cost Gregg most of all. "I really disagreed with him and it hurt me that Duane didn't stand up for me more. I realize that he was looking out for the whole band and its betterment," Gregg reflected, "[but] it ended up costing all of us a shitload of money down the line."[17]

With the benefit of hindsight, Gregg understood the importance of Walden's patronage. "I loved the way my brother would deal with Phil Walden," he said. "He would never be ungracious or anything, because we were fixing to cut a record and have a career together. He would just go in there and say, 'We need this, this, and this.' He wore Walden down so much that Phil eventually stopped asking why and gave us what Duane asked him for."[18]

By late 1970, *Idlewild South* dropped off the charts altogether. Consensus was what musician and writer Tony Glover explained as its great flaw: "It was the Allmans in a studio and live shows of theirs often turn into a whole other trip." On stage, he wrote, "the Brothers can go from powerhouse soaring stomp rock, to fluid and flowing tone poems in sound just like southern mountain water running rough over rocks and smooth on sand. They're into each other's heads. They make a total music that has little to do with ego or flash." The band, Glover continued, "loves to play, and it shows. Some groups come off like they can't wait for the set to end so they can get to the party; with the Allmans, the set is the party."[19]

This success as a live act led Duane to pose an idea for the band's next record. "We need the freedom of a live album," he told Walden. "That'll get people that don't see us in person an opportunity to really hear what the Allman Brothers are all about." It was, the manager recalled, "a brilliant idea."[20]

Idlewild South missed the spark and spontaneity of the live experience that for Duane and his bandmates was the truest measure of the band's approach. Even if the musicians were improvising, studio recordings were simply too polished. Live, Duane explained, "there's rough arrangements, rough layouts of the songs, and then the solos are entirely up to each member of the band. So some nights are really good, and some nights ain't too hot. But the naturalness of a spur-of-the-moment type of thing is what I consider the valuablest asset of our band."[21]

To Duane, playing live was as liberating as studio recording was frustrating. "When bands start to play, they play live," he said. "We haven't got a lot of experience in making records. I do, a little bit, from doing sessions and stuff, but not like a polished session man or anything."[22]

In December 1970 Duane said the ABB would record its next record "partly live, part in Miami" at Criteria Studios. He mentioned that the band had recorded sets at the Atlanta Pop and Love Valley festivals. "If that's any good, we'll use that," he said.[23]

While in hindsight it seems Bill Graham's Fillmore East was the only place the band would even consider recording live, the band had given serious consideration to recording at the Warehouse in New Orleans. After Atlantic's southeastern promo man Philip Rauls introduced Warehouse co-owner Bill Johnston to the band's first album, the Allman Brothers played the venue regularly, including several shows that, through the miracle of bootleg recordings, have since become legendary. Backstage at the Warehouse on New Year's Eve 1970, Duane mentioned they had hoped to record the show, but producer Tom Dowd was unavailable. "We're going to do a live album here," Duane proclaimed. "The next time we play we're going to record it."[24]

A long-circulating recording of the show that night demonstrates a band flexing its muscle. It may not have been a true *At Fillmore East* session rehearsal, but it might as well have been. Duane's open E-tuned slide songs had all moved to the beginning of the set, so retuning didn't slow the set's pace down. The band played five of the seven tracks that made the final album, with only "Done Somebody Wrong" and "Hot 'Lanta" missing from the set that night.

As 1971 dawned, the Allman Brothers Band found themselves at a crossroads. The group had toured relentlessly for nearly two years. They had released two studio albums that had gained critical acclaim but little commercial success. Duane remained undaunted. "I guess success depends on how many people dig you," he reflected. "You play what you feel and hope you're doing the right thing. You've got to do whatever you believe in. If you're wrong, you change and keep making changes till you make it—or till you're happy with the whole thing."[25]

It was Phil Walden who gave Duane Allman the support to chart his own path. Walden nurtured the development of *At Fillmore East*, and the record validated his steadfast belief in Duane's talent. He fought his partner Jerry Wexler's efforts to move the band from the South to break nationally because Duane and his band believed they needed to remain in the South, and Walden believed in Duane's vision. Walden agreed with Duane: a live album was the final piece of the puzzle.

Duane Allman's last appearance in Atlanta, July 17, 1971. The Allman Brothers Band moniker meant more than brothers in the family sense, though
brothers Duane and Gregg Allman anchored the band. This is my favorite
photo of Gregg and Duane. Their concentration says a lot to me about their
relationship and devotion to music. Gregg was the last to join Duane's band
and led it from Duane's 1971 death until the band retired on October 28, 2014.
Courtesy Carter Tomassi.

Left: The band on stage from the wings, in Duane's last Atlanta show, July 17, 1971. All eyes but Jaimoe's are on Dickey as he solos, while Jai seems to be meditating on his drums. Courtesy Carter Tomassi.

Below: Duane's last show in Macon, April 9, 1971. Clear images of the full ABB on stage are somewhat rare, six members and two full drum sets. Berry is watching Duane and Butch is watching Berry, while the other three are deep into their own instruments. Dickey is standing slightly behind the drummers, as he did regularly in this era. Courtesy W. Robert Johnson.

Drummer Jai Johanny "Jaimoe" Johanson, Duane's first recruit. A veteran of the R&B touring circuit, Jaimoe brought the jazz impulse to the band, an influence that set the band apart from its contemporaries and endured for the band's entire forty-five-year career. In this recently discovered photo from a free concert at the University of California–Riverside on January 26, 1970, Jaimoe holds his sticks with traditional grip, as has long been popular in jazz drumming. Courtesy Bruce D. Henderson.

Bassist Berry Oakley, at Birmingham Municipal Auditorium, January 29, 1972. He was the linchpin of the Allman Brothers Band. The ABB's sound revolved around Oakley's bass. The Big House in Macon was his home with his wife, Linda. Oakley was the band's social director and resident hippie, whose psychedelic lead bass brought swing to some of the band's fiercest blues jams. Musician and fan Troy Wilson said of this photo of Berry, "The joy on his face reflects how I feel when I listen to him play." AllmanBrothersBookBySidneySmith.com.

Butch Trucks at the Warehouse in New Orleans on December 31, 1972. Butch provided a rock-solid foundation as Jaimoe's partner on the ABB's backline. Prior to signing up with Duane and crew, Butch had recorded with folk-rock bands the Bitter Ind and the Tiffany System and an album with the 31st of February. Among his many influences, Butch carried a love of classical music, and he used the tympani to bring Allman Brothers jams to dramatic conclusion, as in this shot. AllmanBrothersBookBySidneySmith.com.

Guitarist Dickey Betts in Duane Allman's last show in Macon, April 9, 1971.
The intensity in Dickey's eyes really burns in this photo, a fierceness that fired
Duane's creativity. In Betts, Duane brought in a partner everyone acknowledged
as his equal. A phenomenal and inventive rhythm player, he was also a masterful composer, his instrumentals tailor-made for the band's onstage adventures.
After Duane's death in 1971, Betts took over musical direction of the band, a role
he held until his departure in 2000. Courtesy W. Robert Johnson.

The Allman Brothers Band at the last show at Fillmore East, June 27, 1971. The night before, the band played what everyone—band and crew, audience, promoter—acknowledged as the greatest show the ABB ever played. Duane called it "like leaving church" as he walked offstage to an awestruck crowd. "A brilliant, brilliant set," Bill Graham recalled. "Heavenly music." "The Night They Closed the Fillmore Down," fan Rowland Archer's story of the show, inspired me to seek out more fan accounts of my favorite band. One reason Fillmore East was one of the era's most famous venues was because of Graham's dedication to the audience experience, including psychedelic back-drops by Joshua (later, Joe) Light Show. This image, by famed Fillmore East house photographer Amalie R. Rothschild, shows the band tightly arrayed on the stage. One reason the music of *At Fillmore East* sounds so intimate is because it is. © Amalie R. Rothschild.

Fillmore East, at 105 Second Avenue in New York, May 1970. The auditorium in the heart of the East Village was the city's rock headquarters. When Bill Graham shuttered the venue in June 1971, he chose the Allman Brothers, whom he introduced as "the best of them all," to close the shows. This photo gives a view of the entire building. Guest entered the auditorium under the marquee on Second Avenue. (The black staircase toward the left of the photo is the building's fire escape). The building had several lives after 1971, most notably as the famous gay nightclub The Saint. In 1996 it was razed and replaced with apartments, although the original façade and lobby remained intact as a bank. In 2021 a small photo exhibition on the site's history remained in the lobby. © Amalie R. Rothschild.

The ABB road crew in Macon during a 1971 photo shoot for *At Fillmore East*. Band members considered the road crew as part of the band. This shot is an outtake from the photo sessions with famed rock photographer Jim Marshall. The roadies—(*left to right*) Kim Payne, road manager Willie Perkins (*front*), Joe Dan Petty (*standing*), Mike Callahan, and "Red Dog" Campbell—pose in the band's equipment truck, dubbed the "Black Hearted Woman," after the song from the band's debut album. This photo shows a much more playful side of the crew than the surly-looking outlaws posing on the album's back cover. © Jim Marshall Photography LLC.

The Allman Brothers opening for Love and the Grateful Dead at Fillmore East, February 1970. Dickey Betts is playing a Fender Stratocaster rather than the Gibson Les Paul he and Duane most famously wielded. The Joshua Light Show screen is in the backdrop. This photo is one of several Ira Zadikow took at the show and sent me many years ago, the only copies left. They're significant as documenting the earliest connections between the ABB and the Dead. Photograph by Ira Zadikow, collection of the author.

Dickey Betts on stage during the band's tenth-anniversary tour, Wheeling Civic Center, Wheeling, West Virginia, May 2, 1979. After Duane's death in 1971, Dickey took over the band's slide-guitar role, a position he filled until 1989. Like Duane, Dickey played slide in open-E tuning, though he played with his slide on his middle finger to make it easier for him to chord with his other fingers. Never a fan of playing electric slide to begin with, Betts only played slide in acoustic sets after Warren Haynes joined the band in 1989. Courtesy Art Dobie.

Derek Trucks at New York's Beacon Theatre, October 2014. He's playing Duane's 1957 Les Paul Goldtop at this show during the ABB's final run. Derek is the oldest son of Butch Truck's younger brother, Chris. A gigging musician since age nine, Derek quickly outgrew the child phenom label with a dedication to doing music his way that rivaled Duane's. He formed the Derek Trucks Band in 1994, joined Uncle Butch's psychedelic offshoot Frogwings in 1997, and by 1999 was a full-time member of the Allman Brothers Band. Derek toured the world with Eric Clapton in 2006 before forming the Tedeschi Trucks Band with his wife, Susan Tedeschi, in 2010. Courtesy Derek McCabe.

Guitarist Warren Haynes, drummer Matt Abts, and bassist Allen Woody
(*left to right*), with Kirsten West in the background, at Rose Hill Cemetery
in Macon in 1994. When Gregg, Dickey, Butch, and Jaimoe reunited for the
band's twentieth anniversary in 1989, Warren and Woody powered the front
line with an energy that inspired the original members. They left the ABB in
1997 to devote their full attention to Gov't Mule, the power trio they formed in
1994 with Abts. Photo by Kirk West Photography.

Photo by Bruce D. Henderson

The Allman Brothers Band at a free show at the University of California–Riverside January 26, 1970. During this first trip to the West Coast, they had to panhandle for the fare to cross the bridge into San Francisco. Though in this photo they look like a band rehearsing outside on a nice day, they're actually performing in front of several hundred people. Dickey Betts is leaning back hitting a note as Berry Oakley (*right*) smiles at him. Jaimoe's drums and road case are marked "Jai Johanny Johanson," his stage name at the time. Courtesy Bruce D. Henderson.

The Allman Brothers Band on New Year's Eve 1972 in concert at the Warehouse in New Orleans. The Grateful Dead played the venue the night of the bust they sing about on "Truckin'" and the Allman Brothers Band played legendary shows there. Several exist on tape, including my favorite full Duane show, from September 1971. Capricorn Records broadcast the New Year's Eve 1972 show live on the radio. It would be the band's last gig at the city's premier rock venue. After weathering the deaths of Duane and Berry within one year, the ABB was about to become to biggest band in the land with the lineup shown here that included Chuck Leavell on keyboards and piano, and Jaimoe's childhood friend Lamar Williams on bass. AllmanBrothersBookBy-SidneySmith.com.

The Gray House in Jacksonville's Riverside neighborhood where it all began. On March 23, 2019, fans dedicated this historical marker on the site. Photo by the author.

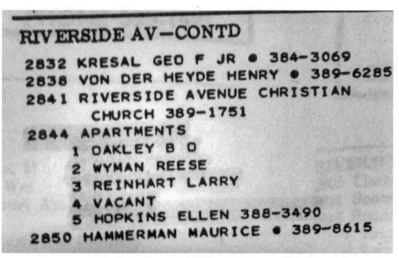

City directory list of renters at the Gray House, 1969. The band first jammed at the communal home of the Second Coming. Berry Oakley and his wife, Linda, lived in apartment 1, keyboardist Reese Wynans in number 2, and guitarist Larry Reinhart in number 3. Duane stayed with Ellen Hopkins in apartment 5 as he assembled the Allman Brothers Band. Courtesy Dennis Price.

Above: Jaimoe's road case on display at the Big House Museum. This is the same case seen on the cover of *At Fillmore East*, (*below*) shot by Jim Marshall in Macon in front of a building near Capricorn Studios. The road cases served as the backdrop for a band the photographer caught mid-laugh. The photo implies a group of friends ready to lay it all out on stage and have a damn good time doing it; the reality was that Duane had just scored drugs from a dealer who happened to be passing by during the photo shoot. Photo by the author.

The Allman plot at Rose Hill Cemetery. The graves (*left to right*) are of Butch Trucks (slightly out of the photo), Gregg Allman, Duane Allman, and Berry Oakley. Rose Hill is very significant to the ABB story. In the band's earliest days in Macon, they would trek from "the Hippie Crash Pad" they shared at 309 College Street to Rose Hill Cemetery, along the Ocmulgee River. Steven Paley took some of the band's first publicity photos there, including the image on the back cover of the group's debut album. Dickey's favorite writing spot inspired the title for "In Memory of Elizabeth Reed." Duane and Berry were buried there in 1972, and by the late 1990s, ongoing vandalism led Candace Oakley, Johnny Sandlin and his wife, Ann, and others to raise money to fence in their gravesites. By 2017 Gregg had purchased multiple plots for his bandmates and paid to have the entire site redesigned for public viewing. In this photo, a group of my friends and yours truly (white shirt and hat) pay our respects to Butch, Gregg, Duane, and Berry in 2019. Gary Barrett's Knucklehead Club.

The Allman Brothers Band in St. Petersburg, Florida, April 18, 1970. The ABB had two paying gigs in St. Petersburg, a daytime concert at Florida Presbyterian (Eckerd) College and an evening show at the Aragon Ballroom. Dickey was still experimenting with his main stage rig, using a guitar he later gave to Duane for slide. Commonly called Duane's SG, it was actually a 1961 Gibson Les Paul model that Duane kept tuned to open E so he didn't have to retune between songs. This photo from the college gig shows original road manager Twiggs Lyndon with a camera at the edge of the stage. Photo from *Logos*, Florida Presbyterian College, 1970, courtesy of the Eckerd College Archives, St. Petersburg, Florida.

Duane's funeral, November 1, 1971, at Snow's Memorial Chapel in Macon. Atlantic's Jerry Wexler gave the eulogy, and the band honored their leader the only way they knew how: with music. Gregg performed a solo version of "Melissa." Thom Doucette and Dr. John joined the band, as did Duane's good friend Delaney Bramlett (*left*). When the music ended, Dickey took off Duane's Les Paul, placed it in its case, and leaned it beside the casket. Jeff Albertson Photograph Collection (PH 57). Department of Special Collections and University Archives, University of Massachusetts Amherst Libraries.

CHAPTER 12

RECORDING *AT FILLMORE EAST* (MARCH 13-14, 1971)

The Allman Brothers did it all. On stage they were giants.
Philip Rauls

Walden agreed that a live album was the best way to build on the audience Duane and the band had worked so hard to develop. The decision was not without risk. While live albums were common, they were typically a way established artists generated sales between studio albums. The Allman Brothers Band had no such credibility and instead used the medium to grow its audience. The live album presented their music at its absolute best. *At Fillmore East* became the quintessential Allman Brothers Band recording, the pinnacle of Duane Allman's meteoric career.

Fillmore East also presented a decidedly American take on contemporary music, critic Bud Scoppa contended. The ABB were "a reminder that rock 'n' roll didn't start out to be a mean but ambiguous kind of music played by fey and mannered young Britishers" like the British blues artists who had actually introduced electric blues to much of white America. "The real rock 'n' roll was hard, blues-rich, powerful, and overtly *virile* stuff."[1]

Atlantic promo men Philip Rauls and John Carter likewise lauded the band's live presence. "The Allman Brothers did it all," Rauls said. "On stage they were giants." As Carter recalled, "Every night was different. I've never seen a band that was so spontaneous and reacted so well to each other. It was absolutely real and spontaneous and driven by greatness." Tony Glover wrote that the Allman Brothers have "their chops together—and know how to use them to create thick smoking tapestries of blues and rock, tempered with a lyrical aching beauty." He found it genuine: "No one is into aerobatics or sex shows, they just stand there and play their heads off." It was the response the band sought.[2]

Scoppa described their music as "powerhouse rock 'n' roll" that combined the electric blues of Muddy Waters and Miles Davis's *Bitches Brew*–era jazz fusion. It made the ABB "the tightest instrumental group I'd ever heard." Audiences loved it. "The force of the whole band playing with that incredible single-mindedness gets people on their feet after practically every number," Scoppa observed. Their music "may get very free and loose and sophisticated at certain points, but it's always got its chest out and its eyes open. Part of the masculine feel comes from the patterned thunder of Jai Johanny's and Butch Trucks's double drumming, part from the two guitars circling each other like a pair of killer falcons."[3]

Rolling Stone's Alex Dubro found the approach "incredibly versatile and highly musical." While jazz left contemporaries in "hopeless befuddlement," Dubro argued, the ABB "grab the latitude allowed by jazz changes and add power."[4]

An August 1970 Allman Brothers concert in Miami captivated Eric Clapton. He recounted,

> The music was unbelievable, because they were doing all that harmony playing. Everything seemed to be, even if they played solos, they were all in harmony. It was fantastically worked out. The impression that I got was how much hard work they'd put into their presentation, and the fact that it wasn't really blasted all over the airwaves, you know? They had just quietly gone about doing a fantastic job of making really, really good music that was really well thought out.[5]

Thus, Duane returned to Clapton some of the inspiration he took from him. "They influenced my music at the time," Clapton said. "They made it okay for a band to be live all the time—their thing was really more about live than [studio]." Clapton cited the Allman Brothers' expansiveness in expressing his frustration with Cream. "We were really limited onstage," he said. "We could go into the studio and make great records by overdubbing—I would play a rhythm part, and then play a lead part with a harmony to it, so you're really talking about three guitar [parts]." The Allman Brothers Band had no such limitations.[6]

Though it was rare for underground artists like the Allman Brothers to release a live record, concert albums otherwise were common. Some artists used the live medium to introduce new material or change musical direction. John Coltrane's *Coltrane "Live" at the Village Vanguard* (1962) is an example of both; Johnny Cash's *At Folsom Prison* (1968) and *At San Quentin* (1969) established Cash as the Man in Black, champion of the underdog. Many live records were attempts at a midstream career boost, such as James Brown's self-funded *Live at the Apollo* (1963). *Live at the Apollo* spent more than a year on the *Billboard* pop albums chart, but most live albums, such as B. B. King's *Live at the Regal* and Muddy Waters's *At Newport* by Muddy Waters, failed to chart altogether.[7]

To the record industry, live albums served as filler material for audiences to purchase between bands' studio recordings. It took until the mid-1960s for label executives to realize that there was a market for live rock albums. The breakthrough was the Beach Boys' *Beach Boys Concert*. Released in 1964, it spent sixty-two weeks on the charts, four of them at number 1. Two years later, the Rolling Stones released *Got Live If You Want It!*, which eventually reached number 6. Both albums are indicative of how the music industry perceived live records at the time. Like James Brown's *Live at the Apollo*, the albums featured hit songs. Unlike Brown's record, Beach Boys and Rolling Stones albums heavily overdubbed tracks. Dickey Betts told *Rolling Stone*'s Corbin Reiff, "There was kind of a running joke in the music business. Nobody said it in public in an interview or anything, but people would say, 'The only thing live on such-and-such record was the audience.' A lot of times they would go back into the studio and redo things; redo vocals and stuff."[8]

Soon rock bands and labels began including live tracks on studio albums. Clapton's career was once again at the forefront of this trend. After he'd wrapped up his tenure with the Yardbirds, his label slapped four of his live cuts on 1965's *Having a Rave Up with the Yardbirds*. By the end of the decade, half of the tracks, among them "Crossroads," were live on Cream's final two albums, *Wheels of Fire* and *Goodbye Cream*.

The Allman Brothers Band used the live album in an altogether new way. Unlike their peers, all of whom were well established in the marketplace, the ABB was an underground phenomenon. Labels supported the live releases as low-cost investments that kept audiences buying records. The Allman Brothers had no such cachet. The live album was a low-cost gamble, however, given that they didn't require months of paying for studio time.

Yet another comparison to the Grateful Dead is useful. Although the Dead was America's premier improvisational and experimental live rock act since its earliest days, they, too, struggled with studio recordings. The Dead's second album, *Anthem of the Sun*, in 1968, included live and studio cuts. Sales flagged, as they did for its follow-up, *Aoxomoxoa*, released in June 1969. In debt to Warner Brothers for $250,000, the Dead doubled down. Rather than recording a studio album and embarking on a tour behind the album, the Dead chose to record their fourth album live. *Live/Dead* proved to be a breakthrough when it appeared in November 1969, and it remains one of the most revered live records of the era. All of the tracks but two, "St. Stephen" and "Dark Star," made their first appearance on the release.[9]

Whether the Allman Brothers Band considered *Live/Dead* when they decided to record their third album live is immaterial. The connection matters most because these two similarly influenced, influential, innovative, improvisational bands decided their best showcase was a live album. The groups believed the excitement of the live experience was how they best expressed themselves musically, and the resulting albums confirmed that instinct. *Live/Dead* didn't sell all that well, only reaching number 64 in fifteen weeks on the charts. But it sounded as close to the experience of a live Grateful Dead concert as possible, and it brought in new fans along the way. The ABB sought the same results.

The live album idea also became part of a campaign to take advantage of the Allman Brothers' reputation as "the People's Band." Jonny Podell, the band's New York–based booking agent, recalled how "the word had got out. The tastemakers—Bill Graham and *Rolling Stone*—had come out forcefully in favor of the Allman Brothers. The network of underground clubs, from Boston Tea Party to the Fillmore West, clearly supported the Allman Brothers, and would play them five times a year if they could." The band's relentless touring schedule had garnered a significant following. Translating the live sound to vinyl was the right next step.[10]

The Allman Brothers would record the album at Fillmore East. The venue at Sixth Street and Second Avenue in New York City's East Village was nearly as important as the music itself. Graham's theaters dissolved the line between musician and audience. "Performers interacted with the audience to form a unit," Fillmore West manager Paul Baratta said, "not just somebody performing at an audience." Graham encouraged the closeness. The dynamic was tailor-made for the Allman Brothers Band, whose concerts were as much a chance for the band to perform for the audience as it was for the band and audience to celebrate life together.[11]

Betts called Fillmore East "the Carnegie Hall of rock 'n' roll. [Graham] made a great presentation of rock 'n' roll with light shows and curtains and presentations of the bands and the set changes." Most importantly, he said, the room sounded fantastic. "The P.A. system was set up correctly. It wasn't too loud, it wasn't too soft, and everyone in the room could hear and see." Jaimoe said, "That stage was smoking."[12]

The *At Fillmore East* sessions spanned six shows over three nights, March 11 through 13, 1971; tapes survive for the latter four shows. The Allman Brothers were not the scheduled headliner; they had the middle slot on a bill between headliner Johnny Winter and opener the Elvin Bishop Group. Tickets cost $5.50 (orchestra), $4.50 (first balcony), $3.50 (second balcony).[13]

The ABB "tore into the early show like it was a Friday night late show," Alan Arkush recalled. The energy stunned the headliner. "Johnny wanted to reverse the order," Arkush said. "He just couldn't top them." Winter's manager insisted the bands switch slots. "Johnny is gonna be opening for the Allman Brothers from now on because we can't have that happen again," Trucks heard him say after the Thursday night shows, which is exactly what happened. The bands traded places, with Winter playing the middle slot for rest of the run.[14]

The lineup change gave the ABB the time and liberty to do what it did best, improvise and expand songs as the muse struck. Graham's bills afforded only ninety minutes to the middle act, not enough time for a band that topped a combined sixty minutes with only four songs on *At Fillmore East*: "You Don't Love Me" (19:06), "Whipping Post" (22:40), "In Memory of Elizabeth Reed" (12:46), and "Stormy Monday" (8:31). If the lineup order hadn't switched, Butch recalled, "we absolutely wouldn't have had all that time to do all the stretching out that led to *At Fillmore East*."[15]

Bud Scoppa reported that the *Fillmore East* sessions caught a band "entering its prime as a performing unit." They arrived in New York well rehearsed and in top form. Arkush said, "The Saturday night shows, early and late, were probably the greatest I ever saw the Allman Brothers play, one of the greatest live performances I've ever witnessed." The bulk of *At Fillmore East* came from these two shows.[16]

At Fillmore East was a carefully planned and brilliantly executed documentation of the band's development. Listeners can hear the closeness of the musicians in their musical conversations, each improvising his part, whether soloing, comping, or both simultaneously. "What made that weekend special is that we had been out on the road, we'd been playing these songs, and you know how sometimes, everything comes together at the right time? When you have the right people in the right place doing the right thing?" Butch reflected. "We were really comfortable with these songs that we were playing. On 'Whipping Post' and 'Mountain Jam,' we had really learned to talk to each other. By the time that weekend came along, we were really communicating."[17]

"We knew those shows were special," Jaimoe said, "but when you're doing it and you're in the middle of it, you're not thinking like that. Great stuff was going on. I didn't want to get hung up over knowing the shows were being recorded. That would not be good, you need to get your mind off of that so you don't get hung up and forget what you're supposed to be doing, which is playing music and connecting with an audience."[18]

The full session recordings, released in 2014 as *The 1971 Fillmore East Recordings*, feature six musicians in deep, constant musical conversation in front of an appreciative audience. Duane's and Dickey's guitars are the most prominent in conversation, but the third guitar, Berry's bass, drives nearly all of it. His runs answer his bandmates' with ideas of his own that spur the entire band in new directions. On Hammond B-3, Gregg is as active as he would ever be in his Allman Brothers Band career, laying down a steady base of sound. Firming up the foundation is an unshakeable rhythmic foundation. The power of the drums is one of the most noticeable differences between *Idlewild South* and *At Fillmore East*. Jaimoe plays as much percussion on *Idlewild* as he does drums, which may be another reason it didn't sell. Jaimoe is a drummer, not a percussionist, and the Allman Brothers was a two-drummer band. The double drumming on *At Fillmore East* makes the rhythm more forceful, which seemed to give the band confidence.

The Fillmore East recordings captured a group at the peak of its powers playing a typically great series of shows. "We were a hell of a band," Betts said, "and we just got a good recording that captured what we sounded like." Trucks recalled, "We knew each other well enough, we knew the material well enough to where we didn't have to think about it and could let it all flow so naturally. We knew what each other was going to do—yet we were constantly wide open to letting it go and taking a dive and seeing what would happen." Jaimoe said, "You went by what the song was dictating as opposed to thinking it out."[19]

It was jazz in a rock context. The ABB's songs were "structured to the point where we'd know who went first," Betts recalled, "but what was going to happen in the middle of it, we never knew." As bandleader, Duane would count off songs, Gregg said. "We would end it when he raised his hand, but in between, the band just let itself go wherever the music would take us." Tunes morphed accordingly, stretching to whatever limits the band and soloist felt in the moment, which Jaimoe cited as Coltrane's influence. "With whatever amount of space you have to do something," he quoted the saxophonist, "that's what you have and the ability to do that just shows the mastery of knowing what you're doing, how to develop it and how to play a song."[20]

The Fillmore East audience was among the ABB's most attentive. "They would kind of play along with us," Gregg recalled. "We'd go from two decibels to a hundred. But when we shut down, they'd shut down. They'd go from screaming and yelling to absolute silence. They were right on top of every single vibration coming from the stage." Dowd captured the vibe well on the recording. Twice on "You Don't Love Me," for example, the band dropped out altogether, leaving Duane soloing alone on stage. Both times, the crowd remained nearly still, as if stirring would disturb the magic. The second time it happened, one dude could hold back no longer. "Play all night!" he burst out, in one of the most famous, joyful fan moments captured live. Duane teased the eighteenth-century Christmas carol "Joy to the World" to signal the end of his solo. Dickey first picked up the cue, then the band followed as the guitarists steered toward the song's thundering conclusion.[21]

The Allman Brothers Band played six shows over the course of the *Fillmore East* sessions. Recordings remain of only four: the early and late shows on March 12 and 13. For the March 11 shows, Duane had invited a three-person horn section including Jaimoe's friend Juicy Carter to guest on a few songs. Following the March 11 early show, Dowd told Duane to cancel the experiment. "This isn't the time to try this out," he argued. Dowd was adamant (and correct) that the unrehearsed, slightly out-of-tune horn section did not belong on the album. Carter demonstrated little feel for the Allman Brothers Band's music, and though he joined the band at least twice more over the weekend, none of the horn section's appearances made the final album.[22]

Convincing Duane to excise the out-of-place jazz horn section from the *At Fillmore East* sessions was perhaps Dowd's most important contribution to the album, as it gave the world a note-perfect, horn-free "In Memory of Elizabeth Reed" that is a highlight of the record and among the best pieces of music the Allman Brothers ever recorded. His suggestion is even more remarkable considering Dowd wasn't even supposed to be in New York for the sessions. He was in Ghana working on the film *Soul to Soul* and had planned a brief vacation before he changed his mind and flew home to New York instead. He called Atlantic when he landed and learned the Allman Brothers were in town recording. He headed straight to Fillmore East.

Given the album's high stakes, the serendipity is puzzling. The band hadn't recorded in New Orleans on New Year's Eve 1970 because Dowd wasn't available, so why then would they book the Fillmore East for recording without their producer? More than likely, the group decided recording at the Fillmore was more important than Dowd's presence at the sessions. Once the band started playing live, the producer's role is less essential. Engineers did the recording.

The Allman Brothers Band played tight set lists over the weekend. By 1971 sets had formalized to the extent that shows began with the songs Duane played on slide. At the Fillmore, this meant four short blues songs: "Statesboro Blues," "Trouble No More," "Don't Keep Me Wonderin'," and "Done Somebody Wrong." Two of the tracks, "Statesboro Blues" and Elmore James's "Done Somebody Wrong," had yet to appear on an Allman Brothers release, though the band had attempted to record the former several times in the studio. By the final show that weekend, the Allman Brothers dropped all but "Statesboro" from the set, satisfied that they'd captured what they needed for the new album. In their place was harmonica player Sonny Boy Williamson's "One Way Out," a somewhat off-kilter take that the band did not release officially until the 2014 box set.

The sessions include three performances of Betts's "In Memory of Elizabeth Reed," two with Carter's out-of-tune sax. The third, recorded at the early show on Saturday, March 13, clocks in at almost thirteen minutes, nearly twice the length of the studio version. It is the definitive version of the band's definitive instrumental. The two guitarists are in command of their instruments, as Betts and Allman confidently channel jazz influence and blues roots in extended solos, with Duane bringing his solo to two climaxes. The *Fillmore East* version is a masterwork, six band members in sync through multiple melodic and tempo changes. A second instrumental, the up-tempo, jazzy "Hot 'Lanta," is the sole full-band co-write. It is the only Allman Brothers instrumental that never appeared on a studio album and that the band never stretched out on stage.[23]

Three extended blues songs rounded out the sessions, two covers—"Stormy Monday" and "You Don't Love Me"—and Gregg's "Whipping Post." The band played "Stormy Monday" just once over the weekend, the Saturday late show, in a performance that made the final album. The group played Willie Cobbs's "You Don't Love Me" three times, in an arrangement they borrowed from Junior Wells's *Hoodoo Man Blues* featuring Buddy Guy on guitar. The Allman Brothers Band made the tune their own. At the Fillmore, "You Don't Love Me" expanded to nearly twenty minutes of musical conversation in a patch of two versions. They also stretched out "Whipping Post"—performed three times—from 5:17 on its debut album to 19:30, 17:30, and 22:53 at the Fillmore.

The third version of "Whipping Post" segued into the last song the full Allman Brothers Band played during the Fillmore run, "Mountain Jam." The jam was a fitting end to a triumphal weekend. The thirty-plus-minute improvisation featured solos from all band members, including a three-minute drum jam. "Sure has been a fine weekend," Duane exclaimed at the jam's conclusion.[24]

"Fine weekend" was an understatement. The music the band recorded at Fillmore East March 12 and 13, 1971, was a band in its element, playing at an absolute peak. And the group knew it. "Last weekend we played in New York," Berry Oakley announced from the Warehouse stage the following week. "We recorded four different shows, and we got enough material that sounds a lot like the really spaced-out stuff that we do when we get down here and we're gonna put it out on record in about six weeks." Capricorn released *At Fillmore East* less than four months after the sessions, on July 6. By September 3, it reached number 13 on the *Billboard* charts. By October 25, *At Fillmore East* had sold 500,000 copies.[25]

CHAPTER 13

AT FILLMORE EAST BREAKS THROUGH (SUMMER AND FALL 1971)

My complaint is this. After listening to your beautiful music, the rest of my records seem irrelevant.

M. Skryp

It is unclear exactly when the ABB decided to issue a double album of new and older songs. The group may have originally conceived of a single album featuring only the former. In this construct, side A would consist of "Statesboro Blues," "Done Somebody Wrong," and "Stormy Monday" and side B including "One Way Out," "Hot 'Lanta," and "You Don't Love Me," with solos edited down to fit on two twenty-minute sides of a record.

Ultimately, the caliber of the March 1971 Fillmore East performances and recordings made the decision an easy one. A single album would have made sense, but Walden argued that the band's performances warranted more, and he fought to release a double album. "I told Wexler that our Fillmore East live album would have to be two LPs and contain at least one sixteen-minute song," Walden said. "Not every note is vital to our heritage," was Wexler's reply. "The boys are pure artists and that's what it's got to be," Walden argued. "Jerry agreed, he understood." What he understood, Wexler later said, "was that I had never heard a guitarist I found as satisfying as Duane."[1]

Walden then presented an additional demand: "Our image is that this is the People's Band. Music is for the people and therefore we want to make this specially priced." He wanted to sell the double album for the cost of a single record. Wexler relented only after Walden agreed to cut a deal on song publishing for the three original Allman Brothers Band songs on the record—"In Memory of Elizabeth Reed," "Hot 'Lanta," and "Whipping Post."[2]

Walden's gamble paid off, and *At Fillmore East* became the breakthrough that the band, its manager, and Atlantic Records had long sought. "I don't think anyone could've predicted the extent of the album's success but we were counting heavily on it," Walden said. Trucks recounted, "Two years of playing every city in the country, we built a following. When that live album came out that's what everybody was waiting for."[3]

The album was as near a representation of the band's live performances as possible. Unlike many live albums of the period, including the Grateful Dead's eponymous live album, *At Fillmore East* had "no overdubs whatsoever," Betts said. "No vocal overdubs, no repair work." Other than a splice of two versions of "You Don't Love Me," he said, "there was nothing done to that. It's just a pure performance." Walden explained, "*At Fillmore East* is absolutely live. We didn't go back and re-record one guitar solo; we didn't add anything to it. The live album gave them an opportunity to play on record as they played in person. That was really the turning point." Critics and consumers responded favorably, engaging with the album on a level far beyond anything the band had experienced with its previous two albums.[4]

"The band had not really found themselves in the studio," Walden said, "but they had in front of live audiences where they had more freedom; they opened up. They weren't a three-minute-cut band." *At Fillmore East* gave the ABB the opportunity to stretch out. "No record [is] as good as hearing the band live," Tony Glover wrote, but *Fillmore East* "comes close to capturing the feelings they generate."[5]

The album features 76:22 of music spread across just seven tracks. Five of the seven songs were new, and only two, "Statesboro Blues" (4:17) and "Done Somebody Wrong" (4:33), were even remotely of the appropriate length to be released as singles, although neither was. Two cuts, "In Memory of Elizabeth Reed" and "Hot 'Lanta," are instrumentals, hybrids of jazz and rock but not the fusion of Miles Davis, Tony Williams Lifetime, and Mahavishnu Orchestra. Song lengths mirrored those from Coltrane's live albums at New York's Village

Vanguard. Five songs top five minutes, three exceed twelve, and two, "You Don't Love Me" and "Whipping Post," are twenty minutes each. *At Fillmore East* was music for serious music listeners; it found an audience on the FM radio format.

In the prestreaming world, most people accessed music through radio. For much of the twentieth century, AM dominated the market; its more powerful, lower-fidelity signal reached a wider geographic audience than later FM's less powerful, higher-quality signal. Because advertisers paid to reach listeners and pop music kept listeners listening, that's what AM stations programmed.

AM's dominance waned after a 1965 Federal Communications Commission ruling that prohibited AM stations from retransmitting programming on FM sister stations. The decision forced hundreds of stations to develop new formats nearly overnight. Many turned to freeform, a format devoid of the influence of the singles chart. FM played tracks that AM programmers ignored altogether. Freeform playlists featured a wider spectrum of music and favored longer album tracks over singles.[6]

New York's WOR was America's first commercial FM rock station. The station turned to freeform in 1966. It was, WOR-FM program director Tommy Reynolds said, "quality music. Rock without the AM shlock." WOR's playlists included banned songs such as "Bend It" by Dave Dee, Dozy, Beaky, Mick & Tich, a hit in Britain but not in the United States because of alleged sexual innuendo, and the Byrds' "Eight Miles High," which many AM stations banned because of its drug-related connotations. The format change drew listeners and, Alfred G. Aronowitz reported in the *Saturday Evening Post*, "was threatening to revolutionize radio by playing pop music for adults in the same dignified format that FM usually reserves for classical music."[7]

San Francisco's KMPX was another influential underground FM station. KMPX was home to Tom "Big Daddy" Donahue, who arrived at the station in 1967 and adapted his show from fellow KMPX DJ Larry Miller's existing format of folk, classical, jazz, and rock. Listeners responded enthusiastically. Soon, Jesse Walker writes, "The hippies took over KMPX." KMPX epitomized the underground FM station. Aimed at the youth audience, the station's "experimental and psychedelic music" addressed openly the cultural zeitgeist of San

Francisco. Its DJs "personified the mellow, often stoned, attitudes of listeners," Todd Coffin argues.[8]

Underground FM radio of the late 1960s and early 1970s was, scholar Michael C. Keith writes, "in step with that of the growing counterculture. It resented the mainstream gestalt of the day regarding social issues (war, drugs, race), but most of all it detested formula radio."[9] FM DJs and their listeners found *At Fillmore East* far from formulaic.

As stations began focusing on album cuts, FM became where true music aficionados tuned in. The Warehouse in New Orleans urged its patrons to support local FM radio as a way to boost the Crescent City's music scene. An advertisement by Beaver Productions, the Warehouse's management company, explained,

> We strongly encourage the switch from AM bubblegum music to New Orleans's two FM stations: WJMR and WRNO. Richard Shanks with some help from his friends, Larry Klein and Mike Roach, have put together one of the nation's finest shows. Joe Costello, owner and general manager of WRNO, along with his staff have been quite helpful in getting the Warehouse off the ground. WJMR-FM, WRNO-FM, and the Warehouse are all trying to bring nice music to this city. Join us in our fight against AM-bubblegum music—switch to FM.[10]

FM was the perfect medium for the music of the Allman Brothers Band; the dial's predilection for album cuts was critical to the breakthrough success of *At Fillmore East*. "The Allman Brothers were an FM radio band," Atlantic's Philip Rauls said. John Carter, also from Atlantic, said, "People couldn't believe the number of records the Allman Brothers were selling on what appeared—to the old school—as no airplay. The small audience that was listening to those FM stations was religious about it." The band knew this. Its instrumentals and "drawn-out pieces were not really commercial," Betts reflected. "If it hadn't been for FM radio that would play these extended pieces of music, we would never have been successful."[11]

Upon release, *At Fillmore East* stormed the charts. The album jumped to number 82 within three weeks of its July 6 release. By September 4, it reached its highest chart position, number 13, and by

October 25, the album had reached gold, at more than 500,000 copies sold. It spent forty-eight weeks on the *Billboard* 200, a mammoth achievement for a band who'd yet to sell 100,000 combined units to date.[12]

With *At Fillmore East*, the excitement of the band's live shows finally translated into record sales. The success was long in coming and well earned. "It went along so slow for so long, none of us really expected a whole lot to happen," Trucks reflected. "When we got that gold record, we realized we were doing something." The band had grown to believe their music was simply too original for the mainstream market. "We knew we were playing music nobody else had played before," Trucks said, "but none of us had thought about it in commercial terms." Success brought additional challenges. "Realizing we were commercially successful, that people were starting to listen to us, we had to keep that from influencing our music, keep the music still the six of us having fun," Trucks said.[13]

Listeners loved the album. On November 10, 1971, M. Skryp of Quebec wrote to the band,

> Please view this letter of complaint. After spending a small fortune in hard-earned money in amassing a very fine record collection, I recently purchased your new live double LP album. After smoking up some excellent home-grown marijuana (one joint only), I then played your album.
>
> My complaint is this. After listening to your beautiful music, the rest of my records seem irrelevant.
>
> Thank you very much for a wonderful performance. Hope to see you live.
>
> Your dedicated fan, M. Skryp.[14]

At Fillmore East, Gary Wishik of the *Statesman* declared, was "the next best thing to actually seeing them," lacking only "the possibility of an encore that quite possibly could last till dawn." *Rolling Stone*'s George Kimball called the album "one of the nicest things that ever happened to any of us. If you've been so unfortunate as to never have caught the Allman Brothers Band live, this recording is certainly the next best thing. Turn the volume up all the way and sit through the concert; by the time it's over you can almost imagine the Allman Band getting high and heading back to Macon." The *Boston Globe*'s Ernie Santosuosso wrote, "The Allmans really stretch out but the 'winging' is done with a sure purpose." Marshall Fine of the *Minneapolis Star* described the album as "electric magic, driving and energetic—beautiful."[15]

The Grateful Dead remained the standard against which reviewers measured all improvisational rock bands of the era, and *At Fillmore East* was no exception. Rich Aregood found that the ABB's album "sustained the Dead's kind of excitement." Marshall Fine said the record "captures the sound, the energy, and the excitement of a live performance as none have since *Live/Dead*." Kimball argued in *Rolling Stone*, "Any comparison is fatuous. Guitarists Duane Allman and Dickey Betts, organist-vocalist Gregg Allman, Berry Oakley on bass, and drummers J.J. Johanson and Butch Trucks comprise the best damn rock and roll band this country has produced in the past five years."[16]

Many reviews detected a sense of urgency in the record's shorter blues numbers "Statesboro Blues" and "Done Somebody Wrong" in comparison to longer tracks such as "You Don't Love Me" and "Whipping Post." Other reviewers drew attention to the instrumentals "Hot 'Lanta" and "In Memory of Elizabeth Reed." Santosuosso contended that "Stormy Monday" was "as good as anything else on the album, a sort of tonic in its decelerated, relaxed manner." In "Stormy Monday," Wishik found "the soft and gentle side of the group. Duane is picking the most fragile notes he can find while Dickey Betts is softly sliding in and out, over and behind him and Gregg Allman is lifting the whole thing very gently with a beautiful rhythm pattern from the mighty Hammond B-3 organ."[17]

Most critics considered *At Fillmore East* an authentic representation of the Allman Brothers Band live. "Musicians' musicians," the Clemson University *Tiger* called the ABB, "one of the best instrumental groups in the country." Jim Conley assured El Paso readers, "You won't be bored, even though there are only seven cuts on the four sides. From soft mellow blues to cooking rock, they just do it all right." Aregood called the album "excellent from beginning to end. The excitement they generate in live performance manages to leak through on the recording."[18]

Glover found Duane Allman's musical vision at the heart of *At Fillmore East*. "In these days of so many groups who are merely competent, and ritualized sets which mostly bore your ass off," he wrote, "it's a real joy to hear a group that loves to play and can communicate their enthusiasm." The album demonstrated that "not only have they got their chops together—but that they know how to use them to create thick, smoking tapestries of blues and rock, tempered with a lyrical aching beauty." Though Duane stood out, "sliding out sinuous solos that coo, with southern soul," he was "only part of the web. Brother Gregg sits high atop his organ, throbbing out long lines of swirling sounds, doing most of the vocal work with a mellow rasp while Dickey Betts plays alternate lead guitar, often in rippling counterpoint to Duane's loping runs. The rhythm section of double drummers Butch Trucks and Jai Johanny Johanson, bottomed by cooking bassist Berry Oakley are always right there, driving it all along with power and a fine sense of dynamics."[19]

On *Fillmore East*, Duane's music speaks for him and his bandmates. "His complete confidence—like the complete confidence of his band—is right out there," Scoppa wrote. "No nonsense. He heads straight for whatever he's after." *Rolling Stone*'s Dubro asked after an ABB run in in California in January 1971, "Where do they want to go from here? Mostly they all seemed to want to do what they're doing. It didn't seem like they wanted to be stars, just musicians." Duane had said as much backstage during the Fillmore East sessions in March 1971 when he told Glover, "We're a *band* man, a band that works like a band. If we could just get people to come out and see us I *know* they'd like what they heard."[20]

The completed album sounds like a band that took immense joy in playing. Duane quotes Robert Johnson's "Come on in My Kitchen" during "You Don't Love Me" and playfully teases the seventeenth-century folk song "Frere Jacques" as "Whipping Post" winds down. Stage banter gives insight into band members' personalities. Duane introduces Elmore James's "Done Somebody Wrong" as "an old, true story" before adding off-mic, "Wonder who?" He introduces "Stormy Monday" as "an old Bobby Bland song" before correcting himself. "Actually, it's a T-Bone Walker song." Oakley announces "Brother Gregg Allman singing the blues!" and as the track fades out "Duane, Dickey, and Ace [Thom Doucette] playing 'em." Duane introduces "In Memory of Elizabeth Reed" as "a song Dickey Betts wrote from our second album" and "Whipping Post" as "a little number from our first album,

Berry starts 'er off." In anticipation of the band's set closer, at least five folks yell out "Whipping Post" before Berry plays a note.

Song introductions and interludes on *Fillmore East* also highlight the decision to market the Allman Brothers Band as the People's Band. Glover called them "natural, no bullshit people." Other recordings from the era prove the band's Fillmore East stage announcements weren't a put-on. Duane and his mates enjoyed themselves on stage, and they let audiences know that.[21]

At Fillmore East also provides the clearest example of Butch Trucks's classical influence on the Allman Brothers Band's sound. The influence might at first seem obscure because while the ABB's music was complex like classical, but it was also improvised, less structured. Butch's classical influences inspired the band's use of tempo changes and dramatic movements in its longer jams. He also translated the "feel" of classical to rock, using the tympani to bring "Hot 'Lanta" and "Whipping Post" to dramatic conclusion. The latter closed the album, fading as the band segued into "Mountain Jam."

After two-plus years of relentless touring, the Allman Brothers Band had finally broken through. The success of *At Fillmore East* proved Duane's theory about the importance of a live album for the Allman Brothers. Sadly, he missed out on the success and widespread acclaim the ABB achieved as a result of his artistic masterpiece. On October 29, 1971, just four days after the album hit gold, Duane died in a motorcycle crash in Macon. He was just shy of his twenty-fifth birthday.

CHAPTER 14

TOURING AND RECORDING WITHOUT DUANE (NOVEMBER 1971-NOVEMBER 1972)

So soon the five-man Allman Brothers began to play again—
what else *could* they do?

Tony Glover

Spirits were high in Macon in fall 1971. As *At Fillmore East* stormed the charts, the group had begun to lay down tracks for its next album. Duane's accident on October 29 happened just after his return from a rehab stint for heroin. The band's fourth album, *Eat a Peach*, is the epilogue to Duane Allman's remarkable career and the final chapter of the original era of the Allman Brothers Band.

Duane's devastated bandmates honored him with an enduring commitment to his vision. They channeled their grief the only way they knew how: through music. On November 1, they played at Duane's memorial service. Three weeks later, they embarked on a ninety-date nationwide tour as a quintet the following February released *Eat a Peach*.

Their leader's absence had a profound effect on his surviving bandmates. In interviews over forty-plus years, Butch, Gregg, Dickey, and to a lesser extent, Jaimoe, have been quite candid about their grief for Duane. All agree Berry Oakley was the most distraught. Duane's death, Butch said, "absolutely destroyed him." Capricorn's Frank Fenter said Oakley was "under tremendous pressure" after Duane's death. He felt like he was responsible for the band. He wasn't, really, but he felt like the mantle had fallen on him." Gregg lamented, "Berry Oakley's life ended with my brother's life. Never have I seen a man collapse like that." Roadie Kim Payne, who was dating Berry's sister Candace at the time, recounted how Oakley "just became totally disoriented. He went from being a perfect family man to being a person who didn't care about nothing."[1]

Oakley blunted his pain in a haze of drugs and alcohol, which more than once affected his playing to such an extent that roadie Joe Dan Petty replaced him on stage several times on the 1972 *Eat a Peach* tour. In yet another chapter in the southern gothic tale that is the Allman Brothers Band, Berry died in a motorcycle accident on November 11, 1972. It was a little more than a year after Duane's own death. Berry's accident occurred a stone's throw from the site of Duane's.

The accident killed Oakley, but Berry really died of a broken heart. Duane's death mortally wounded his spirit, and Oakley died before he recovered from the loss. He and Duane were brothers, musical soulmates. "He could not abide a world without Duane Allman," Butch commented. The bandmates were buried beside each other in Macon's Rose Hill Cemetery, in a section that will eventually hold the graves of all six original ABB members. Nearby is where Betts composed the band's greatest instrumental, the grave of Elizabeth Jones Reed Napier, namesake of Dickey's "In Memory of Elizabeth Reed."[2]

Gregg, too, turned to drugs and alcohol to cope, and he long counted himself fortunate to have survived the aftermath of Duane's death. One of rock's great survivors, Gregg faced alcoholism, drug addiction, federal investigation, and tabloid celebrity as he carried on after his brother died. In 2010 Gregg had a liver transplant, and he lived until May 2017, six months shy of his seventieth birthday.[3]

Duane's death marked the end of Gregg's most productive songwriting period. "In the days and weeks that followed, I began to wonder if I would ever get back that feeling," Gregg wrote. "I wondered if I'd ever find the passion, the energy, the love of making music and making it better—all of that good old stuff." He continued to write regularly for the next five decades but never again at the pace he had in the original era of the Allman Brothers Band. Gregg and Oakley shared credit on "Stand Back," but "Ain't Wastin' Time No More," his tribute to Duane, was his only new song on *Eat a Peach*. "In my grief," Gregg wrote, "I probably didn't help the band too much at all. I tried to play and I tried to sing, but I didn't do too much writing." For one glorious year, his Hammond B-3 became more of a lead instrument than at any other time in Allman Brothers' history, and Gregg's playing helping to fill the Duane-size hole during 1972's five-man band tour.[4]

Duane's accident was never far from Gregg's mind, he wrote.

> Not that I got over it—I still ain't gotten over it. I don't know what getting over it means, really. I don't stand around crying anymore, but I think about him every day of my life. . . . I had the deepest, closest personal relationship with him I've ever had with anyone, because we went through heaven and hell together. Without him, there's no telling how I would have turned out.[5]

Duane's death weighed heavily on Betts as well. "It took me a long time to really accept it. Your mind kind of protects you in that way," Betts said. "It was such a damn surprise that my mind never really accepted it. It was so tough that it's hard to try to explain to somebody." In the immediate aftermath of Duane's death, Betts admitted that he "went through a lot of heavy changes. I don't know if I've nailed them all down yet."[6]

Decades after Duane's death Betts said, "I used to have nightmares all the time. Usually it was the same one. In it, the Allman Brothers Band is on the road, and we end up on a show with Delaney and Bonnie. We see Duane at the show, and everything's all right. Duane says, 'Hey man, how've you been?' And we say, 'Great.' And then we all get together and play, and everything's alright again. That dream probably kept me sane." But eventually, he recalled, "You gradually begin to realize that Duane Allman is not playing with Bonnie and Delaney. He's gone."[7]

Duane's accident was the result of a tragic combination of unbounded, infectious energy and self-destructive tendencies. Duane was as seemingly uninhibited in his personal life as he was while improvising on stage. His death came as no shock to many. "He had literally flirted with death too often to be surprised," Jon Landau wrote.[8]

Duane may not have had a death wish, but his recklessness sure left that impression. Landau observed, "No matter how briefly you knew him or how little, the more you got to know him, the more you realized that underneath the energy, the humor, the mock arrogance, and the real arrogance, was a troubled man who knew just how talented he was, but who didn't know how to live at peace with that talent. In some ways the world wasn't ready for him. And in others, he just wasn't ready for it."[9]

"Don't bet everything on this pony because I'll tell you, I'm going to live on the edge," Duane told Walden. "I'm going to get every damn thing I can out of life every damn day. I'm not a safe bet. I don't think I'll live a real long time." Walden explained, "He wasn't saying it in any morbid way. He was just stating it like a fact of life." When Walden praised Duane at their last meeting, Duane responded, "That's the scary part. I don't know if I can get any better." Trucks recalled that Duane began to talk openly with his bandmates about life without him after he returned from King Curtis's funeral in August 1971. "If anything ever happens to me," he told the band, "you guys better keep it going. Put me in a pine box, throw me in the river, and jam for two or three days," he said.[10]

The relentless pace finally caught up to Duane on October 29, 1971. Three days later, the band performed at Duane's memorial service at Snow's Funeral Home in Macon. It was a fitting tribute to their fallen leader. The set featured "Statesboro Blues," "Stormy Monday," and "In Memory of Elizabeth Reed" from *At Fillmore East* and two blues standards they rarely played again, "Key to the Highway" and "The Sky Is Crying." Delaney Bramlett led mourners in the Carter Family standard "Will the Circle Be Unbroken." Gregg dedicated his ballad "Melissa" to Duane.[11]

Jerry Wexler eulogized Duane for his talent, his spirit, and his moxie:

It was at King Curtis's funeral that I last saw Duane Allman, and Duane with tears in his eyes told me that Curtis's encouragement and praise was valuable to him in the pursuit of his music and career. They were both gifted natural musicians with an unlimited ability for truly melodic improvisation. They were both born in the South, and they both learned their music from great black musicians and blues singers. They were both utterly dedicated to their music, and both intolerant of the faults and the meretricious and they would never permit the incorporation of the commercial compromise to their music—not for love or money. . . .

Those of us who were privileged to know Duane will remember him from all the studios, backstage dressing rooms, the Downtowners, the Holiday Inns, the Sheratons, the late nights, relaxing after the sessions, the whiskey and the music talk, playing back cassettes until night gave way to dawn, the meals and the pool games, and fishing in Miami and Long Island, this young beautiful man who we love so dearly but who is not lost to us, because we have his music, and the music is imperishable.[12]

Immediately following the memorial service, Gregg, Dickey, Berry, Jaimoe, and Butch returned to Criteria Studios in Miami to complete *Eat a Peach*, released February 12, 1972. It was the ABB's second consecutive double album. Duane appears on sides 2, 3, and 4, two of which feature the thirty-minute-plus "Mountain Jam" that faded out at the end of "Whipping Post" on *Fillmore East*. Side 3 has two live tracks, "Trouble No More" from the *Fillmore* sessions and Sonny Boy Williamson's "One Way Out," recorded at a later Fillmore date, and three studio originals, "Stand Back," "Blue Sky," and "Little Martha."

Though the band was in transition, *Eat a Peach* is a fluid, cohesive musical statement. A mixture of live and six studio tracks, the record presents three separate sides of the ABB: the original band live and in the studio and the five-man band in the studio. The record demonstrates maturity and creativity; tracks reflect influences of western swing and country ("Blue Sky"), folk ("Melissa" and "Little Martha"), electric blues ("Stand Back"), jazz-rock ("Les Brers in A Minor"), and psychedelia ("Mountain Jam").[13]

The five-man band opened the record with "Ain't Wastin' Time No More," Gregg's ode to his brother; the Betts instrumental "Les Brers in A Minor"; and Gregg's "Melissa." "Those last three songs kind of floated right on out of us," Gregg wrote. "They prove that the music hadn't died with my brother. The music was still good, it was still rich, and it still had that energy. It was still the Allman Brothers."[14]

In "Ain't Wastin' Time No More" Gregg sings about moving on in the wake of tragedy. Many listeners mistook Dickey Betts's slide solo for Duane's. His emergence as an electric slide player stunned even his bandmates. Astute listeners heard a familiar melody on "Les Brers in A Minor," Betts's instrumental. Betts had teased it in his "Whipping Post" solo more than once in 1971, including on *At Fillmore East*. "Les Brers" sounds like musicians grieving deeply, though there's a determination in their anger. "Melissa" wraps up the first side of *Eat a Peach*. The first song Gregg ever completed, in 1968, it was Duane's favorite; Gregg first played it in public at Duane's memorial service.

"Mountain Jam" appears on sides 2 and 4. It is a masterwork of momentary composition. The jam revolves around the relatively simple major-key melody of Donovan's "First There Is a Mountain." With it, the six musicians created an entirely new song, a fully improvised jam with multiple movements and solos from each band member, including a drum duet between Trucks and Jaimoe. As Berry transitions to a thundering cadence of notes, Duane, Dickey, and Gregg join back in, the next five minutes are some of the finest musical communication the Allman Brothers Band ever recorded. They are so in sync that the result sounds less like six musicians improvising and more like a classical music ensemble. Listening almost feels like eavesdropping on an intense conversation; the music sounds that intimate. As the song draws to a close, the band joins Duane on the melody of "Will the Circle Be Unbroken," a song the Carter Family first recorded in 1935.

Side 3 includes Duane's final three tracks. "Stand Back" was an instrumental called "The Road to Calico," when Duane laid down one of his best slide solos. "Stand Back" was also Jaimoe's only solo turn on drums. "Blue Sky," which Dickey wrote for his soon-to-be wife, Sandy "Bluesky" Wabegijig, Wiikwemkoong First Nation, foreshadowed an entirely new direction for the band. The song was much more country than rock. Duane's and Dickey's harmony guitars sound as much like the Bakersfield Sound of Buck Owens and Don Rich and western swing as they do anything else. *Eat a Peach* ends with Duane's sole writing credit, "Little Martha." The instrumental's quiet, lyrical melody softly closes the book on Duane Allman's remarkable career.

Eat a Peach delivered two important messages. The first was that while they missed their leader, they would carry on without Duane. Gregg sang in the album's opener, "I still have two strong legs, and even wings to fly." Second, they had not forgotten their leader. "Dedicated to a Brother, Duane Allman," read the gatefold.

Forging ahead proved the right decision. *Eat a Peach* spent forty-eight weeks on the charts, reaching number 4, nine spots higher than *At Fillmore East*. "Duane is gone—but the Allman Brothers Band are still cooking," Tony Glover wrote. "Long may they boogie." Hal Pratt found that "Side One, sans Duane, exhibits evidence of the band's immortality and ability to continue in its unique musical tradition. The music is basically unscathed by Duane's death." Dave Sitz said likewise, "The Allman Brothers Band has emerged unscathed and unchanged in their talent for originality."[15]

"The group is not the same without Duane . . . but it's still the Allman Brothers," Glover wrote in his review for *Rolling Stone*. "It's not a question of being 'as good' or 'not as good'—rather it's just a difference." Stephen Lasko wrote, "There is no overt reckoning with Duane's absence. There probably couldn't be a finer tribute either."[16]

Betts's work as the sole guitarist on three cuts and his vocals on "Blue Sky" brought notice. *Eat a Peach*, Sitz wrote, highlighted "Betts's talent for producing some of the most refreshing material the Allmans had done." Dale Rauch declared, "Many feared that perhaps the spirit and drive of the Allman Bros. had passed on with the untimely death of brother Duane. This two-record set confirms that which all Allman Brothers freaks have known all along. Dickey Betts is one fine guitarist." Ernie Kelly wrote, "The Allmans are a great band with or without Duane Allman. His death overshadowed the equally good work of Dickey Betts."[17]

Following Duane's death and even before finishing *Eat a Peach*, the ABB embarked on tour as a quintet. A show at C. W. Post College on November 22 served as a warm-up gig for the band's Carnegie Hall show on November 25, 1971. Jaimoe finally fulfilled his decades-old pledge to his mother, Helen, that he would play the venue.

"The trademark dual guitar harmonies and interplay were missing," Glover observed of that show, the band's second without Duane, "but the band still boogied hard, strong and soaring. It was as if each of the five had expanded some to fill the empty space, and a different kind of internal structure started to grow." Betts recalled, "We *knew* what we had lost. We were trying to console each other and the best way we could do it was to play music. One thing led to another and we slowly realized that the best thing we could do was stay together. There was so much creative power in that group that that's the only way we were able to continue on without Duane." Gregg told his mates at Duane's memorial, "Playing is our only option." Betts said, "The thought of just ending it and being alone was too depressing. Trucks explained, "After three or four weeks, we were all going crazy. The only way a musician can express feelings is playing."[18]

The five-man band tour replaced a previously scheduled extended break after recording *Eat a Peach*. After nearly three years of non-stop touring and recording four albums, two of them double albums, the Allman Brothers had earned the respite. On October 25, 1971, the band learned *At Fillmore East* had gone gold, selling 500,000 copies. Four days later, they lost Duane in a motorcycle accident. On November 22, 1971, just three weeks after Duane's memorial service, the band played its first show as a five-piece group at C. W. Post on Long Island, New York. In April 1972, after an extensive run of West Coast shows in February and March, they headlined Mar y Sol, the inaugural International Puerto Rican Pop Festival, in Manatí, Puerto Rico.[19]

By late August 1972, the five-man ABB had played more than ninety emotionally charged shows in nine months. Duane's bandmates responded to his death by doing what Duane had wanted them to do: playing music. In honor of Duane and the band's commitment to carry on in his absence, Gregg sometimes changed the last line of "Whipping Post" from "Good lord, I feel like I'm dying!" to "There's no such thing as dying!" Butch said, "We played some blues, let me tell you. We still do. There's one place in our set and it's for Duane. I'm not going to tell you exactly what or where it is, but it's always there. I feel it every night we play. We all do."[20]

Audiences loved it. "Sometime after three the band launched into the obligatory finale 'Whipping Post,'" Bill Brina wrote. "And then you knew why they're staying on tour. The music goes on." Glover wrote, "They can still cook and burn with all the flat out *soul* they they've become known for. The band is tight, together, and full—and though it's sad not to hear the dialogue between Duane and Dickey's guitars, you soon realize that a whole new conversation is going on between Dickey and Berry."[21]

Eat a Peach carried "an awful sense of finality" for Andrew Elkind, he wrote in *Yale Daily News*. "At the conclusion of 'Mountain Jam,'

Duane introduces the band to the Fillmore audience—'Berry Oakley, Dickey Betts, Butch Trucks, Jai Johanny Johanson, Gregg Allman, and I'm Duane Allman'—and that is the end, and it really hurts."[22]

Though Duane's death ended their musical collaboration, his bandmates carried his spirit with them musically. It was the way he'd best appreciate. "Most voids ache to be filled, and music can fill many because it can contain so much; sorrow, celebration, anger, love—and always the joy of just plain getting it on," Glover wrote. "So soon the five-man Allman Brothers began to play again—what else *could* they do?"[23]

CHAPTER 15

EPILOGUE
(NOVEMBER 1972-OCTOBER 2021)

Regardless of musical background, these pulses and grooves
are something we have in common and if we're listening we
can make music together naturally.

Oteil Burbridge

Had the five-man band not filled Duane's absence so notably and no-
bly, there is no doubt the Allman Brothers Band would have broken up
for good following Oakley's death in 1972. That the Allman Brothers
Band continued to play music together until retiring from the road
on their own terms in 2014 is a testament to the endurance of the
four survivors' determination to carry on in their bandmates' honor.

Though the ABB rose to great heights without Duane, its popularity declined rapidly in the aftermath of a bitter breakup in 1976.
A tenth-anniversary reunion in 1979 began with much fanfare but
ended with a whimper. Three albums of declining sales followed
(1979's *Enlightened Rogues*, 1980's *Reach for the Sky*, and 1981's *Brothers of the Road*). The band recorded *Brothers* without Jaimoe, Duane's
first recruit, whom they fired that same year. By the mid-1980s the
band was an afterthought to everyone but their most hard-core fans.

The band's fortunes changed in 1989 with a critically, commercially,
and most of all musically successful twentieth-anniversary reunion
tour in support of *Dreams*, a career-spanning box set. Its release put
the Allman Brothers Band again at the forefront of the music industry
as older fans replaced vinyl albums with the crisp sound of a relatively
new format, the compact disc. Younger fans benefited from release of

material that had circulated only on bootleg recordings and out-of-print releases. *Dreams* drew attention to the band, and the reunited Allman Brothers delivered on stage. The reunion lasted twenty-five years.

Dickey Betts took a much greater songwriting and band leadership role after *Eat a Peach* in 1972. He shepherded the musical direction of the band through the band's most commercially successful period in the 1970s and until his acrimonious departure in 2000.

The Allman Brothers Band waited years before adding a second guitar to its lineup. Instead, in November 1972, shortly before Berry Oakley's fatal accident, Chuck Leavell joined on keyboards. The band replaced Oakley with Jaimoe's childhood friend Lamar Williams. The Chuck and Lamar era lasted from 1973 until the band's first breakup, in 1976.

The ABB released a fifth album, *Brothers and Sisters*, in August 1973. By September it was the number 1 album in the country, a position it held for five weeks. It ultimately spent fifty-six weeks on the charts, Betts's "Ramblin' Man," released as a single, reached number 2. The song was another step in the country direction for Dickey, a sound he had foreshadowed on "Blue Sky."

The band was at the peak of popularity in 1973 and 1974. They played legendary shows with the Grateful Dead at RFK Stadium June 9 and 10, 1973, and in July headlined the 1973 Summer Jam at Watkins Glen, New York, on a bill with the Dead and the Band, where an estimated 600,000 attendees made the largest concert audience in history. The next year, the Allman Brothers' "Campaign '74" tour was one of only two times the band would tour Europe. The other was in 1991.

Capricorn released *Win, Lose, or Draw* on August 22, 1975. Eight days later, the Allman Brothers Band headlined the opening concert at the Superdome in New Orleans. Their November 25 benefit concert at the Providence (Rhode Island) Civic Center infused Jimmy Carter's presidential campaign with much-needed cash, money that Carter says kept him in the race to the White House.

Yet *Win, Lose, or Draw* wasn't a hit, and the band struggled on and off stage. On May 4, 1976, the ABB played Roanoke, Virginia. It was the last show of the Chuck and Lamar era. Though the lineup reached the band's commercial heights, the group broke up in a fog of drugs and infighting, Gregg's testimony against a friend in a federal drug case, unwise business decisions, and other trappings of rock-star excess.

The band re-formed in 1978 without Williams and Leavell. Two members of Betts's band Great Southern, which he formed in the wake of the Allman Brothers' 1976 breakup, joined in their place, Dan Toler on guitar and David Goldflies. It was the first lineup to include two guitars since Duane's death in 1971. In 1979 the band released *Enlightened Rogues* on Capricorn and embarked on a tenth-anniversary tour. *Enlightened Rogues* spent twenty-four weeks on the charts, reaching number 9. "Crazy Love," featuring the band's old friend and "Allman Sister" Bonnie Bramlett, peaked at number 29.

When Capricorn Records folded in 1980, the band joined Arista Records, label of their old friends the Grateful Dead. Audiences rejected their attempts to modernize with synthesizers and a keytar on *Reach for the Sky* (1980) and *Brothers of the Road* (1981). Even worse, the group fired Jaimoe before recording *Brothers of the Road*, replacing him with Dan Toler's brother, Frankie. Due to a combination of band turmoil and dwindling public interest, the band broke up again in January 1982, after playing *Saturday Night Live*.

In celebration of its twentieth anniversary, the Allman Brothers Band re-formed in 1989. Jaimoe once again manned his stage-right drum chair. Gone were the players who had joined the band since the tenth reunion. In their place were guitarist Warren Haynes of the Dickey Betts Band and bassist Allen Woody, an unknown at the time whose bass-playing revitalized the group.[1]

The Warren and Woody era spanned a remarkably productive eight years, 1989 through 1997. The band toured annually and recorded three studio albums—*Seven Turns* (1990), *Shades of Two Worlds* (1991), and *Where It All Begins* (1994)—and two live albums, *An Evening with the Allman Brothers Band First Set* (1992) and *Second Set* (1994). Kirk West, a member of the ABB's road crew and Tour Mystic, urged the band to adopt the Grateful Dead's policy of allowing recordings of their shows, a move that opened up the Allman Brothers Band to a new, younger generation of fans. Combined with bootlegs of earlier eras, live tapes brought together a community of Allman Brothers fans not unlike the Dead's, fans who zealously supported the band until its final show. In honor of Duane, sometime in the 1990s the band began broadcasting "Little Martha" on the PA after its concerts. It was just as Gregg had done on his for his first solo album, 1973's *Laid Back*.

The Allman Brothers continued touring with an evolving lineup until 2014. Percussionist Marc Quiñones joined in 1991. Haynes and Woody left in 1997 to concentrate on Gov't Mule, the power trio they had founded in 1994. Guitarist Jack Pearson replaced Haynes, and Oteil Burbridge filled Woody's shoes on bass. When Pearson left in 1999, Butch's nineteen-year-old nephew Derek Trucks joined the ABB and stayed until the band retired in 2014.

Willie Nelson inducted the ABB into the Rock and Roll Hall of Fame in 1995, around the same time the jamband phenomenon began to take root in American music. In 2012 the Allman Brothers Band received a Grammy Lifetime Achievement Award. Cameron Crowe based his 2000 movie *Almost Famous* on his time touring as a journalist with the ABB. In 2003 *Rolling Stone*'s David Fricke ranked Duane number 2, Warren number 23, Dickey number 58, and Derek number 81 in his "100 Greatest Guitarists" list. A subsequent list, issued in 2015, included Duane at number 9, Derek number 16, and Dickey number 61, with Haynes inexplicably left off the list.

In May 2000 Gregg, Butch, and Jaimoe parted ways with Dickey Betts in a bitter divorce. As was typical for the band each time it endured a potentially crippling loss, the Allman Brothers Band returned to its roots. Gregg sang most of the songs as the band fulfilled its summer 2000 touring commitments. Sets were long on instrumentals, including the return of "Mountain Jam," which the band had only played a few times in the nearly thirty years since Duane's death. Guitarist Jimmy Herring stood in for Betts, and he and Derek Trucks communicated beautifully together on stage in extended jams. The following spring, in March 2001, guitarist Warren Haynes rejoined the band permanently. In 2003 the group released its final studio album, *Hittin' the Note*. It was the only ABB studio album without Dickey Betts.

Haynes's return anchored the ABB's longest-lasting and second great lineup. The era spanned 2001 to 2014 and included three original members, Jaimoe, Butch, and Gregg, and four others with long tenures in the band: guitarist and vocalist Warren Haynes (1989–2014), percussionist Marc Quiñones (1991–2014), bassist Oteil Burbridge (1997–2014), and guitarist Derek Trucks (1999–2014). The lineup was an ideal bookend to the band Duane formed decades earlier.

Together with Derek, Warren, Marc, and Oteil, the original band members recaptured the magic of Duane's vision. It was surely one reason the band continued touring. In 2009 the band honored its founder with a series of fortieth-anniversary concerts at New York's Beacon Theatre, where it had played an annual residency since 1989. The shows featured guest appearances by a number of artists Duane played with or influenced, including Eric Clapton.

On March 10, 2020, the Brothers, a group of ABB alumni and family, played a sold-out, fiftieth-anniversary concert at Madison Square Garden. Happening just days before the Covid-19 pandemic shut down the world, the show was the last major concert event of the Beforetimes. The lineup was an Allman Brothers family reunion. It featured the five living members of the final ABB lineup—Jaimoe, Haynes, Derek Trucks, Burbridge, and Quiñones—and a guest appearance by an old friend, former ABB member Chuck Leavell. Derek's brother, Duane Trucks, filled in on drums for Uncle Butch, and Reese Wynans joined on Hammond B-3, just as he had at the band's first jam in Jacksonville almost exactly fifty-one years earlier.

Gregg Allman released his first solo album, *Laid Back*, in 1973 and the live *Gregg Allman Tour* the following year. He became one of the biggest stars in the world with his 1975 marriage to Cher, kept the Allman Brothers on the road until 2014, and toured as a solo artist until 2016, when he retired due to complications from liver cancer. He released seven solo albums total, including *Southern Blood*, recorded at FAME in Muscle Shoals and released posthumously in 2017.

Butch Trucks did most of his work in the context of the Allman Brothers. He studied percussion at Florida State University in the late 1970s, toured with a band called Trucks, and in the 1980s played drums for Betts, Hall, Leavell, Trucks. He also ran a studio in Tallahassee, Florida. In May 1997 Butch formed Frogwings, a band in the mold of the ABB in spirit but with the psychedelic, experimental bent that came directly from its guitarists, his nephew Derek Trucks and Jimmy Herring on guitar and Oteil Burbridge on bass. The band also included Allman Brother Marc Quiñones on percussion, and North

Carolina native Edwin McCain on vocals. When McCain left in 1998, Butch replaced him with John Popper of Blues Traveler and released *Croakin' at Toad's* in 2000.

After the ABB's 2014 retirement, Butch kept two bands on the road. Les Brers included the entire ABB rhythm section, former Allman Brother Jack Pearson on guitar, and Lamar Williams Jr., the late bassist's son, on vocals. Butch Trucks and the Freight Train Band, included Butch's son, Vaylor Trucks, as musical director and Berry Oakley's son, Berry Duane Oakley, on bass. Sadly, Butch died of a self-inflicted gunshot wound in January 2017 at sixty-nine.

When the ABB broke up in 1976, Jaimoe formed Sea Level with Chuck Leavell and Lamar Williams. He rejoined the Allman Brothers Band in 1978, was fired in 1981, and rejoined for good for the 1989 reunion tour. Jaimoe's longest-running musical project outside of the ABB is Jaimoe's Jasssz Band, which has released one studio album, *Renaissance Man* (2012), and continued to tour until the pandemic took them off the road in 2020.

Dickey Betts released his first solo album, *Highway Call*, in 1974. He formed Great Southern after the ABB's 1976 breakup and released two albums, a self-titled debut (1977) and *Atlanta's Burning Down* (1978). He toured with the Dickey Betts Band throughout the 1980s but rarely performed as a solo artist after the ABB reunited in 1989. Following his 2000 departure from the Allmans, Betts released *Let's Get Together* (2001) and the acoustic *Collectors #1* (2002). He toured with Dickey Betts and Great Southern until he, too, retired from active touring in 2014. His son, Duane Betts, played guitar in later incarnations of the band and served as musical director when Dickey briefly came out of retirement for a run of shows in 2018. Duane Betts joined forces with Berry Oakley's son Berry and Gregg's son Devon in the Allman Betts Band. The group is on hiatus as of this writing and Duane has embarked on a solo career with his guitar partner Johnny Stachela.

Unlike what occurred in 1976 and 1982, when the band faded into oblivion, the 2014 lineup of the Allman Brothers Band went out in a stellar marathon show at the Beacon Theatre. The group agreed to hang it up for good in 2014, its forty-fifth anniversary year. That January, guitarists Trucks and Haynes announced their departure from the band. The Allman Brothers Band played its final show on October 28, 2014. While there had been some talk that the band might again reform with new guitar players, that possibility ended with drummer Butch Trucks's suicide on January 24, 2017. Gregg Allman, the sole Allman in the band since his brother's death, died of liver cancer later that year, on May 27, 2017.

Each of the musicians who had joined the Allman Brothers Band since its 1989 reunion carried deep respect for the band's integrity and Duane Allman's vision. "You never take this band for granted," Allen Woody said. "It's like a sacred trust. I know that sounds corny and stupid, but it really is true." The original members left newer players to figure things out for themselves, just like they did when they founded the band. "One of the hallmarks of the band is everybody gets their own voice," Derek Trucks said. "They don't dictate what you play." Jack Pearson reflected, "Usually a musician has to choose between playing the big pop gig and the small, express-yourself gig. This is a very rare situation where it's both at once."[2]

Oteil Burbridge was the ABB's longest-tenured bass player, 1997 to 2014. A jazz musician by training and inclination, Burbridge appreciated that he was allowed to bring a different feel to the Allman Brothers. "Regardless of musical background," he said, "these pulses and grooves are something we have in common and if we're listening we can make music together naturally." Reflecting on his time in the band, Warren Haynes remarked, "I'm most proud that we've been able to carry the mantle of a great tradition. It was based on trying to tap into the vision and proud tradition of the original band."[3]

Thus, though Duane only played in the Allman Brothers Band for less than three years, his vision for the band outlived him by more than four decades. That itself is as much a testament to Duane's legacy as *At Fillmore East* and *Eat a Peach*. Duane founded the Allman Brothers Band as an outlet to best express himself creatively. His bandmates took that idea, made it their own, and carried on for forty-three years without him.

"Not a day goes by that we don't talk about Duane," Gregg said. "It's almost like he's with us. Sometimes when I'm on stage I can feel his presence so strong I can almost smell him. I don't want to get too cosmic, but it's like he's right there next to me."[4]

Duane's story is of his pursuit of musical excellence, of hittin' the note. His band, the Allman Brothers Band, fused multiple elements of southern music into a singular, cohesive rock sound. Doing so from the South, with a racially integrated band, following an uncompromising musical path, sets him apart from contemporaries. Duane bridged 1960s counterculture with southern sensibilities. And he helped open up the South to other young people.

"Duane will always have a place in my heart—an uncompromising musician, and perhaps more importantly, person," Philip Lane, who saw Duane at Piedmont Park, wrote. "Duane was our hero, to us young guys in the South at that time he represented everything positive about the southern countercultural experience."[5]

At Fillmore East, the band's survival for forty-three years without him, the inspiration his success brought a generation of southern rock musicians, these are all significant legacies of Duane Allman's life and career. But the Allman Brothers Band itself is his greatest legacy.

Duane's fierce determination to forge his own path inspired not only his band but every musician who played in it over its forty-five-year history, most notably Warren Haynes and Derek Trucks. At thirteen years, 2001 to 2014, they were the band's longest-tenured guitar partnership. Both were keenly aware of the band's history, and each learned from the Allman Brothers Band how to approach music as players *and* bandleaders, Warren with Gov't Mule, the project he founded in 1997 with the late Allen Woody, and Derek first with the Derek Trucks Band and later with Tedeschi Trucks Band, the group he founded in 2010 with his wife, Susan Tedeschi.

Duane's example taught each ABB member the importance of intent and purpose in life and onstage:

Find a sound *you* like and let the rest take care of itself.
The best music is live music.
Music is a conversation with bandmates and with audiences; improvising makes the conversation more meaningful.
Assemble a band of players who push you and want you to push them.
Play a wide repertoire; make any cover you play your own.
Be uncompromising in the pursuit of your musical vision.
Music is a family affair, and your musical partners are your family also.

Death and the reaction to it is one final lesson I believe Haynes and Derek Trucks learned from the Allman Brothers Band. When a bandmate dies, the survivors are obligated to carry on musically. And playing is how musicians best cope deal with grief. Haynes and Gov't Mule drummer Matt Abts did this in the immediate aftermath of bassist Allen Woody's death in 2000; Derek and Susan did likewise after keyboardist Kofi Burbridge, Oteil's brother, died suddenly in February 2019, taking the stage that very night. Gov't Mule honored Woody, and the Tedeschi Trucks Band honored Kofi by pouring out their grief onstage night after night. As Tony Glover had remarked about the five-man band, "What else could they do?"[6]

Duane Allman built the Allman Brothers Band on the principles of intent, improvisation, the live experience, a band of equals, original music, and musical conversation. Duane's legacy begat a musical family that followed the path he blazed. Derek Trucks said, "I'm all about going on a musical trip and taking it as deep as you can take it. Music is supposed to become a part of your life in a major way. The Allman Brothers have done that and are fully ingrained into many American lives."[7]

It all boils down to this: find your note and find a way to communicate your note with others. Those who hear your note will find from it their own note, which leaves the circle unbroken.

LONG LIVE THE ALLMAN BROTHERS BAND!

ACKNOWLEDGMENTS

Nearly everyone I have met in my life has had an impact on this book in some way. It kind of blows me away when I think about how profound that is, actually. But everything in my life starts with the most important people in my life, my wife, Candy, and our beautiful daughters, Ryan and Tyler, who have lived this journey with me. Candy, you have been with me from the minute I came up with this crazy idea in my head. Thank you for believing in me. To the "Family Unit," you each continue to inspire me to get the most out of my abilities, to show love to the world the way our family loves each other. Thank you to my big sister, Gwynne Beatty, in whose footsteps I've always followed. Love to my dear Mackenzie and Kaelyn Quinn. To Troy Wilson, Brandon Munson, and Steve Marshall: a man is blessed to have one friend as good as each of you, and my cup overflows that I have three. Thank you for helping me on this journey. The same is true of my first best friend, my cousin Brad Beatty, with whom I discovered the Beatles, the blues, and punk rock.

Thank you to Carroll Van West. Your careful shepherding of my research got me here; it's been a life's honor to work with you on this project. I am also grateful to John Dougan, Bren Martin, and Kris McCusker, whose insights into my earliest drafts were invaluable.

Spencer Downing and Susan Ferentinos have each long been among my favorite co-conspirators. Spence, thank you for reading my dissertation and telling me what my book was about! Sue, your suggestions for improvements were exactly what I needed, and your enthusiasm boosted me at just the right time. I appreciate each of you for your friendship and support.

To my friends in the Allman Brothers Band world who encouraged and inspired me to dig deeper into this band and its meaning. The conversations we have had about the ABB and its music helped make sense of this story. I am sure you will see some of your own thoughts reflected here. (And if you found an Easter egg I planted for you, I probably did.) Without y'all, this book is not possible: Andy Beichler, Gary Barrett, Gary "The Chairman" Nagle, Al Booth, Art Dobie, Philip Torrez, Bill Proudfoot (thanks for the editing, Champ), John Page, Cary Hall, John Flynn, Paul Barbieri, Dan Aforismo, Erik Wiggs, Gail and Ira Packer, Ron Everhart, Tim Langan, Bob Johnson, Jon Sawyer, Mike Ummel, Chris King, Becca Fuller, the Trilli boys, Kevin and Mike, Dave and Kim Ashton, Nan Philpot, Jim Kelly, Jeff Kollath, "Young Ryan" Moore, Tom Clareson, Denise Halbe, Ceecee Moore, Ray Hutchison, Rowland and Lana Archer, Josh Chasin, Akira Horiuchi, Matjaz Kumelj, Christine Karatnytsky, Martha Haynes, Pat Henson, Mark Vormittag, Craig Ruskey, Helene Tekulsky, Mark Brimberry, Dave Melton, John Tyra, Andy Van Noy, Dave Davies, Tom Pragliola, Walter Vanderbeken, Hans Van Ryswyk, Paul Kaytes, Cliff Morse, and anyone whose name I missed. You're here, I promise.

I've lost several friends from this family along the way, four in particular: Jules Fothergill, Skip Littlewood, Eliot Spindel, and John Curatolo. Lorna, the night I spent watching Jules play guitar with Jack Pearson is among my most cherished memories. Thank you for including me. I am forever grateful for Skip for his love of the band, particularly the tapes we traded from his "Republic of Tea" sanctuary in Yuma, Arizona. Eliot and John were friends from the Allman Brothers Band listserv I joined in the mid-1990s, one of the ways I first connected with the wider world of ABB fans. I am sorry none of them are here to see this final result.

Thank you, Tom Nolan, Scott Freeman, Alan Paul, and Randy Poe for laying out the parameters of this story in your own books and to all the folks who have contributed to this story with their own memoirs. I'm particularly grateful to Willie Perkins for answering every clarification question I've ever asked him. To Alan, thank you for your friendship and encouragement. To Andrew Wild, looking forward to the ABB *On-Track* book.

To Galadrielle Allman, just as Duane did with his music, you approached *Please Be with Me* fearlessly and openly, and it shows. Your book is among the best books on music I have ever read and remains an inspiration beyond how I approached my own book about Duane. Thank you, also, for the *Skydog* box set that was my front-to-back playlist as I sat in Muscle Shoals and finished the last draft of this book in October 2021.

Shout-outs to Richard Brent and John Lynskey—and Rob Schneck, Greg Potter, and E. J. Devokaitis before them—for their stewardship of the Big House Museum in Macon.

Sincere gratitude is also due to Kirk and Kirsten West, whose efforts resulted in a permanent home for the legacy of the Allman Brothers Band: the Big House Museum. Kirk was among the first people who truly understood the importance of the ABB's history, and he carried the flame for the band through some of its darker days of the 1980s. This book is in many ways a result of his relentless dedication to all things Allman. The museum is as much Kirsten's accomplishment as it is Kirk's. Thank you both so much for your devotion to preserve the past. Your efforts mean so much to me and to so many friends "seen and unseen."

I wrote this book in 2020 and 2021, a pretty tumultuous time in world history. The ideological and biological pandemics took a lot out of me; they took a lot out of all of us. At times I struggled to write, unable to compartmentalize the chaos happening outside my doors from the task at hand.

I thought a lot about my own life and legacy as I wrote about Duane's. What did I learn from him or from this deep dive into his band? I kept coming back to Gregg's words from "Ain't Wastin' Time No More," the first song he wrote after his brother's death: "With the help of God and true friends, I've come to realize, I still have two strong legs and even wings to fly." Duane had taught his brother and his bandmates the responsibility of the living to carry on. Gregg reminded the band and its audience, including me, of that charge. But I never missed how Gregg said you get through whatever this life thing throws at you: God gives you friends to sustain you on the journey. To my friends, particularly my fellow museum nerds and history geeks, thank you from the bottom of my heart. This one's for you.

Finally, as I wrapped up this project, I considered a lifetime of lessons I learned from three very dear people whom I lost before I got here. The lessons were myriad, but one stood out above all others: the commandment to "love thy neighbor." When I think of my parents, Pat and Suzi, and my kid brother, Brian (who died in April 2020 as I worked on the manuscript), this is the inheritance I cherish the most. I miss the three of y'all so much.

Ultimately this book would not have even been possible had it not been for the music of the Allman Brothers Band. Thank you, Duane Allman, for assembling this band whose music has provided such a soundtrack to my life and to all of the band members who played a part in it. Thank you also to their families, who gave up so much of themselves in sacrifice to the music they, too, loved.

NOTES

Preface

1. And before you ask, yes, Fletch fulfilled his membership requirements for the club and is completely debt-free.

2. Scott B. Bomar, *Southbound*, 47.

Introduction

1. Library of Congress, *Recording Registry*, https://www.loc.gov/programs/national-recording-preservation-board/recording-registry/; *Rolling Stone*, "500 Greatest Albums of All Time," https://www.rollingstone.com/music/music-lists/500-greatest-albums-of-all-time-156826/ and https://www.rollingstone.com/music/music-lists/best-albums-of-all-time-1062063/.

2. Allman wanted two drummers, Johanson said, "because Otis Redding and James Brown have two" (in Alan Paul, *One Way Out*, 19).

3. Lester Bangs, "Heavy Metal Brontosaurus M.O.R.," 57; W. J. Cash, *Mind of the South*, 371.

4. The books on this subject are myriad. Here are some resources that have helped shape my understanding of the Lost Cause mythology: David B. Allison's *Controversial Monuments and Memorials*; David W. Blight's *Beyond the Battlefield* and *Race and Reunion*; John M. Coski's *Confederate Battle Flag*; Karen L. Cox's *Dixie's Daughters* and *No Common Ground*; Kevin M. Levin's *Searching for Black Confederates*.

5. Betts, quoted in Mikal Gilmore, *Night Beat*, 128.

6. Gregg, quoted in Alan Paul, "Gregg Allman 1947–2017."

7. "Gregg Allman Praises New Band, Says To Burn Every Confederate Flag," *Live for Life Music*, July 21, 2015.

8. Robert Palmer, "Memphis Underground"; Nik Cohn, *Rock from the Beginning*, 30–31, 51; Al Rudis, "At Fillmore East Review."

9. Scott B. Bomar, *Southbound*, xv.

10. Rankin Sherling. "Southern Rock," 139.

11. Bill C. Malone and David Stricklin, *Southern Music/American Music*, 14–18.

12. Clapton started in the Yardbirds, joined John Mayall's Bluesbreakers, and formed Cream, Blind Faith, and Derek and the Dominos, which included

Duane Allman, all before going out on his own as a solo musician. Beck was in the Yardbirds, founded the Jeff Beck Group, joined up with Beck, Bogert, and Appice, and recorded after that under his own name. Hendrix fronted the Jimi Hendrix Experience and the Band of Gypsys and recorded prodigiously with a variety of artists including Stephen Stills, Jack Casady, Brian Jones, Steve Winwood, and Johnny Winter. Bloomfield played with the Paul Butterfield Blues Band 1964–1967, played on Bob Dylan sessions and on stage at his infamous Newport Folk Festival set in 1966, and founded and played in the Electric Flag 1967–1968 before beginning a somewhat peripatetic career as a solo artist, accompanist, and session musician, a career he began while still with Butterfield.

13. See Patrick Huber, *Linthead Stomp*; Jocelyn R. Neal, *The Songs of Jimmie Rodgers*; Barry Mazor, *Meeting Jimmie Rodgers*. Bill Monroe is another of these antecedents; he took old-time Appalachian mountain and folk music, sped it up, and added lightning-fast, jazzlike breaks to form bluegrass music.

14. Duane Allman, "Last Interview."

15. See Galadrielle Allman, *Please Be with Me*; Gregg Allman, *My Cross to Bear*; Scott Freeman, *Midnight Riders*; Tom Nolan, *Allman Brothers Band*; Alan Paul, *One Way Out*; Willie Perkins, *No Saints, No Saviors*; Randy Poe, *Skydog*.

16. In Bud Scoppa, *The Rock People*, 62; Joel Selvin, "What Southern Boys Can Do with Rock."

Chapter 1. Duane's Musical Ethos

1. Galadrielle Allman, *Please Be with Me*, xii.

2. Gregg Allman, *My Cross to Bear*, 23.

3. Fussell and Petrucciani, in Tom O'Dell, *Song of the South*.

4. Nolan, *Allman Brothers Band*, 10; Paul Hornsby, "Paul Hornsby's Memories with Duane Allman."

5. In John H. Richardson, "What Gregg Allman's Learned About."

6. Jim Shepley, "Young Duane Allman"; Van Harrison and Sylvan Wells, quoted in Freeman, *Midnight Riders*, 16–17.

7. Geraldine Allman, quoted in Galadrielle Allman, *Please Be with Me*, 71; Duane Allman, "Moment Captured in Time," 15.

8. Wells quoted in Dave Kyle, "Remembering Duane Allman"; Jaimoe quoted in John Lynskey, "Lamar Williams," 21.

9. Duane, quoted in Ellen Mandel, "Georgia Peach," 107. Galadrielle Allman shares some accounts of her father's reaction to the Kent State massacre in *Please Be with Me* (249).

10. Duane, quoted in Mandel, "Georgia Peach," 107.

11. Duane Allman, "Moment Captured in Time," 11–12; Duane, quoted in Mandel, "Georgia Peach," 107.

12. Duane, "Ed Shane Interview with Duane Allman."

13. Geraldine Allman, quoted in Nolan, *Allman Brothers Band*, 7.

14. Duane Allman, "Last Interview."

15. Cameron Crowe, "Allman Brothers Story"; Nolan, *Allman Brothers Band*, 10.

16. Duane Allman, "Moment Captured in Time," 15; Allman and Oakley, "Interview with Duane Allman and Berry Oakley."

17. Jimmy Johnson, quoted in Freeman, *Midnight Riders*, 30, 32.

18. Floyd Miles, "Floyd Miles"; Johnny Sandlin, quoted in Smith and Crutcher, *Capricorn Rising*, 91.

19. Joe Marshall, "Duane Allman"; Bruce Hampton, quoted in Tom Lawson and Michael Koepenick, *Basically Frightened*.

20. Jon Landau, "Allman Brothers Band," unpublished; Wexler, *Rhythm and the Blues*, 225. See also Nolan, *Allman Brothers Band*, 14; Ahmet Ertegun, "*What'd I Say?*," 240.

21. Bill Graham quoted in Henry Porter, "First There Is a Mountain"; Wexler, *Rhythm and the Blues*, 225.

22. Wexler, quoted in Ogden, "First There Is a Mountain," 12; Betts, "Duane Allman."

23. Hornsby, cited in Barney Hoskyns, "Southern Men"; Gregg, quoted in Freeman, *Midnight Riders*, 31.

24. Hornsby, quoted in Freeman, 31; Duane, quoted in Randy Poe, *Skydog*, 56–57.

25. Duane Allman, "Last Interview"; Graham, quoted in Porter, "First There Is a Mountain"; Talton, quoted in Nolan, *Allman Brothers Band*, 10.

26. Sandlin, quoted in Nolan, *Allman Brothers Band*, 10; Walden, quoted in Dan Manley, "Blues for a Brother"; Glover, quoted in Cindy Collins, "Tony Glover Brings It on Home"; Jaimoe, "Reflections 2," 24.

27. Landau, "Allman Brothers Band."

28. Duane Allman, "Last Interview."

29. Hampton and Campbell, quoted in Alan Paul, *One Way Out*, 96–97.

30. Betts, quoted in Kirsten West, "Inside Dickey Betts."

31. Doucette and Jaimoe, quoted in Paul, *One Way Out*, 139.

32. Gregg Allman, *My Cross to Bear*, 163, 199. Selvin described his 1971 "Duane Allman" article in *Earth* as "the greatest edit of my career. The editor had Duane coming out the bathroom and looking for a bottle of aspirin on the table, taking two and pounding his chest. Not quite the same thing."

33. Grover Lewis, "Hitting the Note with the Allman Brothers Band," 53.

34. Wexler and Dowd, quoted Gregg Allman, *My Cross to Bear*, 189–191.

35. Duane Allman and Butch Trucks, quoted in Randy Poe, *Skydog*, 203–204. On their drug use see also Paul, *One Way Out*, 135–136.

36. Jaimoe, quoted in Paul, *One Way Out*, 139; Gregg Allman, *My Cross to Bear*, 199.

37. Duane Allman, "A Moment Captured in Time," 11.

38. Wexler, *Rhythm and the Blues*, 253.

39. Duane, quoted in Mandel, "Georgia Peach," 49; Bramlett, "Delaney Bramlett Interviews, Part Two."

40. Ian Dove, "Talent in Action," 26.

41. Eric Clapton, *Clapton*, 112–114.

42. For detailed accounts of the *Layla* sessions see Galadrielle Allman, *Please Be with Me*, 262–273; Freeman, *Midnight Riders*, 76–85; Poe, *Skydog*, 155–170; Paul, *One Way Out*, 81–91.

43. Clapton, *Clapton*, 128; Dowd, "From the Manhattan Project to the Allman Brothers Band"; Whitlock, quoted in Paul, *One Way Out*, 84.

44. Clapton interview by Robert Palmer.

45. Dowd, quoted in Ertegun, *"What'd I Say?,"* 243.

46. Wyker, in "John D. Wyker's Cat Tales."

47. Duane's letter is quoted in Galadrielle Allman, *Please Be with Me*, 369–70; Trucks is quoted in Paul, *One Way Out*, 88.

48. Duane is quoted in Tony Glover, "The Allman Brothers: Saturday Night Fish Fry," a promotional piece Glover wrote for Capricorn Records. Jaimoe, quoted in Paul, *One Way Out*, 89.

49. Jaimoe, quoted in Paul, *One Way Out*, 89; Clapton, *Clapton*, 128.

50. Duane, quoted in Mandel, "Georgia Peach," 49.

51. Gary Wishik, "Sweet Wine," 9; Oakley, quoted in Kim Rogers, "Rock Minstrel's Life Not Rosey."

52. Oakley, quoted in Grover Lewis, "Hitting the Note with the Allman Brothers Band," 54.

53. Duane, "Interview with Duane Allman of the Allman Brothers Band"; Duane, "Last Interview."

54. Duane, "Interview with Duane Allman," *Free Press*.

55. Kowalke, "Pete Kowalke of Cowboy"; Wynn, "Tom Wynn of Cowboy."

56. Duane, quoted in Mandel, "Georgia Peach," 49; Duane, quoted in Tony Glover, "In This Band You Better Come to Pick." There is very little documentation of musicians joining the Allman Brothers Band on stage. Johnny Winter played with the band at the second Atlanta International Pop Festival in July 1970, and Juicy Carter played sax at Fillmore East and a handful of other dates in 1971. Bobby Caldwell of Winter's band and Captain Beefheart played percussion with the band in March and October 1971, and some remember Peter Green of Fleetwood Mac joining the Allmans on stage at the Warehouse. Allman and some bandmates also sat in with Jerry Garcia and the Grateful Dead on April 26, 1971.

57. Wynn, "Tom Wynn of Cowboy"; Oakley, quoted in Kim Rogers, "Rock Minstrel's Life Not Rosey."

58. There were several bands boasting two lead guitarists prior to the formation of Allman Brothers Band in March 1969. Two British bands, the Yardbirds

and Fleetwood Mac, each used the technique. In 1966 Jeff Beck and Jimmy Page played some dual leads while in the Yardbirds. In 1967 the original Fleetwood Mac included two lead players, Peter Green and Jeremy Spencer, and in 1969 the band added a third guitarist in Danny Kirwan. Stateside, Stephen Stills and Neil Young played lead together in Buffalo Springfield from 1966 to 1968 and in Crosby, Stills, Nash, and Young beginning in 1970. From 1965 to 1969, John Cipollina and Gary Duncan each played lead in Quicksilver Messenger Service.

59. Doucette, quoted in Paul, *One Way Out*, 61; Betts quoted in Bomar, 51.

60. Doucette, quoted in Alan Paul, "Why Duane Allman Didn't Want to Be the Next Hendrix."

61. Betts, quoted in Nolan, *Allman Brothers Band*, 38 (emphasis in the original); Duane, quoted in Eric Snider, "Brothers Forever."

62. Betts, quoted in Nolan, *Allman Brothers Band*, 38.

63. Campbell, quoted in Paul, *One Way Out*, 62.

64. Betts, quoted in Snider, "Brothers Forever."

65. Duane, quoted in Richard Gold, "The Allman Brothers Band," 16.

66. Duane, quoted in Paul, *One Way Out*, 144. Also see Eric Snider, "Brothers Forever."

67. Trucks, quoted in Malcolm X. Abram, "30 Years Down the Road."

68. Gregg Allman, *My Cross to Bear*, 129.

69. Duane, quoted in Glover, "In This Band You Better Come to Pick"; Landau.

70. Crowe, "Duane Allman—The Day the Music Died."

71. Jaimoe, afterword to *One Way Out*, 424–425.

72. Duane, "Last Interview."

Chapter 2. Living and Playing Music in the South (1960–1965)

1. Glenn C. Altschuler, *All Shook Up: How Rock 'n' Roll Changed America* (New York: Oxford University Press, 2005); James Miller, *Flowers in the Dustbin: The Rise of Rock and Roll 1947–1977* (New York: Simon and Schuster, 2000); David P. Szatmary, *Rockin' in Time: A Social History of Rock-and-Roll* (Upper Saddle River, NJ: Prentice Hall, 1996).

2. Malone and Stricklin, *Southern Music/American Music*, 14–18.

3. *Country Soul: Making Music and Making Race in the American South* by Charles L. Hughes is a masterful, in-depth study of southern musicians and racial dynamics in this period.

4. Robert Palmer, *Rock 'n' Roll*, 22. Duane Allman was in two racially integrated bands, the House Rockers early in his career in Daytona Beach and the Allman Brothers Band.

5. For more on the British invasion and its impact see Jonathan Gould, *Can't Buy Me Love*; Barry Miles, *British Invasion*; Bob Spitz, *The Beatles*. Many books have detailed chapters on the British invasion, among them Jack Hamilton's

chapter "The White Atlantic: Cultural Origins of the 'British Invasion,'" in his book *Just around Midnight*; Miller, *Flowers in the Dustbin*; Szatmary, *Rockin' in Time*; Brad Tolinski and Alan Di Perna, *Play It Loud*.

6. Tom Petty, quoted in Marty Jourard, *Music Everywhere*, 30–31.

7. Incidentally, three of these bands—the Yardbirds, the Bluesbreakers, and Cream—featured future Duane Allman collaborator Eric Clapton on guitar.

8. Duane, quoted in June Harris, "Getting Together with the Allman Brothers," *Hit Parader*, September 1970.

9. Palmer, *Rock 'n' Roll*, 6.

10. Galadrielle Allman, *Please Be with Me,* 48–49. Hers is the most lyrical description of the occasion. See also Gregg Allman, *My Cross to Bear*, 32; Poe, *Skydog*, 8; Ray Waddell, "American Classic," 22. Gregg Allman long reported that this show happened at the Nashville Municipal Auditorium in summer 1960; however, the venue opened in October 1962, and Jackie Wilson did not play there for the first time until 1966 ("Municipal Auditorium Concerts: A Complete List from 1963–1999," Tennessee Concerts, https://tennesseeconcerts.com/).

11. Bud Scoppa, *Rock People*, 61; Gregg Allman, *My Cross to Bear*, 33–34; Poe, *Skydog*, 8; Paul, *One Way Out*, 1–2.

12. Gregg Allman, *My Cross to Bear*, 42.

13. Gregg Allman, *My Cross to Bear*, 42; Duane, quoted in Mandel, "Georgia Peach," 49.

14. Shepley, "Young Duane Allman."

15. Fussell recounts the Uniques' beginnings in director Tom O'Dell's film *Song of the South*. Some accounts call this early band the Y-Teens, a misnomer that refers to the youth organization affiliated with the YMCA (Scoppa, *Rock People*, 66). The Uniques were not the first band Duane joined. Randy Poe documents Duane's early attempts at forming bands while he and Gregg attended Castle Heights military school in Lebanon, Tennessee (*Skydog*, 9–13).

16. O'Dell, *Song of the South*. See also Howard Thurman, *With Head and Heart*; Denny Bowden, "Early Daytona's Forgotten African American Communities."

17. Floyd Miles, "Young Duane Allman."

18. O'Dell, *Song of the South.*

19. Shepley, "Young Duane Allman."

20. Wells, quoted in Poe, *Skydog*, 15–16.

21. John Bozzo, "Beat Went on Despite Segregation"; Floyd Miles, "Young Duane Allman."

22. Miles, "Floyd Miles"; Gregg, quoted in Crowe, "Allman Brothers Story."

23. Freeman, *Midnight Riders*, 10–11; Alan Paul, "Lowdown and Dirty: Gregg Allman," 48; Robert Palmer, "Allman Brothers Band: A Great Southern Revival"; Miles, "Floyd Miles."

24. Gregg Allman, *My Cross to Bear*, 45, 49; Miles, "Young Duane Allman."

25. Hazen, quoted in Dave Kyle, "Remembering Duane Allman"; Wells, quoted in Freeman, *Midnight Riders*, 13.

26. Miles, "Floyd Miles."

27. Kyle, "Remembering Duane Allman"; Freeman, *Midnight Riders*, 13; Poe, *Skydog*, 21. In 2012, Rounder Records released "No Name Instrumental," the only original the Escorts recorded for Hazen.

28. Robert Palmer, "Memphis Underground," 15; Gregg Allman, *My Cross to Bear*, 62.

29. Harrison, quoted in Poe, *Skydog*, 22–23.

Chapter 3. Allman Joys Take the Highway (1965–1967)

1. These recordings appeared in 2013 for the first time on *Skydog: The Duane Allman Retrospective*, a CD produced by Duane's daughter, Galadrielle Allman, on the Rounder/Concord Music Group label, B0017877–02. Gregg Allman released a live version of "Turn on Your Love Light" on *The Gregg Allman Tour* album in 1974. Poe says the band's second recordings with Hazen were under the Allman Joys moniker. *Skydog: The Duane Allman Retrospective* documents them as the Escorts. Duane had dropped out of high school a year or two earlier, telling his family, "I can read. I can write, what more do I need?" He often did Gregg's homework for him so he could focus on music (Galadrielle Allman, *Please Be with Me*, 69; Hoskyns, "Interview with Gregg Allman").

2. Poe, *Skydog*, 28; Glover, "Allman Brothers: Saturday Night Fish Fry"; Kyle, "Remembering Duane Allman."

3. Crowe, "Allman Brothers Story," 47; Gregg Allman, *My Cross to Bear*, 65–66.

4. Atkins, quoted in Bozzo, "Beat Went on Despite Segregation"; McCorkle, quoted in Smith and Crutcher, *Capricorn Rising*, 216; Palmer, *Rock 'n' Roll*, 1–2.

5. Jourard, *Music Everywhere*, 38; "The Allman Brothers: A Local Legend That Keeps on Growing," *Daytona Beach Morning Journal*, August 4, 1973.

6. Steve Knopper, "The Rope." For an examination of rhythm and blues music and social change see Michael T. Bertrand, *Race, Rock, and Elvis*; Robert Gordon, *Respect Yourself*; Peter Guralnick, *Sweet Soul Music*; Brian Ward, *Just My Soul Responding*.

7. Johnson, quoted in Steve Knopper, "The Rope."

8. Tommy Roe, *From Cabbagetown to Tinseltown*, 89.

9. Whitlock, *Bobby Whitlock*, 31.

10. Jon Landau, untitled essay, May–June 1969, author's personal collection; Jaimoe, "Allman Brothers Drummer Jaimoe Remembers Gregg Allman."

11. Duane, "Interview with Duane Allman," *Free Press*.

12. Gregg Allman, *My Cross to Bear*, 66.

13. Warren Zanes, *Petty*, 26.

14. Tucker is quoted in "The Allman Brothers: A Local Legend That Keeps on

Growing," *Daytona Beach Morning Journal*, August 4, 1973. Hornsby spoke in O'Dell's film *Song of the South*.

15. Rossington, quoted in Jas Obrecht, "Duane Allman Remembered," 46; Sandlin, quoted in Paul, "Lowdown and Dirty: Gregg Allman," 47.

16. Rossington, quoted in Paul, "Lowdown and Dirty: Gregg Allman," 47; Sandlin, quoted in Nolan, *Allman Brothers Band*, 7.

17. Hornsby, in O'Dell, *Song of the South*; Sandlin, quoted in Anathalee Sandlin, *Never-Ending Groove*, 21–22. Advertisements for the show in the *Pensacola News Journal* co-bill the Allman Joys with the 5 Men-Its. Before eventually settling on the Minutes, the band had various names including the 5-Men-Its and the 5 Minutes (Sandlin, *Never-Ending Groove*, 15–20).

18. Note 183, Duaneallman.info.

19. Note 183, Duaneallman.info; Shepley, "Young Duane Allman." See also Jeff Lemlich, "All Over but the Crying"; Nic Schuck, "Allman Brothers Band Classic Penned in Pensacola."

20. Loudermilk, quoted in Poe, *Skydog*, 32.

21. Poe, *Skydog*, 32–33. The songs are on the 2013 release *Skydog: The Duane Allman Retrospective*.

22. "The Allman Joys (Dial 4046)," *Cashbox*, November 5, 1966; Duane, quoted in Poe, *Skydog*, 33, 36; Killen, quoted in Glover, "The Allman Brothers: Saturday Night Fish Fry."

23. Loudermilk, quoted in Poe, *Skydog*, 33, 36.

Chapter 4. Frustration in California (1967–1968)

1. Poe, *Skydog*, 34–35, 39.

2. Hornsby, "Paul Hornsby," 14–15. See also O'Dell, *Song of the South*.

3. Hornsby, quoted in Poe, *Skydog*, 39–40. See also Freeman, *Midnight Riders*, 21–22; Sandlin, *Never-Ending Groove*, 25–27.

4. Nolan, *Allman Brothers Band*, 7. Also see O'Dell, *Song of the South*; Poe, Skydog, 41.

5. Tim O'Neil, "A Look Back"; Sandlin, quoted in Freeman, *Midnight Riders*, 22.

6. Bill McEuen, quoted in Richard Albero, "*Guitar Player* Tribute." See also O'Dell, *Song of the South*.

7. Crowe, "Allman Brothers Story"; 47; Sandlin, *Never-Ending Groove*, 29–30; Gregg Allman, *My Cross to Bear*, 77.

8. Gregg Allman also remembered other bands from the L.A. scene: Spirit, the Seeds, Love, Electric Flag (with blues guitar phenom Mike Bloomfield), Jackson Browne, Tim Buckley, and Moby Grape. The movement from the dance-oriented rock 'n' roll to the more artist-focused rock is one that several scholars have written about extensively. Elijah Wald affixes blame for this trend on the Beatles and their release of *Sgt. Pepper's Lonely Hearts Club Band* in sum-

mer 1967 (Wald, *How the Beatles Destroyed Rock 'n' Roll*). Jack Hamilton devotes an entire chapter to this discussion and cites Bob Dylan's 1965 recording of "Like a Rolling Stone," released as a single and on Dylan's *Highway 61 Revisited*, as the point where rock diverged from rock 'n' roll (Hamilton, "Darkness at the Break of Noon: Sam Cooke, Bob Dylan, and the Birth of Sixties Music," in his book *Just around Midnight*). Theodore Gracyk moves the timetable further back for both Bob Dylan and the Beatles, citing Dylan's March 1965 release of *Bringing It All Back Home* and the Beatles' release of *Rubber Soul* in December 1965 (Gracyk, *Rhythm and Noise*, 12.

9. "Youth: The Hippies," *Time*, July 7, 1967.

10. Mark Harris, "The Flowering of the Hippies," *Atlantic*, September 1967.

11. Sandlin, quoted in Nolan, *Allman Brothers Band*, 7.

12. Sandlin, quoted in Ray Townley, "Makin' It in Macon," 17; Gregg Allman, *My Cross to Bear*, 82.

13. Many authors have discussed the rise of the teen idols in books on the history of rock 'n' roll. See Altschuler, *All Shook Up*; Anthony DeCurtis, James Henke, and Holly George-Warren, *Rolling Stone Illustrated History of Rock 'n' Roll*; Miller, *Flowers in the Dustbin*; Palmer, *Rock 'n' Roll*; Szatmary, *Rockin' in Time*; Ed Ward, *History of Rock 'n' Roll*, vol. 1; Ed Ward, Geoffrey Stokes, and Ken Tucker, *Rock of Ages*.

14. John McEuen, quoted in Poe, *Skydog*, 41; Altschuler, *All Shook Up*, 161–162.

15. Xander Zellner, "Bobby Vee's Top 10 Biggest Billboard Hits," *Billboard*, October 24, 2016; Hornsby, "I Need More Respect than This." Dallas Smith's experience as Vee's producer was in a music business strongly geared toward the major players: the labels, publishers, and songwriters. He was part of a long trend in American music stretching back to the late nineteenth and early twentieth centuries in New York City, where song publishers and songwriters worked in an area dubbed Tin Pan Alley. By the mid-twentieth century, much of this activity centered around the Brill Building, a few blocks north of Tin Pan Alley, also in Manhattan. See Philip Furia, *Poets of Tin Pan Alley*; Ken Emerson, *Always Magic in the Air*; Mitchell K. Hall, *Emergence of Rock and Roll*; Marc Myers, *Anatomy of a Song*; Timothy E. Scheurer, *Age of Rock*; John Shepherd and David Horn, *Genres: North America*, 91–94.

16. Sandlin, quoted in Paul, *One Way Out*, 5; Hornsby, in O'Dell, *Song of the South*.

17. Townley, "Makin' It in Macon," 17.

18. Hornsby, quoted in O'Dell, *Song of the South*; Gregg Allman, *My Cross to Bear*, 83.

19. Gregg Allman, *My Cross to Bear*, 83–84, 91.

20. John McEuen, quoted in Paul, *One Way Out*, 5.

21. Gregg Allman, *My Cross to Bear*, 85, 88 (Stills quote); Townsend, quoted in Poe, *Skydog*, 45; Hornsby, quoted in *Song of the South*.

22. Bill McEuen, quoted in Richard Albero, "*Guitar Player* Tribute."

23. O'Dell, *Song of the South*; Poe, *Skydog*, 52.

24. Carr, "The Most Important Things in Life."

25. Bill McEuen, quoted in Albero, "*Guitar Player* Tribute."

26. Gregg, quoted in Paul, *One Way Out*, 5.

Chapter 5. Duane Returns South for Good (April–September 1968)

1. Hornsby, "I Need More Respect Than This"; Poe, *Skydog*, 59. FAME was the first of two studios that operated in the Muscle Shoals area (Rick Hall, *Man from Muscle Shoals*). It was also one in a long line of independent studios throughout the South that recorded and nurtured southern musicians in the early blues, rhythm and blues, and rock 'n' roll eras. Here are some of my other favorite books on the subject: Peter Guralnick *Careless Love*, *Last Train to Memphis*, *Sam Phillips*, and *Sweet Soul Music*; Altschuler, *All Shook Up*; Bertrand, *Race, Rock, and Elvis*; Gordon, *Respect Yourself*; Hughes, *Country Soul*.

2. Sandlin, *Never-Ending Groove*, 62. The website Duaneallman.info, which I consider the definitive site for information about Duane's career, lists the date as April 22, 1968.

3. Gregg Allman, *My Cross to Bear*, 95; Sandlin, quoted in Poe, *Skydog*, 60–61. Perhaps burdened by Dallas Smith's reception to his work Los Angeles, Johnny Wyker recalls Gregg's insecurity about his performance.

4. Hornsby, "I Need More Respect than This"; Gregg Allman, *My Cross to Bear*, 95; Carr, quoted in Poe, *Skydog*, 63.

5. Hornsby, in O'Dell, *Song of the South*. For more on the development of Motown see Suzanne E. Smith, *Dancing in the Street*.

6. Bill McEuen, in O'Dell, *Song of the South*; Hornsby, quoted in Poe, *Skydog*, 42.

7. John McEuen, "John McEuen"; Carr, in O'Dell, *Song of the South*.

8. Hornsby, quoted in Poe, *Skydog*, 64; Duane, quoted in Hornsby, "I Need More Respect than This."

9. Duane, quoted in Gregg Allman, *My Cross to Bear*, 96. Other accounts of the band's break from Liberty and California include Freeman, *Midnight Riders*, 37; Glover, "Allman Brothers: Saturday Night Fish Fry"; Obrecht, "Duane Allman Remembered."

10. Galadrielle Allman, *Please Be with Me*, 125–128; Paul, *One Way Out*, xix–xx. For discussion of the evolution from rock 'n' roll to rock music see Hamilton, *Just around Midnight*; Wald, *How the Beatles Destroyed Rock 'n' Roll*.

11. Kevin Spangler and Ron Currens, "Butch Trucks, the Different Drummer," 6–7.

12. Butch Trucks, quoted in Spangler and Currens, "Butch Trucks," 6–7; Gregg Allman, *My Cross to Bear*, 100.

13. Geraldine Allman, quoted in Galadrielle Allman, 125–128.

14. Nolan, *Allman Brothers Band*, 10; Poe, *Skydog*, 66–67; Smith and Crutcher, *Capricorn Rising*, 140; Spangler and Currens, "Butch Trucks," 6–7. Duane later recorded "Nobody Knows When You're Down and Out" with Eric Clapton on the *Layla* album. The Allman Brothers recorded "Melissa," sans Duane, for 1972's *Eat a Peach*.

15. Butch Trucks, foreword to Paul, *One Way Out*, xx–xxi; Hornsby, quoted in Poe, *Skydog*, 66.

Chapter 6. Duane in Muscle Shoals (September 1968–March 1969)

1. Randy Poe reports the first trip as sometime in 1967. The second was the April 1968 Hour Glass recordings. For years, Hall shared a story that Allman lived in a pup tent in the studio parking lot until Hall gave him a shot on a session, a story I've always found implausible but never verified. A few months later, members of Hall's studio band at FAME purchased the building and re-named it Muscle Shoals Sound. The Bleus recordings remain Duane's only documented session in a Memphis studio. How Duane found himself playing with the Bleus is unclear, though it probably came at the invitation of his old friend Eddie Hinton, who was a producer (Rick Hall, *Man from Muscle Shoals*; Poe, *Skydog*, 77; Fentress, *American Revolutions*.

2. Galadrielle Allman, *Please Be with Me*, 129.

3. Crowe, "Allman Brothers Story"; Duane, quoted in Glover, "Allman Brothers: Saturday Night Fish Fry"; Glover, "In This Band You Better Come to Pick"; Spangler and Currens, "Butch Trucks, the Different Drummer," 6.

4. Hall, quoted in Nolan, *Allman Brothers Band*, 14; Hood and Johnson, in Fentress, *American Revolutions*; Hall, quoted in Poe, *Skydog*, 83.

5. Hood, in Fentress, *American Revolutions*.

6. Tony Fletcher, *In the Midnight Hour*, 40; Hall and Duane, quoted in Ertegun, *"What'd I Say?,"* 238.

7. Fentress, *American Revolutions*.

8. Johnson, quoted in O'Dell, *Song of the South*; Pickett, quoted in Fletcher, *In the Midnight Hour*, 141.

9. Hall, *Man from Muscle Shoals*, 281–282; Wexler, *Rhythm and the Blues*, 224–225.

10. Johnson, quoted in Ertegun, *"What'd I Say?,"* 238.

11. Hall, quoted in J. Harris, "Getting Together with the Allman Brothers"; Galadrielle Allman, *Please Be with Me*, 132; Glover, "Allman Brothers: Saturday Night Fish Fry."

12. Duane, quoted in Glover, "Allman Brothers: Saturday Night Fish Fry."

13. Duane, "Last Interview"; Glover, "Allman Brothers: Saturday Night Fish Fry."

14. Rick Hall, *Man from Muscle Shoals*, 281–282, 287.

15. Rick Hall, *Man from Muscle Shoals*, 281–282.

16. For more detail on Redding's career see Jonathan Gould, *Otis Redding: An Unfinished Life* (New York: Crown/Archetype, 2017). Redding had served as Jenkins's driver earlier in the latter's career—leaving Jenkins for his own success after driving him to Memphis for a session at Stax that Redding ended up recording in.

17. Walden, quoted in Ertegun, *"What'd I Say?,"* 239; Wexler, quoted in Marley Brant, *Southern Rockers*, 41.

18. In Galadrielle Allman, *Please Be with Me*, 141, 143. Walden never managed Aretha Franklin.

19. Landau, quoted in Paul, *One Way Out*, 10; Duane, quoted in Galadrielle Allman, *Please Be with Me*, 142.

20. In O'Dell, *Song of the South*.

21. Duane recorded at least two other songs during his aborted solo project, songwriter Jackie Avery's "Voodoo in You" and Bob Dylan's "Down along the Cove," both of which later appeared as backing tracks on Johnny Jenkins's *Ton Ton Macoute* record for Capricorn.

22. Hornsby, "Paul Hornsby"; Sandlin, quoted in Freeman, *Midnight Riders*, 37.

23. Duane, quoted in J. Harris, "Getting Together with the Allman Brothers."

24. Hornsby, in O'Dell, *Song of the South*.

25. Joel Selvin, "Duane Allman"; Duane's letter, quoted in Galadrielle Allman, *Please Be with Me*, 140. See also Patrick Snyder-Scumpy, "Allman Brothers: Boogie or Bust!"; June Harris, "Getting Together with the Allman Brothers."

26. Duane, quoted in J. Harris, "Getting Together with the Allman Brothers."

27. Walden, quoted in Brant, *Southern Rockers*, 43.

28. Walden, quoted in Ertegun, *"What'd I Say?,"* 239.

Chapter 7. The Birth of the Allman Brothers Band, Jacksonville (March 1969)

1. Betts, quoted in Crowe, "Allman Brothers Story."

2. Betts, "Gibson Legend Dickey Betts"; Paul, *One Way Out*, 25; Johanson, "Allman Joy."

3. Palmer, *Rock {ap?}n' Roll*, 114–115.

4. Duane Allman, "Ed Shane Interview with Duane Allman." Also see Duane Allman, "Moment Captured in Time"; Gregg Allman, *Cross to Bear*, 63; Gregg Allman, "Interview with Gregg Allman"; Betts, "Complete 1981 Dickey Betts Interview."

5. Clapton, quoted in Palmer, *Rock 'n' Roll*, 121; Eric Clapton, quoted in interview by Robert Palmer, n.d.

6. Jaimoe, quoted in Crowe, "Allman Brothers Story"; Johanson, "Reflections," 25; Helen Johnson, quoted in Lynne Bernabei, "Mother to an Allman Brother."

7. Johanson, "Reflections," 26; Johanson, "Interview: Jaimoe."

8. Johanson, "Reflections," 26; Johanson, "Jaimoe Johanson Interview"; Robin Tolleson, "Jaimoe."

9. Lynskey, "Lamar Williams," 21; Johanson, "Reflections," 25.

10. Jaimoe, quoted in Freeman, *Midnight Riders*, 34.

11. Jaimoe, quoted in Freeman, *Midnight Riders*, 34. Also see Gavin Edwards, "Allman Brothers Band."

12. Jaimoe, quoted in Palmer, "Allman Brothers Band," unpublished essay.

13. Jaimoe, quoted in Paul, *One Way Out*, 13; "Roots of the ABB Part 4: Jaimoe," *Les Brers*, no. 16; Jim Beaugez, "Jaimoe Johnson Marches to His Own Beat."

14. Beaugez, "Jaimoe Johnson Marches to His Own Beat."

15. Jai Johanny "Jaimoe" Johanson to Twiggs Lyndon, April 28, 1968, Allman Brothers Band Museum at the Big House, Macon, GA. Also see Brian Whitley, "Jaimoe."

16. Jaimoe, quoted in Paul, *One Way Out*, 13; Johanson, "Allman Brothers Drummer Jaimoe Remembers Gregg Allman"; Jaimoe, "Reflections," 27; Edwards, "Allman Brothers Band."

17. Johanson, "Allman Brothers Drummer Jaimoe Remembers Gregg Allman."

18. Jaimoe, quoted in Mikal Gilmore, *Night Beat*, 120.

19. Quotes in Kirk West, "Col. Bruce Reflects on Jaimoe," 31; Mandel, *Georgia Peach*.

20. Jaimoe, quoted in Lynskey, "Lamar Williams," 21; Freeman, *Midnight Riders*, 35.

21. Delvyn Case, quoted in Wesley Morris, "Why Is Everyone Always Stealing Black Music?."

22. Morris, "Why Is Everyone Always Stealing Black Music?."

23. Duane, quoted in Freeman, *Midnight Riders*, 35.

24. Jaimoe, quoted in: Paul, *One Way Out*, 15; Beaugez, "Jaimoe Johnson Marches to His Own Beat."

25. Jaimoe, quoted in: Paul, *One Way Out*, 13–15; Freeman, *Midnight Riders*, 35–36; Johanson, "Reflections," 27.

26. Lyndon, quoted in Nolan, *Allman Brothers Band*, 14–18.

27. Jaimoe, quoted in Paul, *One Way Out*, 15; Gregg Allman, *My Cross to Bear*, 61.

28. Oakley, quoted in Galadrielle Allman, *Please Be with Me*, 84, 129; Poe, *Skydog*, 72.

29. Scoppa, *Rock People*, 62; Nolan, *Allman Brothers Band*, 18; Candace Oakley, quoted in Freeman, *Midnight Riders*, 36. Two undated fliers from the events are "Parish Talent Show" and "To Play for Canteen" (duaneallman.info/family-tree.htm).

30. Roe, *From Cabbagetown to Tinseltown*, 100–103; Bo Glover and Mike Dugo, "The Roemans," *Beyond the Beat Generation*, https://web.archive.org/web/20170119121539/home.unet.nl/kesteloo/roemans.html; Tommy Roe, phone interview by the author, April 14, 2017.

31. Candace Oakley, "Memories of a Brother." See also "The Roemans," *Tampa Times*, April 27, 1966; Glover, "Allman Brothers: Saturday Night Fish Fry"; Nolan, *Allman Brothers Band*, 18; Scoppa, *Rock People*, 62.

32. Roe, interview by author. Also see Dave Kyle, "Berry Oakley"; Scoppa, *Rock People*, 62; Joel Selvin, "What Southern Boys Can Do with Rock."

33. Betts, quoted in Michael Ray FitzGerald, *Jacksonville and the Roots of Southern Rock*, 46.

34. Betts, quoted in Poe, *Skydog*, 69; Betts, quoted in Aledort, "Dickey Betts on Writing the Timeless Classic."

35. Betts, quoted in Michael Brooks, "Meet Dick Betts." See also Andy Aledort, Alan Paul, and Jimmy Brown, "The Allman Brothers Band's 25 All-Time Greatest Songs"; Michael Watts, "The Allmans Are to America Now What the Grateful Dead Were in '67."

36. Betts, quoted in Edwards, "Allman Brothers Band"; Michelizzi, "Dickey Betts at the Hall of Fame."

37. Betts, quoted in Michelizzi, "Dickey Betts at the Hall of Fame."

38. Oakley, quoted in Michelizzi, "Dickey Betts at the Hall of Fame."

39. Betts, quoted in Smith and Crutcher, *Capricorn Rising*, 10.

40. John Meeks, "Tale of the Second Coming," 36.

41. "Roots of the Allman Brothers Band Part 2: The Second Coming," *Les Brers*, no. 14; Poe, *Skydog*, 72.

42. Meeks, "Tale of the Second Coming," 36.

43. Betts is quoted in Aledort, Paul, and Brown, "The Allman Brothers Band's 25 All-Time Greatest Songs."

44. Gilmore, *Night Beat*, 127; Petty, quoted in Nolan, *Allman Brothers Band*, 18; Betts, quoted in Bill Ector, "Allman Brothers Band Hall of Fame Induction."

45. Betts, quoted in Michelizzi, "Dickey Betts at the Hall of Fame"; "Roots of the Allman Brothers Band Part 2," *Les Brers*; FitzGerald, *Jacksonville and the Roots of Southern Rock*, 46. On March 23, 2019, the owner of the home installed a State of Florida Historic Marker on the site.

46. FitzGerald, *Jacksonville and the Roots of Southern Rock*, ix–x, 49 (Price quote).

47. Petty, quoted in Nolan, *Allman Brothers Band*, 22; Scott Bernarde, "Rock's Ramblin' Man"; Betts and Trucks, "Rock Influence (Official)";

48. Betts, "Gibson Legend Dickey Betts"; Paul, *One Way Out*, 70.

49. Betts, "Gibson Legend Dickey Betts"; Betts, "Complete 1981 Dickey Betts Interview"; Wynans, quoted in Paul, *One Way Out*, 67–68;

50. Malone and Stricklin, *Southern Music/American Music*, 95–97.

51. Betts, quoted in Michelizzi, "Dickey Betts at the Hall of Fame"; Paul, *One Way Out*, 17–18.

52. Betts and Price, quoted in Paul, *One Way Out*, 19–20.

53. Freeman, *Midnight Riders*, 39; Spangler and Currens, "Butch Trucks," 5; Janet Gibson, "Butch Trucks"; Trucks, quoted in Marty Racine, "Allman Brothers"; Butch Trucks, "Who Influenced Butch?."

54. Racine, "Allman Brothers"; Trucks, quoted in Spangler and Currens, "Butch Trucks," 5.

55. Betts, quoted in Paul, *One Way Out*, 16–17; Price, quoted in Paul, *One Way Out*, 20.

56. Wynans, quoted in Paul, *One Way Out*, 22.

57. Duane Allman and Berry Oakley, interview; Trucks, quoted in Palmer, "Allman Brothers Band," unpublished essay.

58. Trucks, quoted in Palmer, "Allman Brothers Band," unpublished essay.

59. Wynans, quoted in Paul, *One Way Out*, 23.

60. Dennis McNally, email to author, April 3, 2021.

61. Betts, quoted in Gilmore, *Night Beat*, 126.

62. Duane, quoted in Glover, "Allman Brothers: Saturday Night Fish Fry"; Jaimoe, quoted in "Roots of the Allman Brothers Band Part 3: The 31st of February," *Les Brers*, 15; Butch Trucks, quoted in Palmer, "Allman Brothers Band," unpublished essay; Spangler and Currens, "Butch Trucks," 8.

63. Duane, quoted in Bomar, *Southbound*, 23; Trucks, quoted in Spangler and Currens, "Butch Trucks," 8; Betts, quoted in Jim Dorman, "Dickey Betts Describes How It All Began," filmed 2003, YouTube video, 2:55, posted May 2013, https://www.youtube.com/watch?v=pXJqr8yKWDE.

64. Linda Oakley, quoted in Paul, *One Way Out*, 25; Johanson, "Allman Brothers Drummer Jaimoe Remembers Gregg Allman."

65. Duane, quoted in Snyder-Scumpy, "Allman Brothers," 41; Gregg Allman, quoted in "Inner-View"; Ken Hey, *Southern Voices*.

66. "Special Merit Spotlight: Spotlighting New Singles Deserving Special Attention of Programmers and Dealers," *Billboard*, July 13, 1968, 70; Gregg Allman, *My Cross to Bear*, 97.

67. Geraldine, quoted in Galadrielle Allman, *Please Be with Me*, 75; Duane, in Berry Oakley and Duane Allman, "Houston, TX Interview."

68. Johanson, "Allman Brothers Drummer Jaimoe Remembers Gregg Allman." Also see Paul, "Complete 2015 Interview with Gregg Allman."

69. Gregg Allman, *My Cross to Bear*, 74–75; John McEuen, quoted in Paul, *One Way Out*, 42; Gregg, quoted in Paul, *One Way Out*, 148; Jaimoe, quoted in Alan Paul, "Gregg Allman 1947–2017."

70. Gregg, quoted in Fentress, *American Revolutions*; Johanson, "Allman Brothers Drummer Jaimoe Remembers Gregg Allman."

71. Johanson, "Reflections," 27; Johanson, "Allman Brothers Drummer Jaimoe Remembers Gregg Allman."

72. Betts, quoted in "Gibson Legend Dickey Betts"; Betts, quoted in, "Dickey Betts Describes How It All Began"; Hornsby, quoted in O'Dell, *Song of the South*; Johanson, "Reflections," 16; Johanson, "Allman Brothers Drummer Jaimoe Remembers Gregg Allman."

73. Gregg Allman, *My Cross to Bear,* 111.

74. Duane Allman, "Ed Shane Interview with Duane Allman"; Betts, "Gibson Legend Dickey Betts."

75. Betts, quoted in Paul, *One Way Out*, 23–24.

Chapter 8. A Home in Macon (Spring and Summer 1969)

1. Jonathan Gould refutes this traditional understanding of Redding's relationship with Walden in *Otis Redding: An Unfinished Life*, 344–353.

2. Bomar, *Southbound*, 20–21.

3. Hall, quoted in Paul, *One Way Out*, 10–11.

4. Hall, quoted in Glover, "In This Band You Better Come to Pick"; Duane, quoted in Roger St. Pierre, "Allman Brothers." Members of the band eventually successfully sued Walden for a variety of financial conflicts he had as the band's manager, booking agent, publisher, and record-label owner (Gregg Allman, *My Cross to Bear*, 285–286, 291; Freeman, *Midnight Riders*, 137–138, 263–268; Paul, *One Way Out*, 262–263).

5. Betts, quoted in Jonathan Takiff, "Allman Brothers Sounding Better"; Oakley, quoted in Paul, *One Way Out*, 57.

6. Gregg Allman, *My Cross to Bear*, 122.

7. Duane, "Last Interview"; Berry, quoted in Glover, "In This Band You Better Come to Pick."

8. Wexler, quoted in Nolan, *Allman Brothers Band*, 34.

9. Trucks, quoted in Jon Dale, "Butch Trucks on the Allmans' Wild Times"; Duane, "Interview with Duane Allman."

10. Gregg Allman, *My Cross to Bear*, 123.

11. Willie Perkins and Jack Weston, *Allman Brothers Band*, 17–18; Powell, quoted in Paul, *One Way Out*, 39; Gregg Allman, *My Cross to Bear*, 123.

12. Trucks, quoted in Barry Kerzner, "Butch Trucks Proud of Allman Brothers Legacy."

13. Craig Werner, *Change Is Gonna Come*, Ellison quote, 132. See also Malone and Stricklin, *Southern Music/American Music*, 51; Burton W. Peretti, *Jazz in*

American Culture, 5; Michael Stephans, *Experiencing Jazz*, 4–6. William J. Shafer's entry "Jazz" in *The New Encyclopedia of Southern Culture* offers a more specific discussion.

14. Betts and Trucks, "Rock Influence (Official)"; Betts, quoted in Freeman, *Midnight Riders*, 49.

15. Gregg, quoted in Paul, "Lowdown and Dirty: Gregg Allman," 51.

16. Aledort, Paul, and Brown, "Allman Brothers Band's 25 All-Time Greatest Songs."

17. Betts, quoted in Aledort, Paul, and Brown, "Allman Brothers Band's 25 All-Time Greatest Songs." For a more in-depth discussion of harmony in popular music see David Nicholls, *Cambridge History of American Music*, 314–315.

18. Gregg, quoted in Paul, "Lowdown and Dirty: Gregg Allman," 51; Johanson, "Reflections 2," 29.

19. Paul, *One Way Out*, 53; Edwards, "Allman Brothers Band"; Betts, "Complete 1981 Dickey Betts Interview."

20. Trucks, quoted in Gilmore, *Night Beat*, 133; Gregg Allman, *My Cross to Bear*, 107, 166; Jaimoe, quoted in Lynskey, "Lamar Williams," 23–24.

21. Betts, quoted in Lynskey, "Lamar Williams," 23–24; Gilmore, *Night Beat*, 127.

22. Malone and Stricklin, *Southern Music/American Music*, 109.

23. Richard Meltzer, *Aesthetics of Rock*, 151.

24. Garcia, quoted in Palmer, *Rock 'n' Roll*, 161, 165.

25. Betts, quoted in Michelizzi, "Dickey Betts at the Hall of Fame"; Gregg Allman, *My Cross to Bear*, 114.

26. Jaimoe, quoted in Galadrielle Allman, *Please Be with Me*, 300–301.

27. Atlantic Records Recording Ledgers, 1969, archived at duaneallman.info.

28. Gregg, quoted in Paul, "Lowdown and Dirty: Gregg Allman," 51; Jaimoe, quoted in Paul, *One Way Out*, 60; Ertegun, *"What'd I Say?,"* 239; Grover Lewis, "Hitting the Note with the Allman Brothers Band," 53; Duane Allman and Berry Oakley, "Interview"; Duane, "Interview with Duane Allman."

29. Duane, "Moment Captured in Time," 10. Gregg Allman, *My Cross to Bear*, 150; Paul, "Lowdown and Dirty: Gregg Allman," 51; Palmer, "Allman Brothers Band: A Great Southern Revival"; Betts, quoted in Brooks, "Meet Dick Betts," 24.

30. Trucks, quoted in Corbin Reiff, "Allman Brothers Band's Legendary 1971 Fillmore East Run."

31. Jaimoe, quoted in Nolan, *Allman Brothers Band*, 47; Betts, quoted in Lewis, "Hitting the Note with the Allman Brothers Band," 53. Although I've left the phrase "hittin' the note" intact, out of respect for the band I have changed Lewis's transcription from phrases such as "gettin' down," "all the actin'," and "lettin' it."

32. Betts, "Gibson Legend Dickey Betts"; Ertegun, *"What'd I Say?,"* 239.

33. National Center for Education Statistics, "Table 101.10"; Landon Y. Jones, "Swinging 60s?"; Betts, quoted in Brant, *Southern Rockers*, 58. Duane, "Ed Shane Interview with Duane Allman."

34. Betts, quoted in Dave Hickey, "Why the Allmans Died Young."

Chapter 9. The Journey Begins (May–December 1969)

1. College Discotheque flyer for May 2–3, 1969.

2. College Discotheque flyer; Galadrielle Allman, *Please Be with Me*, 167; Nolan, *Allman Brothers Band*, 22.

3. Patrick Edmondson, "A Bus Stops in Piedmont Park"; Patrick Edmondson, "May 11 Be-In in Piedmont"; Meeks, "Tale of the Second Coming," 34–36; John Ogden, "First There Is a Mountain," 10.

4. Hampton, quoted in Paul, *One Way Out*, 40–41; Cooley, quoted in Kirk Anderson, *"Hittin' the Note* Presents," 21.

5. A Friend and Reader, letter to the editor, *Great Speckled Bird*, May 26, 1969, 4; Steve Wise, "Non-Event," *Great Speckled Bird*, May 19, 1969, 3; Philip Lane, post, July 25, 2016, Friends and Not Necessarily Stoned, but Beautiful: Hippies of the 60s and Beyond, Facebook page, https://www.facebook.com/hippiesofthe60sandbeyond/posts/729683123836256.

6. Miller Francis Jr., "Allman Brothers Band," 10.

7. Walden, quoted in Brant, *Southern Rockers*, 52; Walden, quoted in Russell Hall, "Capricorn Records"; Landau, "Allman Brothers Band," 16.

8. Walden and Duane, quoted in Russell Hall, "Capricorn Records."

9. Law, quoted in Paul, *One Way Out*, 48–49; Betts, "Gibson Legend Dickey Betts"; Odum, quoted in Nolan, *Allman Brothers Band*, 25.

10. Jaimoe, quoted in Lynskey, "Lamar Williams," 21; Betts, quoted in Ogden, "Berry Oakley," 31–33; Betts, quoted in Paul, *One Way Out*, 130.

11. Betts, quoted in Bomar, *Southbound*, 36; Gregg, quoted in Brant, *Southern Rockers*, 85.

12. Francis, "Allman Brothers Band," cover; Bommba, "Prepared, Rehearsed, or Repeated"; Mankin, "We Can All Join In."

13. Betts, quoted in the unsigned *Rolling Stone* article "The Allman Brothers Band: The Fillmore East, New York City, March 11th-13th, 1971," June 4, 1987," 79–80.

14. On the Grateful Dead see Dennis McNally, *Long Strange Trip*; Peter Richardson, *No Simple Highway*.

15. University of California–Riverside, "50th Anniversary Timeline," 2005, https://web.archive.org/web/20050311091252/newsroom.ucr.edu/timeline.html; Bruce Harvie, "I Just Read This on the Telecaster Board," Allmanbrothers.com forum post, June 17, 2008, https://allmanbrothersband.com/community/. The *New Orleans Express* quote is in a photo caption posted in "The Allman Brothers Band Free Concert at The 'Butterfly' Audubon Park, New Orleans,

La. Sunday, August 23, 1970," The Warehouse Concerts List 1970–1982, http://blackstrat.net/Allman-Audubon/Allman-Audubon.htm.

16. Gregg Allman, *My Cross to Bear*, 134.

17. Lyndon, quoted in Nolan, *Allman Brothers Band*, 25; Cooley, quoted in Anderson, *"Hittin' the Note* Presents," 22.

18. Trucks, quoted in Nolan, *Allman Brothers Band*, 25.

19. Odum, quoted in Nolan, *Allman Brothers Band*, 25.

20. Betts, quoted in Newton, "Dickey Betts."

21. Jourard, *Music Everywhere*, 77–80.

22. Jourard, *Music Everywhere*, 77–81; Rory O'Connor, "Allman Brothers Shake Electric Zoo."

23. Steven Rose, "How the Ludlow Garage Transformed Cincinnati's Youth Culture"; Betts, quoted in Ben Sandmel, liner notes.

24. Duane Allman, "Ed Shane Interview with Duane Allman"; Betts, "Complete 1981 Dickey Betts"; Gregg Allman, *My Cross to Bear*, 140–141; Betts, quoted in Watts, "Allmans Are to America."

25. Ed Ochs, "Tomorrow"; John Wren, "Records"; Ben Edmonds, "Allman Brothers Band."

26. Dan Vining, "Good Blues Music"; Roy Eure, "Vibrations."

27. Edmonds, "Allman Brothers Band."

28. Lester Bangs, "Allman Brothers Band."

29. Bangs, "Allman Brothers Band"; "New LP: The Allman Brothers Band," *Anomaly*, April 9, 1970, 3; Edmonds, "Allman Brothers Band."

30. Duane, "Moment Captured in Time," 10; Malone and Stricklin, *Southern Music/American Music*, 14.

31. Bangs, "Allman Brothers Band." For an explanation of modal jazz in relation to Miles Davis's *Kind of Blue* album see Stephans, *Experiencing Jazz*, 170–171; Geoffrey Jacques, "Listening to Jazz."

32. Jim Gillespie, "Muscle Shoals Has Newest Sound Around."

33. Rory O'Connor, "Allman Brothers: Power and Energy."

34. In Fentress, *American Revolutions*.

35. Law, quoted in Paul, *One Way Out*, 94–95; O'Connor, "Allman Brothers: Power and Energy."

Chapter 10. The ABB Builds Its Reputation (December 1969–September 1970)

1. Bill Graham, *Bill Graham Presents*, 172; Garcia quote, 202.

2. Graham, *Bill Graham Presents*, 172–175; Walden quote, 173. Emphasis is in the original source.

3. Graham, *Bill Graham Presents*, 172–173, 206; Clapton quotes, 214, 217; White quote, 340.

4. Graham, quoted in Nolan, *Allman Brothers Band*, 28.

5. Arkush, quoted in Graham, *Bill Graham Presents*, 306–307.

6. Graham, *Bill Graham Presents*, 306–307; Gregg Allman, *My Cross to Bear*, 142; Lyndon, quoted in Nolan, *Allman Brothers Band*, 28.

7. Graham, quoted in Nolan, *Allman Brothers Band*, 28.

8. Gregg Allman, *My Cross to Bear*, 142.

9. Johanson, "Reflections 2," 24.

10. Betts, quoted in Nolan, *Allman Brothers Band*, 48.

11. In Paul, *One Way Out*, Campbell quote, 94; Gregg quote, 95. Campbell gained renown in two *Rolling Stone* articles on the band, including those by Grover Lewis in 1971, "Hitting the Note with the Allman Brothers Band," and Cameron Crowe in 1973, "Allman Brothers Story." Crowe also named a roadie character Red Dog in his 2000 movie *Almost Famous*.

12. Hampton, quoted in Paul, *One Way Out*, 35; Betts, quoted in Gilmore, *Night Beat*, 128.

13. Doucette, quoted in Paul, *One Way Out*, 114–115.

14. Jim Cox, "Allman Brothers Band." See also Gregg Allman, *My Cross to Bear*, 174–177; Freeman, *Midnight Riders*, 95–96; Paul, *One Way Out*, 130–133.

15. Brian Ward, *Just My Soul Responding*, 113–116, 225–232.

16. Ward, *Just My Soul Responding*, 257; Brian Ward, email to the author, April 5, 2021.

17. Gregg, quoted in Hoskyns, "Southern Men"; Joseph L. "Red Dog" Campbell, *Legendary Red Dog*, 75; Betts, quoted in Gilmore, *Night Beat*, 128.

18. Richard Price, "Richard 'Hombre' Price July 11, 2017," comment in the Facebook group Duane Allman—Skydog Fan Page, https://www.facebook.com/groups/Skydog/permalink/1145030282265653/.

19. ABB contract paperwork of November 23, 1970, is posted at "Let's Explore a Treasure Trove of 1970s Memorabilia from Alabama Concert Promoter," AL.com, https://www.al.com/entertainment/index.ssf/2017/08/lynyrd_skynyrd_emmylou_harris.html; Willie Perkins, Facebook message to the author, March 16, 2018.

20. Gregg Allman, *My Cross to Bear*, 128.

21. Paul, *One Way Out*, 33–35; Hudson quote, 34; Lyndon quote, 33.

22. Betts, quoted in Freeman, *Midnight Riders*, 47. For more on Macon in this era see Andrew Michael Manis, *Macon Black and White*. Sadly, Manis makes no mention of the Allman Brothers Band or Capricorn Records in his book.

23. Johanson, "Reflections," 24.

24. Recording details come from the album *Skydog: The Duane Allman Retrospective*.

25. Dowd, quoted in Dave Hogerty, "Eulogy to a Friend," 36.

26. Liner notes, *Idlewild South Super Deluxe Edition*, Allman Brothers Band, Mercury Records, 2015.

27. Betts, quoted in Aledort, Paul, and Brown, "Allman Brothers Band's 25 All-Time Greatest Songs"; Betts, quoted in Wade Tatangelo, "Dickey Betts."

28. Dickey Betts, "Revival" lyrics on *Idlewild South*, original release, 1970.

29. Trucks, quoted in Freeman, 40; Galadrielle Allman, *Please Be with Me*, 85–89; Gregg Allman, *My Cross to Bear*, 55–61.

30. Gregg Allman, *My Cross to Bear*, 173; Duane, "Interview with Duane Allman," *Free Press*.

31. Exact numbers for the event are unverified. Promoter Alex Cooley said he estimated a crowd of 100,000 as he planned the event, but shortly after it began, tens of thousands crashed the gates and attended for free. Cooley's website estimates around 200,000 ultimately attended, while the *Atlanta Journal Constitution* estimated between 350,000 and 500,000 attendees at the time (Cooley, "2nd Atlanta International Pop Festival"; Richard L. Eldredge, "What a Splash). See also Ben Standifer, "Top 5 Facts"; Christina M. Wright, "Historical Marker."

32. "Love Valley Rock Festival July 17," *N.C. Anvil*, July 4, 1970; James Neal, "47 Years Ago This Weekend"; Porter, "First There Is a Mountain"; Duane Allman and Berry Oakley, "Interview."

33. "Festival!," *Inquisition*, July 17, 1970.

34. Dowd, quoted in Poe, *Skydog*, 143–144.

35. Nolan, *Allman Brothers Band*, 28.

36. "Blues Neglected for Rock," *Kentucky Kernel*, November 12, 1970; Leimbacher, "Review: *Idlewild South*"; Stuart Stevens, "Allman Brothers Introduce New Abilities"; Rory O'Connor, "*Idlewild South* Is a Hit."

37. "Spring Music," *The Guilfordian*, April 16, 1971; Dick Hartsook, "Off the Record"; Leimbacher, "Review: *Idlewild South*"; Butch Ochsenreiter, "Plastic Rap." Ochsenreiter, "Plastic Rap."

38. Francis, "*Idlewild South*."

39. Francis, "*Idlewild South*."

40. "Top Tape Cartridges (Based on Best-Selling LP's)," *Billboard*, December 19, 1970, 18.

41. "The Allman Brothers Band Chart History: 'Revival (Love Is Everywhere)," Billboard.com.

42. Walden, quoted in Paul, *One Way Out*, 94.

43. Leimbacher, "Review: *Idlewild South*"; Francis, "*Idlewild South*."

44. Nolan, *Allman Brothers Band*, 28, 32; Ben Edmonds, "Snapshots of the South"; Duane, "An Interview with Duane Allman." Radio programming data are found in "Campus News," *Billboard*, December 5, 1970, 39, and in "Campus Programming Aids," *Billboard*, October 31, 1970, 43; January 16, 1971, 35; February 6, 1971, 43.

45. Walden, quoted in Paul, *One Way Out*, 94; Edmonds, "Snapshots of the South."

Chapter 11. Phil Walden and Capricorn Records (1969–1971)

1. Michael T. Bertrand, *Race, Rock, and Elvis*, 64; Robert Gordon, *Respect Yourself*, 36.

2. Walden, quoted in Edmonds, "Snapshots of the South."

3. Wexler, quoted in Brant, *Southern Rockers*, 48; Johanson, "Jaimoe—Founding Member."

4. Edmonds, "Snapshots of the South." Fenter died of a heart attack on July 21, 1983, during Capricorn Records' bankruptcy case.

5. Wooley, quoted in Bomar, *Southbound*, 65; Ertegun, quoted in Kirk West, "Ahmet Ertegun," 24.

6. Walden, quoted in Bob Hamilton, *Operating Manual for Starship Radio '73*, 367; Fenter, quoted in Cameron Crowe, "Sound of the South," 26.

7. Duane, in Allman and Oakley, "Interview"; Duane, quoted in Glover, "Allman Brothers: Saturday Night Fish Fry."

8. Duane, "Moment Captured in Time," 16; Duane Allman to Jerry Wexler, January 2, 1970, https://duaneallman.info/images/postcard01021970b.jpg.

9. Walden, quoted in Brant, *Southern Rockers*, 50; Betts and Walden, in Fentress, *American Revolutions*.

10. Odum, quoted in Paul, *One Way Out*, 100.

11. Betts, in Hey, *Southern Voices*; Betts, quoted in Paul, "Lowdown and Dirty: Shades of Dickey Betts."

12. Kirsten West, "History of the Big House."

13. Candace Oakley, quoted in Poe, *Skydog*, 138; Doucette, quoted in Paul, *One Way Out*, 71; Willie Perkins, *No Saints, No Saviors*, 15; Gregg Allman, *My Cross to Bear*, 148–149; Freeman, *Midnight Riders*, 67–68.

14. Butch Trucks, quoted in Crowe, "Allman Brothers Story," 52; Sandlin, quoted in Hoskyns, "Southern Men"; Betts, quoted in Paul, "Lowdown and Dirty: Shades of Dickey Betts," 51.

15. Walden, quoted in Russell Hall, "How the Allman Brothers Band Launched Southern Rock"; Steve Dollar, "Duane Allman Left Tragic but Lasting Musical Legacy."

16. Gregg Allman, *My Cross to Bear*, 116; Freeman, *Midnight Riders*, 53.

17. Gregg Allman, *My Cross to Bear*, 117.

18. Gregg Allman, *My Cross to Bear*, 129.

19. Glover, "Allman Brothers Band: Saturday Night Fish Fry"; Glover, "In this Band, You Better Come to Pick."

20. Duane and Walden, in Fentress, *American Revolutions*.

21. Duane Allman, "Ed Shane Interview with Duane Allman."

22. Duane Allman, "Ed Shane Interview with Duane Allman."

23. Duane, in Allman and Oakley, "Interview."

24. Duane, "Interview with Duane Allman of the Allman Brothers Band"; Philip Rauls, phone interview by the author, October 7, 2016.

25. Duane, quoted in June Harris, "Getting Together with the Allman Brothers."

Chapter 12. Recording *At Fillmore East* (March 13–14, 1971)

1. Scoppa, *Rock People*, 66–67.

2. Rauls, phone interview by the author, October 7, 2016; Carter, quoted in Poe, *Skydog*, 198; Glover, "Allman Brothers Band: Saturday Night Fish Fry."

3. Scoppa, *Rock People*, 58, 66–67.

4. Alex Dubro, "Them Vino-Lovin' Allman Brothers."

5. Clapton, "Slowhand Remembers Skydog," 19.

6. Clapton, "Slowhand Remembers Skydog," 19.

7. Guralnick, *Sweet Soul Music*, 234–238.

8. Betts, quoted in Corbin Reiff, "Allman Brothers Band's Legendary 1971 Fillmore East Run."

9. Dennis McNally, emails to the author, March 30, 2020, and February 7, 2021.

10. Podell, "Jon Podell," 35; Ray Waddell, "American Classic."

11. Baratta, quoted in Graham, *Bill Graham Presents*, 206.

12. Betts, in Gregg Allman and Dickey Betts, "In the Studio with Redbeard"; Betts, quoted in Corbin Reiff, "Allman Brothers Band's Legendary 1971 Fillmore East Run"; Jaimoe, quoted in Freeman, *Midnight Riders*, 88.

13. Ticket prices are from http://duaneallman.info/chronologypart4.htm.

14. Arkush, quoted in Graham, *Bill Graham Presents*, 307; Butch Trucks, quoted in Dale, "Butch Trucks."

15. Trucks, quoted in Reiff, "Allman Brothers Band's Legendary 1971 Fillmore East Run."

16. Scoppa, *Rock People*, 58, 66–67; Arkush, quoted in Graham, *Bill Graham Presents*, 307.

17. Trucks, "Butch Trucks."

18. Johanson, "Allman Joy."

19. Betts and Trucks, quoted in Reiff, "Allman Brothers Band's Legendary 1971 Fillmore East Run"; Johanson, "Allman Joy."

20. Betts, quoted in "Allman Brothers Band: The Fillmore East," *Rolling Stone*, June 4, 1987; Gregg, quoted in Reiff, "Allman Brothers Band's Legendary 1971 Fillmore East Run"; Johanson, "Allman Joy."

21. Gregg, quoted in "Allman Brothers Band: The Fillmore East," *Rolling Stone*, June 4, 1987.

22. Paul, *One Way Out*, 116–124, Dowd quote on p. 120.

23. "Hot 'Lanta" is also the one ABB song that all surviving original band members played in their solo bands.

24. Duane Allman in "Mountain Jam," *Eat a Peach*, CD, Allman Brothers Band, 1992, PolyGram.

25. Oakley and Duane are quoted from audio recording of the concert at the Warehouse in New Orleans on March 20, 1971.

Chapter 13. *At Fillmore East* Breaks Through (Summer and Fall 1971)

1. Wexler and Walden, quoted in Ertegun, *"What'd I Say?,"* 240.

2. Walden, in Fentress, *American Revolutions*; Russell Hall, "How the Allman Brothers Band Launched Southern Rock."

3. Walden, quoted in Hall, "How the Allman Brothers Band Launched Southern Rock"; Trucks, in Betts and Trucks, "Interview—11/4/1984."

4. Betts, "Complete 1981 Dickey Betts Interview"; Walden, quoted in Nolan, *Allman Brothers Band*, 32; Glover, "Allman Brothers Band: Saturday Night Fish Fry."

5. Walden, quoted in Nolan, 32; Glover, "Allman Brothers Band: Saturday Night Fish Fry."

6. See Jesse Walker, *Rebels on the Air*, 48–51; WFMU, "A Brief History of Freeform Radio," 1998, https://web.archive.org/web/20220124235012/http://www.wfmu.org/LCD/21/freeform.html. For more comprehensive histories of FM radio see Michael C. Keith's works *Sounds in the Dark* and *Voices in the Purple Haze*; Richard Neer, *FM*; Dave Pierce, *Riding on the Ether Express*; Rick Sklar, *Rocking America*; Christopher H. Sterling and Michael C. Keith, *Sounds of Change*.

7. Reynolds, quoted in Keith, *Sounds in the Dark,* 94; Todd Coffin, "Birth of Community Rock Radio"; Richard Goldstein, "Pop Eye"; Alfred G. Aronowitz, "Pop Music."

8. Walker, *Rebels on the Air*, 92–93; Coffin, "Birth of Community Rock Radio."

9. Keith, *Sounds in the Dark*, 94.

10. Untitled clipping, July 28, 2013, The Warehouse Concerts List 1970–1982, http://www.blackstrat.net/warehouse/70-04-bb-an.jpg.

11. Rauls, phone interview with the author, October 7, 2016; Carter, quoted in Poe, *Skydog*, 197; Betts, quoted in Ertegun, *"What'd I Say?,"* 239. Data regarding radio play derives from *Billboard*: "Special Merit Picks, Programming Aids: Progressive Rock," *Billboard*, December 20, 1969, 39. "Campus Programming Aids," *Billboard*, October 31, 1970, 43; November 7, 1970, 30; November 14, 1970, 31; January 16, 1971, 35; (Bob Glassenberg) January 23, 1971, 38; February 6, 1971, 43; February 20, 1971, 36. "Campus News," *Billboard*, November 7, 1970, 28; November 14, 1970, 29; December 5, 1970, 39.

12. "Action Records: National Breakouts," *Billboard*, July 24, 1971, 50; "Top LP's A-Z (Listed by Artist)," *Billboard*, July 24, 1971, 60; "The Allman Brothers Band Chart History," *Billboard*, https://www.billboard.com/artist/the-allman-brothers-band/; Paul, *One Way Out*, 143.

13. Trucks, quoted in Nolan, *Allman Brothers Band*, 34, 38. The album re-

flected some changes in the music industry as well, in a turn toward double albums. See Paul Ackerman, "Output of 2-LP Sets up, Spurs Multiple Pricing."

14. M. Skryp to the Allman Brothers Band, c/o Atlantic Recording Corp., November 10, 1971, in the archives of the Allman Brothers Band Museum at the Big House.

15. Gary Wishik, "S.B. 'House' Band Rivaled by Live Album"; George Kimball, "Allman Brothers Band"; Ernie Santosuosso, "Allman Blues Superior Stuff"; Marshall Fine, "Allman Live Recording Best."

16. Rich Aregood, *At Fillmore East* Review"; Fine, "Allman Live Recording Best"; Kimball, "Allman Brothers Band."

17. Santosuosso, "Allman Blues Superior Stuff"; Wishik, "S.B. 'House' Band Rivaled by Live Album."

18. "Review: *At Fillmore East*," *The Tiger*, September 17, 1971, 14; Jim Conley, "Platter Chatter"; Aregood, "*At Fillmore East* Review."

19. Glover, "Allman Brothers Band: Saturday Night Fish Fry."

20. Scoppa, *Rock People*, 66; Dubro, "Them Vino-Lovin' Allman Brothers"; Duane, quoted in Glover, "In This Band You Better Come to Pick."

21. Wexler and Ritz, *Rhythm and the Blues*, 256–257; Glover, "Allman Brothers Band: Saturday Night Fish Fry."

Chapter 14. Touring and Recording without Duane (November 1971– November 1972)

1. Trucks, quoted in Hoskyns, "Southern Men"; Fenter, quoted in William Chaze, "Allman Brothers' House Now Empty"; Gregg Allman, *My Cross to Bear*, 207; Payne, quoted in Freeman, *Midnight Riders*, 114.

2. Trucks, "Butch Trucks on Berry Oakley." Gregg had yet to arrange to bury Duane's body, and it lay in cold storage for a year until Linda Oakley and Duane's widow, Donna Allman, had their late husbands buried side by side.

3. Keith Richards gets credit as rock's greatest survivor, but my choice is Gregg Allman.

4. Gregg Allman, *My Cross to Bear*, 197.

5. Gregg Allman, *My Cross to Bear*, 200.

6. Betts, quoted in Betts and Trucks, "Interview—11/4/1984"; Betts, quoted in Freeman, *Midnight Riders*, 114.

7. Betts, quoted in Crowe, "Duane Allman"; Betts, quoted in Freeman, *Midnight Riders*, 114.

8. Jon Landau, "More on Duane Allman."

9. Jon Landau, "Loose Ends."

10. Walden, quoted in "Sky Man Played Last Tune 25 Years Ago for Allmans," *Augusta Chronicle*, November 17, 1996; Duane, quoted in Kyle, "Remembering Duane Allman"; Trucks, quoted in Gilmore, *Night Beat*, 132.

11. Gregg Allman, "Inner-View."

12. Wexler, quoted in Landau, "Bandleader Duane Allman Dies in Bike Crash."

13. "Billboard Album Reviews," *Billboard*, March 18, 1972, 46, 48.

14. Gregg Allman, *My Cross to Bear*, 204.

15. Tony Glover, "The Allman Brothers Band: Did They Grieve?"; Hal Pratt, "The Critic's Opinion: *Eat a Peach*"; Dave Sitz, "Allman Brothers Overcome Tragedy." Chart ratings are from *Billboard*'s "Allman Brothers Band Chart History."

16. Glover, "The Allman Brothers Band: *Eat a Peach*"; Stephen Lasko, "Allman Brothers Rock on without Duane."

17. Sitz, "Allman Brothers Overcome Tragedy"; Dale Rauch, "In One Ear"; Ernie Kelly, "Presenting."

18. Glover, "Allman Brothers Band: Did They Grieve?"; Betts, quoted in Gilmore, *Night Beat*, 130, 132; Gregg Allman, *My Cross to Bear*, 196–197; Betts, quoted in Paul, *One Way Out*, 60; Trucks, "Interview: Allman Brothers Butch Trucks."

19. Reniet Ramirez Rivera, "History-Intro."

20. Trucks, quoted in Crowe, "Allman Brothers Story."

21. Bill Brina, "That Allman-Geils Show"; Glover, "Allman Brothers Band: Did They Grieve?"

22. Andrew Elkind, "Off the Record: *Eat a Peach*," *Yale Daily News*, March 7, 1972.

23. Glover, "Allman Brothers Band: *Eat a Peach*."

Chapter 15. Epilogue (November 1972–October 2021)

1. Keyboard player Johnny Neel also served a short stint with the band for the 1989 *Dreams* tour.

2. Woody, "Allen Woody Interview"; Derek Trucks, quoted in Paul, *One Way Out*, 333; Pearson, quoted in Paul, *One Way Out*, 329.

3. Burbridge, quoted in Paul, *One Way Out*, 329; Haynes, quoted in Paul, *One Way Out*, 2nd ed., 414.

4. Gregg, quoted in Paul, *One Way Out*, 397.

5. Lane, post, July 25, 2016, Not Necessarily Stoned, but Beautiful, Facebook page.

6. Glover, "Allman Brothers Band: *Eat a Peach*."

7. Derek Trucks, quoted in Paul, *One Way Out*, 329.

REFERENCES

Abram, Malcolm X. "30 Years Down the Road." *Macon Telegraph*, October 21, 2001.

Ackerman, Paul. "Output of 2-LP Sets Up, Spurs Multiple Pricing." *Billboard*, October 16, 1971, 1, 62.

Albero, Richard. "A *Guitar Player* Tribute: Duane Allman 'Just Rock On, and Have You a Good Time.'" *Guitar Player*, June 1973.

Aledort, Andy. "Dickey Betts on Writing the Timeless Classic, 'Jessica.'" *Music Aficionado*, July 12, 2016.

Aledort, Andy, Alan Paul, and Jimmy Brown. "The Allman Brothers Band's 25 All-Time Greatest Songs." *Guitar World*, July 28, 2017.

Allison, David B. *Controversial Monuments and Memorials: A Guide for Community Leaders*. Lanham, MD: Rowman and Littlefield, 2018.

Allman, Duane. "Ed Shane Interview with Duane Allman (WPLO FM, 1970)." Audio recording. *The Duane Allman Dialogs*. Capricorn PRO-545, 1972.

———. "An Interview with Duane Allman of the Allman Brothers Band." *Free Press*, February 1, 1971.

———. "The Last Interview with Duane Allman." Interview by Laurel Dann. *Creem*, December 1973.

———. "A Moment Captured in Time: The *Crawdaddy* Interview with Duane Allman." *Hittin' the Note*, no. 26 (n.d.), 9–18.

Allman, Duane, and Berry Oakley. "Interview with Duane Allman and Berry Oakley." Interview by Jon Tiven. *New Haven Rock Press*, December 10, 1970.

Allman, Galadrielle. *Please Be with Me: A Song for My Father, Duane Allman*. New York: Random House, 2014.

Allman, Gregg. "Complete 2015 Interview with Gregg Allman." Interview by Alan Paul, June 5, 2017. Alanpaul.net.

———. "Gregg Allman—The 1977 'Inner-View' Radio Interview." 1977. YouTube video, 45:66, posted by jaxflfreebird. https://www.youtu.be/DUDux025Qro.

———. "Interview with Gregg Allman, May 27, 2002." Interview by Barney Hoskyns. Rock's Backpages. https://rocksbackpages.com.

———. *My Cross to Bear*. With Alan Light. New York: William Morrow, 2012.

Allman, Gregg, and Dickey Betts. "In the Studio with Redbeard: Allman Brothers Band—Live at Fillmore East." Interview, n.d. Redbeard's Blog. https://www.inthestudio.net/redbeards-blog/allman-brothers-band-live-fillmore-east-gregg-allman-dickey-betts/.

Allman Joys. "Allman Joys—Pensacola Beach 1966: Spanish Village Patio Pensacola Beach Friday July 22nd 1966." YouTube video, 32:44, posted December 2015 by mlbloverock. https://youtube.com/watch?v=IUoR3Ouzsuo.

Altschuler, Glenn C. *All Shook Up: How Rock 'n' Roll Changed America*. New York: Oxford University Press, 2005.

Anderson, Kirk. "*Hittin' the Note* Presents: Alex Cooley." *Hittin' the Note*, no. 12 (June 1995), 19–23.

Archer, Rowland. "The Night They Closed the Fillmore Down." *Hittin' the Note*, no. 12 (June 1995), 11–14.

Aregood, Rich. "*At Fillmore East* Review." *Philadelphia Daily News*, July 30, 1971.

Aronowitz, Alfred G. "Pop Music: The Most or Just the Mess?." *Saturday Evening Post*, July 15, 1967, 72.

Bangs, Lester. "The Allman Brothers Band: *The Allman Brothers Band*." *Rolling Stone*, February 21, 1970.

———. "Heavy Metal Brontosaurus M.O.R." *Creem*, May 1976.

Beaugez, Jim. "Jaimoe Johnson Marches to His Own Beat." *Mississippi Today*, February 17, 2017. https://mississippitoday.org/2017/02/17/jaimoe-johnson-marches-to-his-own-beat/.

Bernabei, Lynne. "Mother to an Allman Brother." *South Mississippi Sun*, June 4, 1974.

Bernarde, Scott. "Rock's Ramblin' Man." *Palm Beach Post*, January 12, 1995.

Bershaw, Alan. "Cream, Winterland, March 10, 1968 Early Show." Wolfgang's Vault. https://www.wolfgangs.com/music/cream/audio/408-1446.html?tid=23268.

Bertrand, Michael T. *Race, Rock, and Elvis*. Urbana: University of Illinois Press, 2005.

Betts, Dickey. "The Complete 1981 Dickey Betts Interview." Interview by Jas Obrecht, July 16, 1981.

———. "Dickey Betts Describes How It All Began." Interview by Jim Dorman. 2003. YouTube video, 2:54, posted by Jim Dorman. http://youtube.com/watch?v=pXJqr8yKWDE.

———. "Gibson Legend Dickey Betts Talks about Duane Allman and Southern Rock." Interview by Ted Drozdowski. *Gibson.com*, May 21, 2014.

Betts, Dickey, and Butch Trucks. "Interview—11/4/1984—Rock Influence (Official)." Interview by Pete Fornatale, November 4, 1984. YouTube video, 18:39, posted by Allman Brothers on MV. https://youtube.com/watch?v=rDDkDhCnh7E.

Blight, David W. *Beyond the Battlefield: Race, Memory and the American Civil War*. Amherst: University of Massachusetts Press, 2002.

———. *Race and Reunion: The Civil War in American Memory*. Cambridge, MA: Belknap Press of Harvard University Press, 2003.

Bomar, Scott B. *Southbound: An Illustrated History of Southern Rock*. San Francisco: Backbeat, 2014.

Bommba, E. Jr. "Prepared, Rehearsed, or Repeated." Letter to the editor. *Great Speckled Bird*, May 19, 1969, 6.

Bowden, Denny. "Early Daytona's Forgotten African American Communities— Waycross, Newtown, Midway, and Silver Hill." Blog post, February 15, 2004. *Volusia History: Retracing Florida's Past*. http://volusiahistory.wordpress. com/2014/02/15/early-daytonas-forgotten-african-american-communities- waycross-newtown-midway-and-silver-hill/.

Bozzo, John. "Beat Went on Despite Segregation." *Daytona Beach News Journal*, October 17, 2007.

Bramlett, Delaney. "The Delaney Bramlett Interviews 2008 (Part Two)." Interview by Michael Buffalo Smith. Swampland.com. http://swampland. com/articles/view/title:the_delaney_bramlett_interviews_2008_part_two_ duane_janis_and_eric.

Brant, Marley. *Southern Rockers: The Roots and Legacy of Southern Rock*. New York: Billboard, 1999.

Brina, Bill. "That Allman-Geils Show." *Albany Student Press*, December 3, 1971.

Brooks, Michael. "Meet Dick Betts." *Guitar Player*, October 1972, 20–24.

Campbell, Joseph L. "Red Dog." *The Legendary Red Dog: A Book of Tails*. Joseph L. Campbell, 2001.

Carr, Pete. "The Most Important Things in Life Are Rock and Roll, and a Hot Carr: An Interview with Muscle Shoals Guitar Legend, Pete Carr." Interview by Michael Buffalo Smith. Swampland.com, May 2000, http://swampland. com/articles/view/title:pete_carr.

Carr, Roy. "First Person Present 1972." *Hit Parader*, November 1972, 11.

Cash, W. J. *The Mind of the South*. New York: Alfred A. Knopf, 1941.

Charlton, Katherine. *Rock Music Styles: A History*. Boston: McGraw-Hill, 2003.

Chaze, William. "Allman Brothers' House Now Empty." *Tuscaloosa News*, January 26, 1973.

Clapton, Eric. *Clapton: The Autobiography*. New York: Broadway, 2007.

———. Interview by Robert Palmer. N.d. Robert Palmer Papers. Tulane University Hogan Jazz Archive, New Orleans, LA.

———. "Slowhand Remembers Skydog." Interview by Sam Hare. *Hittin' the Note*, no. 26 (n.d.), 19–23.

Coffin, Todd. "Birth of Community Rock Radio: A Brief History of KMPX and KSAN-FM; Historical Essay." *Found SF*, January 21, 2010. https://www. foundsf.org/index.php?title=Birth_of_Community_Rock_Radio:_A_brief_ history_of_KMPX_and_KSAN-FM.

Cohn, Nik. *Rock from the Beginning*. New York: Stein and Day, 1969.

Collins, Cindy. "Tony Glover Brings It on Home." Twin Cities Media Alliance, September 5, 2005. http://www.tcdailyplanet.net/tonygloverbringsithome/.

Conley, Jim. "Platter Chatter: Allmans, Canned Heat Cut Great New Albums." *El Paso Prospector*, July 1971.

Cooley, Alex. "The 2nd Atlanta International Pop Festival." N.d. http://alex-cooley.com/fest-atlpop2.html.

Coski, John M. *The Confederate Battle Flag: America's Most Embattled Emblem.* Cambridge, MA: Belknap, 2006.

Cox, Jim. "The Allman Brothers Band: Famous Band Arrested in Jackson, Spent the Night in the Clarke County Jail in 1971." *Clarke County Historical Society Quarterly*, 2016.

Cox, Karen L. *Dixie's Daughters: The United Daughters of the Confederacy and the Preservation of Confederate Culture.* Gainesville: University Press of Florida, 2004.

———. *No Common Ground: Confederate Monuments and the Ongoing Fight for Racial Justice.* Chapel Hill: University of North Carolina Press, 2021.

Crowe, Cameron. "The Allman Brothers Story." *Rolling Stone*, December 6, 1973: 46–54.

———. "Duane Allman—The Day the Music Died." *The Uncool: The Official Site for Everything Cameron Crowe.* 1989. https://www.theuncool.com/journalism/duane-allman-the-day-the-music-died/.

———. "The Sound of the South Sounds Fine." *Circular*, August 12, 1974.

Dale, Jon. "Butch Trucks on the Allmans' Wild Times at the Fillmore East." *Uncut*, September 14, 2014.

DeCurtis, Anthony, James Henke, and Holly George-Warren, eds. *The Rolling Stone Illustrated History of Rock 'n' Roll: The Definitive History of the Most Important Artists and Their Music.* 3rd ed. New York: Random House, 1992.

Dollar, Steve. "Duane Allman Left Tragic but Lasting Musical Legacy," *Wilmington Star-News*, November 17, 1996.

Dove, Ian. "Talent in Action: Delaney and Bonnie and Friends Carnegie Hall, New York." *Billboard*, October 17, 1970, 26.

Dowd, Tom. "From the Manhattan Project to the Allman Brothers Band: An Interview with Tom Dowd." Interview by Michael Buffalo Smith. Swampland.com, Fall 2002. http://swampland.com/articles/view/title:tom_dowd.

Dubro, Alex. "Them Vino-Lovin' Allman Brothers." *Rolling Stone*, March 4, 1971.

Ector, Bill. "The Allman Brothers Band Hall of Fame Induction," *Hittin' the Note*, n.d.

Edmonds, Ben. "The Allman Brothers Band: *The Allman Brothers Band.*" *Fusion*, February 20, 1970.

———. "Snapshots of the South: The Allman Brothers and Capricorn Records." *Creem*, November 1972.

Edmondson, Patrick. "A Bus Stops in Piedmont Park July 7, 1969." Strip Project, February 20, 2014. http://www.thestripproject.com/a-bus-stops-in-piedmont-park-july-7–1969/.

———. "May 11 Be-In in Piedmont—Meet The Allman Brothers Atlanta!" Strip Project, February 27, 2014.

Edwards, Gavin. "The Allman Brothers Band: 30 Years of Ups and Downs; The Music Got Them, and after Three Decades They're Still Going Wherever It Takes to Play." *Rolling Stone*, November 25, 1999.

Eldredge, Richard L. "What a Splash: Recalling Georgia's 'Woodstock.'" *Atlanta Journal-Constitution*, July 4, 1995.

Elkind, Andrew. "Off the Record: *Eat a Peach*." *Yale Daily News*, March 7, 1972, 2.

Emerson, Ken. *Always Magic in the Air: The Bomp and Brilliance of the Brill Building Era*. New York: Penguin, 2006.

Ertegun, Ahmet. *"What'd I Say?" The Atlantic Story: 50 Years of Music*. New York: Welcome Rain, 2001.

Eure, Roy. "Vibrations." *Hattiesburg American*, April 18, 1970.

Fentress, Anne, dir. *American Revolutions: Southern Rock*. Film. CMT, 2005.

Fine, Marshall. "Allman Live Recording Best." *The Minneapolis Star*, August 3, 1971.

FitzGerald, Michael Ray. *Jacksonville and the Roots of Southern Rock*. Gainesville: University Press of Florida, 2020.

Fletcher, Tony. *In the Midnight Hour: The Life & Soul of Wilson Pickett*. New York: Oxford University Press, 2017.

Francis, Miller Jr. "The Allman Brothers Band." *Great Speckled Bird*, May 19, 1969, cover, 10–11.

———. "Records: The Allman Brothers Band: *Idlewild South* (Atco Capricorn SD 33–342)." *Great Speckled Bird*, November 9, 1970, 8.

Freeman, Scott. *Midnight Riders: The Story of the Allman Brothers Band*. Boston: Little, Brown, 1995.

Furia, Philip. *The Poets of Tin Pan Alley: A History of America's Great Lyricists*. Oxford, England: Oxford University Press, 1992.

Gibson, Janet. "Butch Trucks." *Gamecock*, September 29, 1978.

Gillespie, Jim. "Bassist Paces Allman Brothers before Appreciative Audience." *Minneapolis Star*, October 1, 1971.

———. "Muscle Shoals Has Newest Sound Around." *Minneapolis Star*, June 18, 1970.

Gilmore, Mikal. *Night Beat: A Shadow History of Rock 'n' Roll*. New York: Anchor, 1999.

Glassenberg, Bob. "Campus Programming Aids." *Billboard*, January 23, 1971, 38.

Glover, Bo, and Mike Dugo. "The Roemans." *Beyond the Beat Generation*. N.d. http://www.beyondthebeatgeneration.com/roemans.html.

Glover, Tony. "The Allman Brothers: Saturday Night Fish Fry." Capricorn Records, July 1971.

———. "The Allman Brothers Band: Did They Grieve?" *Circus*, May 5, 1972.

———. "The Allman Brothers Band: *Eat a Peach*." *Rolling Stone*, April 13, 1972.

———. "In This Band You Better Come to Pick." *Circus*, March 1971.

Gold, Richard. "The Allman Brothers Band: The People Still Want Them to Play All Night." *Rock*, June 19, 1972: 16–18.

Goldstein, Richard. "Pop Eye: 69 with a Bullet, Part II." From *Village Voice* December 1, 1966. New York Radio Archive. http://www.nyradioarchive.com/images/radioscans/WORFM_VV_19661201.pdf.

Gordon, Robert. *Respect Yourself: Stax Records and the Soul Explosion*. New York: Bloomsbury, 2013.

Gould, Jonathan. *Can't Buy Me Love: The Beatles, Britain, and America*. New York: Three Rivers, 2008.

———. *Otis Redding: An Unfinished Life* New York: Crown Archetype, 2017.

Gracyk, Theodore. *Rhythm and Noise: An Aesthetics of Rock*. Durham, NC: Duke University Press, 1996.

Graham, Bill. With Robert Greenfield. *Bill Graham Presents: My Life Inside Rock and Out*. New York: Doubleday, 1992.

Guralnick, Peter. *Careless Love: The Unmaking of Elvis Presley*. Boston: Back Bay, 2000.

———. *Last Train to Memphis: The Rise of Elvis Presley*. Boston: Little, Brown, 1994.

———. *Sam Phillips: The Man Who Invented Rock 'n' Roll*. New York: Little, Brown, 2015.

———. *Sweet Soul Music: Rhythm and Blues and the Southern Dream of Freedom*. Boston: Little, Brown, 1999.

Hall, Mitchell K. *The Emergence of Rock and Roll: Music and the Rise of American Youth Culture*. London: Routledge, 2014.

Hall, Rick. *The Man from Muscle Shoals: My Journey from Shame to Fame*. Monterey, CA: Heritage Builders, 2015.

Hall, Russell. "Capricorn Records." Swampland.com, April 2004. http://www.swampland.com/articles/view/title:capricorn_records.

———. "How the Allman Brothers Band Launched Southern Rock." *Gibson.com*, June 11, 2013. http://www.gibson.com/news-lifestyle/features/en-us/allman-brothers-band-launched-southern-rock.aspx/.

Hamilton, Bob. "Capricorn Records." *Operating Manual for Starship Radio '73*, 367. Los Angeles: Bob D. Hamilton, 1973. Page posted at http://americanradiohistory.com/hd2/IDX-Business/Music/Archive-Tip-Sheets/IDX/Hamilton/Starship-Radio-1973-Full-OCR-Page-0369.pdf#search=%22allman%22.

Hamilton, Jack. *Just around Midnight: Rock and Roll and the Racial Imagination*. Cambridge, MA: Harvard University Press, 2016.

Harris, June. "Getting Together with the Allman Brothers." *Hit Parader*, September 1970.

Harris, Mark. "The Flowering of the Hippies." *Atlantic*, September 1967.

Hartsook, Dick. "Off the Record." *Abilene* (TX) *Reporter-News*, October 18, 1970.

Hey, Ken, dir. *Southern Voices, American Dream*. Film. 1976.

Hickey, Dave. "Why the Allmans Died Young." *Village Voice*, October 11, 1976, 12–13.

Hogerty, Dave. "Eulogy to a Friend: Tom Dowd, the Language of Music." *Hittin' the Note*, no. 43 (2004), 34–37.

Hornsby, Paul. "I Need More Respect Than This." Interview by Jake Feinberg. *Jake Feinberg Show*, June 3, 2017.

———. "Paul Hornsby: The *Kudzoo* Interview." Interview by Michael Buffalo Smith. *Kudzoo*, March 2017, 9–31.

———. "Paul Hornsby's Memories with Duane Allman." Big House Museum, November 19, 2016. YouTube video, 2:29. https://www.youtube.com/watch?v=2PMfEiCSUL4.

Hoskyns, Barney. "Southern Men: The Long Tall Saga of the Allman Brothers Band." *Mojo*, December 2002.

Huber, Patrick. *Linthead Stomp: The Creation of Country Music in the Piedmont South.* Chapel Hill: University of North Carolina Press, 2008.

Hughes, Charles L. *Country Soul: Making Music and Making Race in the American South.* Chapel Hill: University of North Carolina Press, 2015.

Jacques, Geoffrey. "Listening to Jazz." In *American Popular Music: New Approaches to the Twentieth Century*, edited by Rachel Rubin and Jeffrey Paul Melnick, 87–90. Amherst: University of Massachusetts Press, 2001.

Johanson, Jai Johanny "Jaimoe." Afterword to *One Way Out: The Inside History of the Allman Brothers Band*, by Alan Paul. New York: St. Martin's Griffin, 2nd edition, 2015, 424–425.

———. "Allman Brothers Drummer Jaimoe Remembers Gregg Allman." Interview by Paul Alan. *Rolling Stone*, June 2, 2017. http://www.rollingstone.com/music/news/allman-brothers-drummer-jaimoe-remembers-gregg-allman-w485240.

———. "Allman Joy: Jai Johanny 'Jaimoe' Johanson on The Allman Brothers Band's Legacy." Interview by Ken Sharp. *Rock Cellar Magazine*, December 10, 2014.

———. "Interview: Jaimoe." Interview by McClain Johnson. Bands That Jam, November 12, 2014. Posted at https://web.archive.org/web/20170531163505/http://www.bandsthatjam.com/bands-that-jam-jam-bands/allman-brothers-band/interview-jaimoe/.

———. "Jaimoe—Founding Member of the Allman Brothers Band." Interview by Brian Whitley. 11th Hour Online, March 21, 2016. http://11thhouronline.com/2016/03/21/jaimo-founding-member-of-the-allman-brothers-band/.

———. "Jaimoe Johanson Interview." February 2009. YouTube video, 2:26, posted by moogisvideo. https://youtube.com/watch?v=Wo-qqND1t5U.

———. "Reflections: The World According to Jaimoe." Interview by John Lynskey, Kirk West, and Glenn White. *Hittin' the Note*, no. 21 (1998), 18–30.

———. "Reflections 2: The World According to Jaimoe." Interview by John Lynskey. *Hittin' the Note*, no. 22 (n.d.), 23–29.

Jones, Landon Y. "Swinging 60s?" *Smithsonian*, January 2006, 102.

Jourard, Marty. *Music Everywhere: The Rock and Roll Roots of a Southern Town.* Gainesville: University Press of Florida, 2016.

Keith, Michael C. *Sounds in the Dark: All-Night Radio in American Life.* Ames: Iowa State University Press, 2001.

———. *Voices in the Purple Haze: Underground Radio and the Sixties.* Westport, CT: Praeger, 1997.

Kelly, Ernie. "Presenting: The Allmans Rocking thru Four Sides." *Denisonian*, March 17, 1972.

Kerzner, Barry. "Butch Trucks Proud of Allman Brothers Legacy and His Freight Train." *American Blues Scene* January 26, 2017. https://www.americanblues-cene.com/2017/01/butch-trucks-proud-allman-brothers-legacy-freight-train/.

Kimball, George. "The Allman Brothers Band: *At Fillmore East*." *Rolling Stone*, August 19, 1971.

Knopper, Steve. "The Rope: The Forgotten History of Segregated Rock 'n' Roll Concerts." *Rolling Stone*, November 16, 2017. http://www.rollingstone.com/music/features/rocks-early-segregated-days-the-forgotten-history-w509481.

Kowalke, Pete. "Pete Kowalke of Cowboy: The GRITZ Interview." Interview by Michael Buffalo Smith. Swampland.com, n.d. http://swampland.com/articles/view/title:pete_kowalke_of_cowboy_the_gritz_interview.

Kyle, Dave. "Berry Oakley." *Vintage Guitar Magazine*, December 1996, retrieved from http://www.duaneallman.info/berryoakley.htm.

———. "Remembering Duane Allman." *Vintage Guitar Magazine*, January 1997, retrieved from http://www.duaneallman.info/rememberingduaneallman.htm.

Landau, Jon. "Allman Brothers Band: Homage to the King." *The Phoenix*, August 24, 1971, 16.

———. "Bandleader Duane Allman Dies in Bike Crash." *Rolling Stone*, November 25, 1971, 5–6.

———. "Loose Ends: Duane Allman, the Sky Is Crying." *The Phoenix*, November 10, 1971, 46.

———. "More on Duane Allman." *The Phoenix*, December 3, 1971, 47.

Lasko, Stephen. "Allman Brothers Rock on without Duane." *Commonwealth Times*, April 6, 1972, 3.

Lawson, Tom, and Michael Koepenick. *Basically Frightened: The Musical Madness of Colonel Bruce Hampton*. DVD, 2012.

Leimbacher, Ed. "Review: *Idlewild South*." *Rolling Stone*, December 24, 1970.

Lemlich, Jeff. "All Over but the Crying: The Sandpipers Story." *Soul Up North*, no. 43. Posted to Spectropop, http://spectropop.com/Sandpipers/.

———. *Savage Lost: Florida Garage Bands, the '60s and Beyond*. Plantation, FL: Distinctive, 1992.

Levin, Kevin M. *Searching for Black Confederates: The Civil War's Most Persistent Myth*. Chapel Hill: University of North Carolina Press, 2019.

Lewis, Grover. "Hitting the Note with the Allman Brothers Band." *Rolling Stone*, November 25, 1971, 52–55.

Live for Live Music. "Gregg Allman Praises New Band, Says to Burn Every Confederate Flag." July 21, 2015. https://liveforlivemusic.com/news/gregg-allman-new-band-burn-every-confederate-flag/.

Lynskey, John. "Lamar Williams: Out of the Shadows." *Hittin' the Note*, no. 17, n.d., 20–28.

Malone, Bill C., and David Stricklin. *Southern Music/American Music*. Lexington: University Press of Kentucky, 2003.

Mandel, Ellen. "The Georgia Peach." *Guitar World*, November 1991, 47–49, 73, 107.

Manis, Andrew Michael. *Macon Black and White: An Unutterable Separation in the American Century*. Macon, GA: Mercer University Press, 2004.

Mankin, Bill. "We Can All Join In: How Rock Festivals Helped Change America." *Like the Dew*, 2011.

Manley, Dan. "Blues for a Brother." *Macon Telegraph*, October 29, 1971.

Marshall, Joe. "Duane Allman: Memories from His Friend, Joe Marshall." Interview by Russell Hall. *Gibson Brands Features, Articles, and Interviews*, July 26, 2013. http://www.gibson.com/news-lifestyle/features/en-us/duane-allman-memories-from-his-friend-joe-marshall.aspx.

Mazor, Barry. *Meeting Jimmie Rodgers: How America's Original Roots Music Hero Changed the Pop Sounds of a Century*. Oxford, England: Oxford University Press, 2009.

McEuen, John. "John McEuen." Interview by Derek Halsey. Swampland.com, January 2002. http://swampland.com/articles/view/title:john_mceuen.

McNally, Dennis. *A Long Strange Trip: The Inside History of the Grateful Dead*. New York: Bantam, 2002.

Meeks, John. "A Tale of the Second Coming." *Hittin' the Note*, no. 21 (1998), 34–36.

Meltzer, Richard. *The Aesthetics of Rock*. New York: Something Else, 1970.

Miles, Barry. *The British Invasion: The Music, the Times, the Era*. New York: Sterling, 2009.

Miles, Floyd. "Floyd Miles." Interview by Michael Buffalo Smith. Swampland. com, October 2004. http://swampland.com/articles/view/title:floyd_miles.

———. "Young Duane Allman: The Floyd Miles Interview." Interview by Jas Obrecht, May 18, 1982. At http://jasobrecht.com/young-duane-allman-floyd-miles-interview/.

Miller, James. *Flowers in the Dustbin: The Rise of Rock and Roll 1947–1977*. New York: Simon and Schuster, 2000.

Morris, Wesley. "Why Is Everyone Always Stealing Black Music?." *New York Times Magazine*, August 14, 2019. https://www.nytimes.com/interactive/2019/08/14/magazine/music-black-culture-appropriation.html.

Myers, Marc. *Anatomy of a Song: The Oral History of 45 Iconic Hits That Changed Rock, R&B, and Pop*. New York: Grove, Atlantic, 2016.

National Center for Education Statistics. "Table 101.10. Estimates of Resident Population, by Age Group: 1970 through 2018." *Digest of Education Statistics, 2018*. http://nces.ed.gov/programs/digest/d18/tables/dt18_101.10.asp.

Neal, James. "47 Years Ago This Weekend, Love Valley Hosted Its Version of

Woodstock. This Is What It Looked Like." *Statesville (NC) Record and Land-mark*, July 15, 2017.

Neal, Jocelyn R. *The Songs of Jimmie Rodgers: A Legacy in Country Music*. Bloom-ington: Indiana University Press, 2009.

Neer, Richard. *FM: The Rise and Fall of Rock Radio*. New York: Villard, 2001.

Newton, Steve. "Dickey Betts Figures Duane Allman Is Playing 'Dreams' in Heaven with Hendrix." Ear of Newt, April 12, 2014. https://earofnewt.com/2014/04/12/dickey-betts-figures-duane-allman-is-playing-dreams-in-heaven-with-hendrix/.

Nicholls, David, ed. *The Cambridge History of American Music*. New York: Cam-bridge University Press, 1998.

Nolan, Tom. *The Allman Brothers Band: A Biography in Words and Pictures*. New York: Sire Books and Chappell Music, 1976.

Oakley, Berry, and Duane Allman. "Berry Oakley and Duane Allman 06/06/71 Houston, TX Interview." *Down in Texas '71*. Allman Brothers Band Recording, 2021.

Oakley, Candace. "Memories of a Brother." *Hittin' the Note*, no. 3 (Winter 1993), 13–14.

Obrecht, Jas. "Duane Allman Remembered." *Guitar Player*, October 1981, 33–36, 42–54.

Ochs, Ed. "Tomorrow: The Allman Brothers Band." *Billboard*, December 27, 1969.

O'Connor, Rory. "The Allman Brothers: Power and Energy." *Tampa Tribune*, November 28, 1969.

———. "Allman Brothers Shake Electric Zoo." *Tampa Tribune*, August 30, 1969.

———. "*Idlewild South* Is a Hit." *Tampa Tribune*, October 31, 1970.

Ogden, John. "Berry Oakley: The Hoochie Coochie Man." *Hittin' the Note*, no. 22 (n.d.), 30–35.

———. "First There Is a Mountain." *Hittin' the Note*, no. 22 (n.d.), 9–22.

Olszewski, Mike. *Radio Daze: Stories from the Front in Cleveland's FM Air Wars*. Kent, OH: Kent State University Press, 2003.

O'Neil, Tim. "A Look Back: Gaslight Square in St. Louis Burned Brightly but Briefly in the 1960s." *St. Louis Post-Dispatch*, March 23, 2013.

Ochsenreiter, Butch. "Plastic Rap." *The Ridgerunner*, November 4, 1970, 11.

O'Dell, Tom, dir. *Song of the South: Duane Allman and the Rise of the Allman Brothers*. Prism Films, 2013.

Palmer, Robert. "Allman Brothers Band." Unpublished essay, 1979. Robert Palmer Papers, Tulane University Hogan Jazz Archive, New Orleans, LA.

———. "Allman Brothers Band: A Great Southern Revival." *Rolling Stone*, May 3, 1979.

———. *Deep Blues*. New York: Penguin, 1982.

———. Liner notes in *Kind of Blue*, Miles Davis. Album. Columbia/Legacy, CK 64935, 1997.

———. "Memphis Underground." *Changes* 1, no. 13 (1969), 14–15, 27. At Robert Palmer Papers, Tulane University Hogan Jazz Archive, New Orleans, LA.

————. *Rock 'n' Roll: An Unruly History*. New York: Harmony, 1995.

Paul, Alan. "Gregg Allman 1947–2017: Bidding Farewell to a Southern Rock Legend." *Guitar World*, July 25, 2017. https://www.guitarworld.com/artists/gregg-allman-1947–2017-bidding-farewell-southern-rock-legend.

————. "Lowdown and Dirty: Gregg Allman; Looking Back . . . Looking Forward." *Hittin' the Note*, no. 26 (n.d.), 46–54.

————. "Lowdown and Dirty: Shades of Dickey Betts." *Hittin' the Note*, no. 22 (n.d.), 51.

————. *One Way Out: The Inside History of the Allman Brothers Band*. New York: St. Martin's, 2014; St. Martin's Griffin, 2nd edition, 2015.

————. "Why Duane Allman Didn't Want to Be the Next Hendrix." Musicaficionado.com, November 15, 2016. https://web.musicaficionado.com/main.html#!/article/duane_allmans_greatest_talent_was_his_generosity_by_alanpaul?invitedBy=concordmusicgroup&utm_source=facebook&utm_campaign=fanpage.

Peretti, Burton W. *Jazz in American Culture*. Chicago: Ivan R. Dee, 1997.

Perkins, Willie. *No Saints, No Saviors: My Years with the Allman Brothers Band*. Macon, GA: Mercer University Press, 2005.

Perkins, Willie, and Jack Weston. *The Allman Brothers Band: Classic Memorabilia 1969–1976*. Macon, GA: Mercer University Press, 2015.

Pierce, Dave. *Riding on the Ether Express: A Memoir of 1960s Los Angeles, the Rise of Freeform Underground Radio, and the Legendary KPPC-FM*. Lafayette: Center for Louisiana Studies, University of Louisiana, 2008.

Podell, Jon. "Jon Podell: Booking the Best Band in the Land." Interview by Kirk West. *Hittin' the Note*, no. 25 (n.d.), 30–41.

Poe, Randy. *Skydog: The Duane Allman Story*. San Francisco: Backbeat, 2006.

Porter, Henry. "First There Is a Mountain." *Creative Loafing*, December 28, 1981.

Pratt, Hal. "The Critic's Opinion: *Eat a Peach*." *Daily Illini*, April 11, 1972, 15.

Racine, Marty. "The Allman Brothers: The Road Back Was No Paved Interstate." *Milwaukee Sentinel*, June 15, 1979.

Ramirez Rivera, Reniet. "History-Intro." Mar y Sol Pop Festival, Puerto Rico, 1972. http://marysol-festival.com/history-intro/.

Rauch, Dale. "In One Ear: Review of *Eat a Peach*." *Ithacan*, April 6, 1972, 13.

Richardson, John H. "What Gregg Allman's Learned about Life, Music, and Women." *Esquire*, October 30, 2013. http://www.esquire.com/blogs/news/gregg-allman-interview-0114.

Richardson, Peter. *No Simple Highway: A Cultural History of the Grateful Dead*. New York: St. Martin's, 2015.

Roe, Tommy. *From Cabbagetown to Tinseltown and Places in Between: The Autobiography of Tommy Roe*. North Charleston, SC: Tommy Roe, on CreateSpace, 2016.

Rogers, Kim. "Rock Minstrel's Life Not Rosey." *Florida State Flambeau*, October 12, 1970, 1, 8.

Rose, Steven. "How the Ludlow Garage Transformed Cincinnati's Youth Culture." *Cincinnati Magazine*, September 16, 2019. https://www.cincinnatimagazine.com/article/how-the-ludlow-garage-transformed-cincinnatis-youth-culture/.

Rudis, Al. "*At Fillmore East* Review." *Corpus Christi Times*, September 25, 1971.

Sandlin, Anathalee. *A Never-Ending Groove: Johnny Sandlin's Musical Odyssey.* Macon, GA: Mercer University Press, 2012.

Sandmel, Ben. Liner notes in *Live at Ludlow Garage: 1970.* Allman Brothers Band, Polydor Records, 843 260–2, 1990.

Santosuosso, Ernie. "Allman Blues Superior Stuff." *Boston Globe*, August 15, 1971.

Scheurer, Timothy E., ed. *The Age of Rock: Readings from the Popular Press.* Volume 2 of *American Popular Music.* Bowling Green, OH: Bowling Green University Popular Press, 1989.

Schuck, Nic. "Allman Brothers Band Classic Penned in Pensacola." Sands Paper, n.d.

Scoppa, Bud. *The Rock People: Interviews with 13 Top Stars and Groups.* New York: Scholastic, 1973.

Selvin, Joel. "Duane Allman." *Earth*, January 1971.

———. "What Southern Boys Can Do with Rock." *San Francisco Chronicle*, February 14, 1971.

Shafer, William J. "Jazz." In *The New Encyclopedia of Southern Culture: Music*, edited by Bill C. Malone, 83–88. Chapel Hill: University of North Carolina Press, 2008.

Shepherd, John, and David Horn, eds. *Genres: North America.* Volume 8 of *Continuum Encyclopedia of Popular Music of the World.* New York: Continuum International, 2012.

Shepley, Jim. "Young Duane Allman: The Jim Shepley Interview." Interview by Jas Obrecht, May 12, 1982. http://jasobrecht.com/.

Sherling, Rankin. "Southern Rock." In *The New Encyclopedia of Southern Culture: Music*, edited by Bill C. Malone. Chapel Hill: University of North Carolina Press, 2008.

Silver, Ward H. "*Win, Lose, or Draw*." *Great Speckled Bird*, October 2, 1975, 12.

Sitz, Dave. "Allman Brothers Overcome Tragedy." *Daily Iowan*, September 28, 1973.

Sklar, Rick. *Rocking America: An Insider's Story—How the All-Hit Radio Stations Took Over* (New York: St. Martin's, 1984).

Smith, Michael Buffalo, and Roxanne Crutcher. *Capricorn Rising: Conversations in Southern Rock.* Macon, GA: Mercer University Press, 2016.

Smith, Suzanne E. *Dancing in the Street: Motown and the Cultural Politics of Detroit.* Cambridge, MA: Harvard University Press, 1999.

Snider, Eric. "Brothers Forever." *Sarasota Herald-Tribune*, January 11, 1995.

Snyder-Scumpy, Patrick. "The Allman Brothers: Boogie or Bust!" *Crawdaddy*, October 1973.

Reiff, Corbin. "Allman Brothers Band's Legendary 1971 Fillmore East Run: An Oral History." *Rolling Stone*, March 11, 2016.

Spangler, Kevin, and Ron Currens. "Butch Trucks, the Different Drummer." *Hittin' the Note*, no. 15 (Fall 1996), 4–14.

Spitz, Bob. *The Beatles: The Biography*. New York: Little, Brown, 2005.

St. Pierre, Roger. "The Allman Brothers: A Rock Tragedy." *New Musical Express*, December 9, 1972.

Stephans, Michael. *Experiencing Jazz: A Listener's Companion*. Lanham, MD: Scarecrow, 2013.

Sterling, Christopher H., and Michael C. Keith. *Sounds of Change: A History of FM Broadcasting in America*. Chapel Hill: University of North Carolina Press, 2008.

Stevens, Stuart. "Allman Brothers Introduce New Abilities in *Idlewild South*." *The Catalyst*, October 23, 1970.

Szatmary, David P. *Rockin' in Time: A Social History of Rock-and-Roll*. 3rd ed. Upper Saddle River, NJ: Prentice Hall, 1996.

Takiff, Jonathan. "Allman Brothers Sounding Better All the Time to an Ex-Skeptic." *Philadelphia Daily News*, August 27, 1970.

Tatangelo, Wade. "Dickey Betts on His Most Famous Allman Brothers Songs." *Sarasota Herald-Tribune*, October 30, 2014.

Thurman, Howard. *With Head and Heart: The Autobiography of Howard Thurman*. New York: Harcourt Brace Jovanovich, 1979.

Tolinski Brad, and Alan Di Perna. *Play It Loud: An Epic History of the Style, Sound, and Revolution of the Electric Guitar*. New York: Doubleday, 2016.

Tolleson, Robin. "Jaimoe." *Modern Drummer*, January 2018.

Townley, Ray. "Makin' It in Macon." *Downbeat*, September 12, 1974, 16–17, 36, 40.

Trucks, Butch. "Butch Trucks on Berry Oakley." Duane Allman—Skydog Fan Page, February 17, 2016. https://www.facebook.com/groups/Skydog/?fref=nf.

———. Foreword to *One Way Out: The Inside History of the Allman Brothers Band*, by Alan Paul, xx–xxi. New York: St. Martin's, 2014.

———. "Interview: Allman Brothers Butch Trucks on Closing Fillmore East, Favorite ABB Tunes." Interview by Jim Clash. Forbes.com, April 9, 2016.

Vining, Dan. "Good Blues Music 'Thanks to the South': Allman Bros. Band Disk; It Moves." *Florida Alligator*, January 15, 1970.

Waddell, Ray. "An American Classic: The Allman Brothers Band *Billboard* Salute." *Billboard*, December 18, 1999, 19–21, 30–34.

Wald, Elijah. *How the Beatles Destroyed Rock 'n' Roll: An Alternative History of American Popular Music*. New York: Oxford University Press, 2009.

Walker, Jesse. *Rebels on the Air: An Alternative History of Radio in America*. New York: New York University Press, 2001.

Ward, Brian. *Just My Soul Responding: Rhythm and Blues, Black Consciousness, and Race Relations*. Berkeley: University of California Press, 1998.

Ward, Ed. *The History of Rock 'n' Roll. Volume 1: 1920–1963*. New York: Flatiron, 2016.

Ward, Ed, Geoffrey Stokes, and Ken Tucker. *Rock of Ages: The Rolling Stone History of Rock 'n' Roll*. New York: Rolling Stone, Fireside, 1993.

Watts, Michael. "The Allmans Are to America Now What the Grateful Dead Were in '67." *Melody Maker*, August 25, 1973.

Werner, Craig. *A Change Is Gonna Come: Music, Race, and Soul of America*. Ann Arbor: University of Michigan Press, 2006.

West, Kirk. "Ahmet Ertegun: A Six-Point Perspective." *Hittin' the Note*, no. 50 (2006), 24–25.

———. "Col. Bruce Reflects on Jaimoe." *Hittin' the Note*, no. 21 (1998), 30–32.

West, Kirsten. "History of the Big House." The Big House: The Allman Brothers Museum, April 29, 2009. http://web.archive.org/web/20090429065212/www.thebighousemuseum.org:80/history.htm.

———. "Inside Dickey Betts." *Hittin' the Note*, no. 10 (Fall 1994), 10.

Wexler, Jerry. With David Ritz. *Rhythm and the Blues: A Life in American Music*. New York: St. Martin's, 1994.

Whitlock, Bobby, with Marc Roberty. *Bobby Whitlock: A Rock 'n' Roll Autobiography*. Jefferson, NC: McFarland, 2011.

Wise, Steve. "Non-Event." *Great Speckled Bird*, May 19, 1969, 3.

Wishik, Gary. "S.B. 'House' Band Rivaled by Live Album." *Statesman*, September 17, 1971.

———. "Sweet Wine: Delaney & Bonnie *Motel Shot*." *Statesman*, April 27, 1971, 14.

Woody, Allen. "Allen Woody Interview." Interview by Bill Ector. *Hittin' the Note*, Fall 1993.

Wren, John. "Records." *The Technician*, January 14, 1970, 3, 8.

Wright, Christina M. "Historical Marker to Recognize 1970 Byron Pop Festival." *Macon Telegraph*, September 11, 2012.

Wyker, John D. "John D. Wyker's Cat Tales—Macon & Capricorn Records." Swampland.com, n.d. http://www.swampland.com/articles/view/title:john_d_wykers_cat_tales__macon__capricorn_records.

Wynn, Tom. "Tom Wynn of Cowboy: The GRITZ Interview." Swampland.com, n.d. http://swampland.com/articles/view/title:tom_wynn_of_cowboy_the_gritz_interview.

Zanes, Warren. *Petty: The Biography*. New York: Henry Holt, 2016.

Zellner, Xander. "Bobby Vee's Top 10 Biggest Billboard Hits." *Billboard*, October 24, 2016. https://www.billboard.com/articles/columns/chart-beat/7550125/bobby-vee-biggest-billboard-hits.

INDEX

Oteil; Coltrane, John; Davis, Miles; Johanson, Jai Johanny "Jaimoe"

Jefferson Airplane, 57, 61, 91

Johanson, Jai Johanny "Jaimoe": Carnegie Hall and, 83, 194; as drummer, 8, 79, 94–96, 108, *150, 152, 163, 166*, 175–76, 193, 200–201; Duane's death and, 188, 192; early career, 8, 83–85; firing of, 197 199; jazz music's influence on, 83–86, 105, 112, 123, 176; musical bond with Duane, 14, 86; official name, 10; projects after ABB, 202; race and racism, 87, 99–100, 129, 131–32

Johnson, Helen, 83

Johnson, Jimmy, 22, 54, 72–74

Johnson, Robert, 9, 30, 41, 90, 112. "Come on in My Kitchen," 29, 186; "Crossroads," 52; slide guitar and, 82

Johnson, Terry, 48–49

Jones, Elvin, 84, 86

Joplin, Janis, 57–58

Jourard, Marty, 48, 120

Keller, Bob, 56

Killen, Buddy, 53, 77

Kimball, George, 184–85

Kowalke, Pete, 33

Landau, Jon, 23, 25, 36, 49–50, 72, 77, 116, 190

Law, Don, 116–17, 120

Leavell, Chuck, 12, *164*, 198, 201–2

Lebanon, TN: Bradley's Barn studio, 52; Castle Heights Military Academy, 18, 216n15

Led Zeppelin, 41, 77, 91, 121, 137, 140–41

Leimbacher, Ed, 137–38

"Les Brers in A Minor," 192–93, 202

Lesh, Phil, 92, 110

Lewis, Grover, 26–27

Liberty Records: Gregg and, 69, 98; *Hour Glass* and, 60–61; onerous contract and, 13, 57–58, 66–67; *Power of Love* and, 62; rejection of FAME sessions, 65–66. *See also* Smith, Dallas

Lipham, Buster, 120. *See also* Gainesville, FL

"Little Martha," 192–93, 200

Live at Ludlow Garage 1970 (1990), 135

Los Angeles, CA: ABB and, 55–62; West Coast rock scene and, 45, 53

Lost Cause, 5

Loudermilk, John D., 18, 47, 52–53, 55, 60

Love Valley, NC: Love Valley Festival, 135, 147

Lyndon, Twiggs, 87, *168;* arrest and, 129–30; Johanson and, 84–85; as road manager, 103, 119, 127; Vietnam and, 134

Lynyrd Skynyrd, 4, 7, 51

Macon, GA: ABB road crew and, *158;* Betts's last show in, *155;* Big House, 10, 144, *153;* Big House Museum, *166*, 209; Central City Park, 111; College Discotheque, 114; Duane's death and funeral, *169*, 187, 191; Duane's last show in, *151;* Gregg and, 108; as home base, 116, 135, 145; *Idlewild South* and, 132–33; Jaimoe and, 84–85; integration and, 132; relocation to, 14, 102–3; Rose Hill Cemetery, *162, 167*, 188; southern rock scene and, 39. *See also* Walden, Phil

Marks, Jan, 12

Marshall, Jim, *158, 166*

Marshall, Joe, 22

McEuen, Bill, 57, 61–62, 65

McEuen, John, 56, 59, 61, 66, 99

McKinney, Mabron, 57

"Melissa," 68, 70, *169*, 191–93, 221n14

"Midnight Rider," 133, 138

Miles, Floyd, 43–45. *See also* Daytona Beach, FL

Monterey International Pop Festival, 58, 102

"Mountain Jam," 29, 111, 128, 135–36, 175, 192–93, 195, 200; *At Fillmore East* and, 178, 187; folk influence on, 1, 110

Muscle Shoals, AL, 39, 50, 71; FAME Studios, 7, 18, 62, 64–67, 72–79, 87, 201; Muscle Shoals Sound, 71, 221n1

Music critics. *See* Dubro, Alex; Edmonds, Ben; Francis, Miller, Jr.; Glover, Tony; Harris, Mark; Kimball, George; Landau, Jon; Leimbacher, Ed; Lewis, Grover; Ochs, Ed; O'Connor, Rory; Scoppa, Bud; Selvin, Joel; Stevens, Stuart

Music industry: centrality of Chicago, New York, Nashville, and Los Angeles, 3, 45; double albums and, 234–35n13; drug culture and, 105; live albums and, 172–74; Motown and, 65; race and, 58, 103; Southern rock and, 3–7, 142; Teen Idols, 59–60. *See also* Atlantic Records; Capricorn Records; Liberty Records; Vanguard Records

Music obsessive. History geek. Southerner. Guitar player. Public historian. Teacher. Writer. Fan. Bob Beatty grew up devouring his mom's Beatles and dad's Hank Williams and bluegrass records. Throughout his life he's interwoven his love of punk rock, the Allman Brothers Band, and his band Jam Depression as a historian, fan, and musician. It was only a matter of time that enduring passion culminated in a PhD and publication of *Play All Night! Duane Allman and the Journey to Fillmore East*. A cultural entrepreneur, Bob spent more than twenty-five years working in nonprofits and museums in senior leadership roles before he founded the Lyndhurst Group in 2016. As a public historian, musician, storyteller, and family man, Bob focuses on what brings people together as a community and as citizens of the world through the unending conversation. You can reach him on Twitter @ Lyndhurst_Group or https://www.atfillmoreeastbook.com.